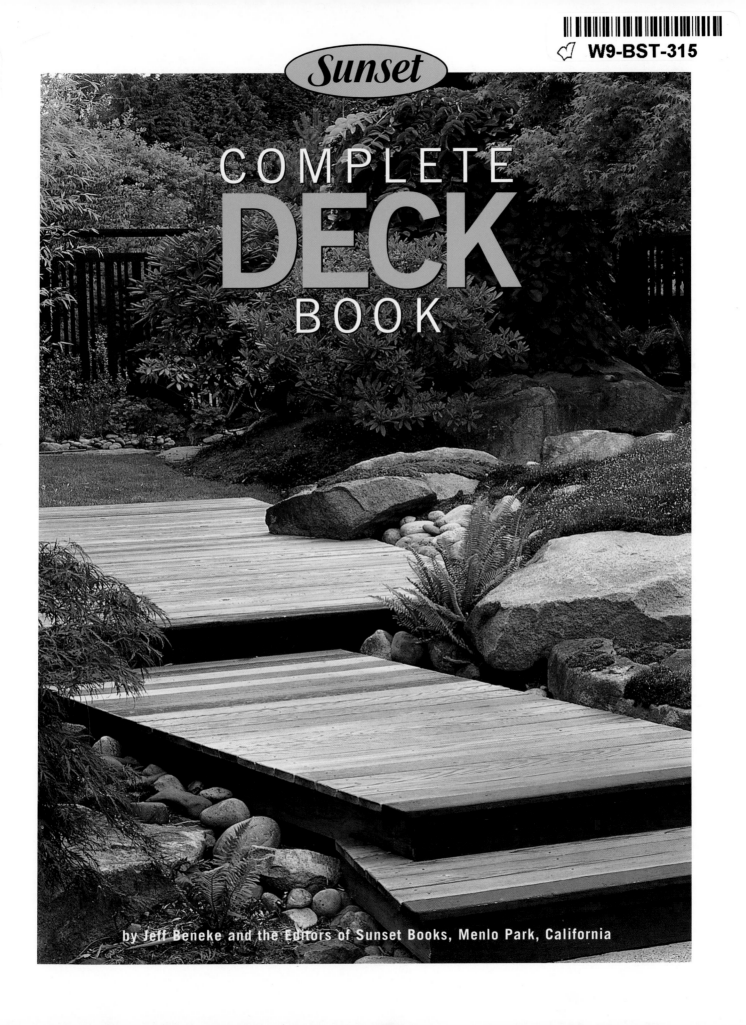

Sunset

COMPLETE
DECK
BOOK

by Jeff Beneke and the Editors of Sunset Books, Menlo Park, California

SUNSET BOOKS

Vice President & General Manager: Richard A. Smeby
Vice President & Editorial Director: Bob Doyle
Production Director: Lory Day
Director of Operations: Rosann Sutherland
Sales Development Director: Linda Barker
Art Director: Vasken Guiragossian

STAFF FOR THIS BOOK:

Managing Editor: Esther Ferington
Senior Editor, Sunset Books: Bridget Biscotti Bradley
Writer: Jeff Beneke
Art Director: Alice Rogers
Photo Editor/Contributing Writer: Scott Fitzgerrell
Illustrator: Jim Kopp, Kopp Illustration, Inc.
Principal Photographer: Mark Rutherford
Technical Consultant: Jeff Palumbo
Page Production: Linda M. Bouchard
Copy Editor: Carol Whiteley
Contributing Photo Editor: Jane Martin
Proofreader: David Sweet
Production Coordinator: Eligio Hernandez
Indexer: Nanette Cardon

Cover: Photography by Ernest Braun, courtesy of
the California Redwood Association. Deck designed
and built by Gary Cushenberry.

ISBN: 0-376-01107-6
Library of Congress Catalog Card Number: 2002108858
Printed in the United States.

For additional copies of the *Complete Deck Book* or any
other Sunset book, call 1-800-526-5111 or visit us at
www.sunset.com.

how to use this book

Decks have clearly become a "must have" feature for many homeowners. Not so many years ago, the front porch was the focal point of warm-weather activity and neighborly interaction. As foot traffic gave way to cars, however, the backyard gained popularity as a quiet retreat, and the affordable, easy-to-build deck became its centerpiece.

In many areas, professional contractors can be found who keep busy year-round doing little else but building decks. But one of the most appealing aspects of decks is that they are great do-it-yourself projects. With only basic carpentry skills, a modest budget, a little patience, and some time, you can design and build your own deck, one that can rival a professional job.

This book is designed to walk you through each step of the deck-building process. It begins with an opening chapter of deck photographs that will help you to think about the size and style of deck that would be best for your house. The middle section of the book covers the design and construction process in depth, with a focus on good-quality materials and techniques that will help ensure a long life for your deck. The final chapter presents plans for 16 unique decks, each of which may inspire your own planning regardless of how different the deck you have in mind may be.

While the how-to section of this book follows the normal sequence of construction, it will be a more useful tool if you read the entire book before you begin designing and constructing your deck. That way you will better understand the steps involved and the many options that are available to you. Built-in seating, for example, is discussed in Chapter 9, but if you want to incorporate this type of seating into your own plan, you will need to make proper adjustments in the framing, which is covered in Chapter 5. And for at least a few readers, a new deck project will begin with the removal of an old deck, a subject that is covered on page 196.

a wealth of good ideas

THE WELL-DESIGNED DECKS IN the following pages offer plenty of inspiration for whatever project you are considering. Decks are nothing if not

adaptable, and these examples prove the point, showcasing a variety of sizes, styles, and materials in settings that range from grassy lawns to rocky hillsides. Despite their differences, all were built to fit into a landscape, complement a house, and suit their owners' interests—just as yours will be. Take some

time to explore this chapter for design elements that suit your needs, including the distinctive details that can really bring a deck to life. ■ The decks that follow are grouped into categories, beginning with room-like decks attached directly to a house. Next come decks set away from a house, followed by decks that connect a house with another area, such as a garage or garden. Sections on pool and spa decks and unique deck details round out the chapter.

outdoor rooms

Attached directly to a house wall, a traditional deck serves as an extension of the interior space, becoming an outdoor room. A deck beside a house also can offer a space in which family members and guests mingle and circulate between house and garden, and even between adjacent rooms. On a fine day, with the doors wide open, the free flow in and out can be positively enchanting.

▲ **SEA-VIEW SPECTACULAR** *Stretched across the length of a house, this multilevel deck offers a large social space with a stunning vista. Railings built with tempered-glass panels preserve the view, while a step-down design breaks up the deck's broad expanse.*

◀ **UNDER THE TREES** *Well suited to its woodland setting, this rustic deck ends in a relaxed S-curve with built-in benches over a stone base. Old-fashioned turned posts support a roof overhang that protects deck and house alike from bad weather or hot sunlight, and a single large stone serves as a casual step to the lawn.*

TIMELESS SIMPLICITY *A classic low-level deck filled with welcoming Adirondack chairs complements the formal symmetry of this gabled wing. The deck's tapered second level offers a step down to the sloping yard. Since railings were not required for this low-lying design, there is no interruption in flow from one space to the other.*

UP IN THE AIR *A striking combination of white steel railings and hardwood decking, with gleaming white cantilevered joists visible below, this stylish deck serves as an elevated backyard for a house on a hill. Low walls create areas for sitting, dining, and entertaining. A deck this high requires special engineering; supports below include steel beams, braces, and posts set in deep footings.*

SPACE-SHAPING CURVES

Two decks in wooded settings show the beauty and versatility of curved designs. At left, a complex shape creates separate dining and sitting areas, the latter with built-in bench seating that matches the diagonal decking; a rounded cap rail accentuates the deck's curves. Below, levels and curving Clear Heart redwood railings help separate areas for dining and visiting.

▲ **WOOD, STONE, AND METAL**
In an effective mix of materials, a curving redwood deck with a built-in laminated bench steps down from the slate surface beside this modern house. To further preserve the view, a simple pipe rail caps the low wall.

◄ **EVERGREEN AND WATERY BLUE**
Sturdy but slender welded steel railings are easy to ignore on this high deck with a terrific view over the treetops. Still more trees grow through the deck, adding dramatic color and moderating breezes off the water.

ARCHITECTURAL SOLUTION *Tightly integrated with the house, this elegantly simple deck is a literal extension of the room it surrounds, shown here with its large sliding doors retracted. A flush perimeter drain prevents rain from flowing back into the inside living space. Outside, a solid railing provides privacy while admitting the distant view.*

OUTDOOR DINING *Above, large windows bring together a modern kitchen and the outdoor barbecue station beside it; because they are built above living spaces in the house, the decks in this project required professional design and engineering. At left, an octagonal deck serves as a backyard family room and eating area. A screened-in gazebo offers a bug-proof retreat for warm summer months.*

▲ **ON THE TERRACE** *A cleanly designed deck creates a broad, sunny terrace a few steps up from the lawn, with a columned veranda at the rear for shade.*

◀ **AT HOME WITH THE HOUSE** *Complemented by dark-stained cedar decking, clapboard siding and matching risers tightly integrate this small, well-crafted deck with the house beside it. Four steps down from a main level used for dining and socializing, a ground-level section bridges a dry bed of river rocks on the way to the yard.*

▲ **THIS WAY TO THE GARDEN**

A wide, low deck makes an ideal viewing stage for a flower-filled backyard. A shingled wall helps make the deck a visual extension of the house. Broad steps invite entry into the garden, while an adjoining notch in the plan brings the garden into the deck itself.

◄ **NESTLED IN THE TREES**

Small and cozy, with a hillside view, this snug aerie makes a marvelous outdoor space for sitting and relaxing. Sofa-like seating provides solid comfort, and slim balusters pull in the view.

◀ **CUL-DE-SAC** *Positioned beside an entry stair, this cozy nook is a natural spot for sitting and relaxing. White-painted window trim, columns, overhead, stair risers, deck skirting, and even the furniture tie everything together.*

▼ **INTO THE WOODS** *Taking the idea of an "outdoor room" a little further than most decks, this open-air garden bedroom with a moss-covered roof offers the ultimate in outdoor comfort. In the foreground, a casual sitting area joins the house and the bedroom retreat.*

ROCK CLIMBER *Built over an adaptable post-and-beam structure, this rugged redwood deck on an otherwise unusable site provides a light, airy living space with a view. Rather than trying to conquer the few large boulders above deck level, the designer chose to work around them, adding to the deck's visual appeal.*

OPEN AND SHUT CASES *When the lay of the land literally sets a deck apart, the design can be open and expansive, as shown in the large deck above. Combining an upper seating section with a stepped-down strolling area offers still more access to the view without blocking it from the house. In the deck at left, the opposite solution was needed. Tall Craftsman-style fences topped with a simple overhead provide privacy for the neighbors.*

destination decks

Not every deck is built up against a house in the classic style. Instead, a deck can be a place to go, a destination in itself. If the site is a special place already—or needs to become special— designing a deck for it can provide extraordinary freedom. Since there is rarely a direct house connection, many choices present themselves.

WORTH THE TRIP *At the bottom of a lovely garden, this secluded deck can be discovered from above by winding steps cut into the hillside, or through the charming gate and path behind it. Diagonal decking leads the eye into the space, and a built-in bench lends a sense of enclosure.*

◀ **HOME PORT** *Reaching out into a country pond, this hybrid retreat consists of a railed decking surface that rests on dock floats below. The broad decking boards, simple shape, and cantilevered design enhance the nautical theme, and a ladder provides access for swimmers.*

▼ **SAILING ON A SEA OF GREEN**
Shrubs grow right up to the skirting on this woodsy peninsula deck, making the structures seem to float above the forest floor. The decking pattern—a single large parquet— provides a sense of arrival. Built-in benches serve as railings and help to keep the plants in check.

▲ UP ON THE ROOF An unusual deck for an unusual place, this very modern design offers a sweeping view from atop a sod-roof house. A post-and-beam overhead structure suggests enclosure while remaining open to light and air. Banquette seating complements the simple forms of the walls.

◄ OVER THE WAVES Hovering over surf and rocks, this dramatic deck makes the most of its spectacular site, providing a lookout point over the crashing waves below. Pipe balusters maximize the experience. A stone stairway leads to the lawn below, enclosed with the same style of railing to integrate the design.

FOCAL POINT A beautiful tree provides the focus for a two-level deck that nearly fills the yard. The inviting composition of angled, wraparound decks and a central bench provides flexible space for relaxing and entertaining.

◀ **PROMONTORY SEATING**

Two platforms with crisply designed, built-in benches create a natural gathering place beside a landscaped backyard. The angular, asymmetrical composition provides a striking contrast to the greenery beyond.

▼ **A PERFECT PENINSULA**

The graceful swoop of this stepped deck becomes a peaceful peninsula in a wooded garden. The lowered main level, combined with a curved, laminated bench, creates a sense of intimacy while remaining completely open to the yard.

▲ **TRANQUILITY BASE** *Softly weathered decking, a simple gazebo, and a koi pond create a perfect spot for peaceful contemplation. Vertical decking keeps the framing out of sight and the scale small and unobtrusive.*

▶ **PRIVATE ISLAND** *A versatile do-it-yourself project, this stand-alone deck combines built-in seats, latticework walls, decorative overheads, and even side tables for books and refreshments. The highly compact design can fit into almost any level backyard.*

ONE WITH NATURE *This square platform rests its feet in a plant-filled pond, providing just enough space to comfortably fit two chairs and a small table. Herringbone decking is the only decorative element, aside from the peaceful view. Large pressure-treated posts handle the load—and the watery environment.*

ON THE ROCKS *Built of robust timbers, this deck-gazebo combination fits right into a rugged garden in which casual, dry-laid walls of massive stone are the theme. A retaining wall at the rear keeps the earth at bay, and the stepped-down design creates a transition to the lower level in the foreground, cantilevered over still more stones.*

connector decks

*Because they are endlessly adaptable—
suited to almost any shape or size—
decks make a great way to tie things
together outdoors, whether as broad,
decked pathways or larger spaces.
Even those that serve mainly to move
people from one spot to another can
also be planned as a place worth
visiting along the way.*

▼ **STEPS AND LEVELS** *The stairway platforms below
vary in size from pure steps to pure decks—with several
variations in between. Ornamented with ample planters
and an appealing bench at the rear, the whole scheme
creates an inviting, leisurely stairway that offers plenty
of time to take in the garden.*

◀ **_A WINDING WAY_** _This elevated pathway is built as a deck on low foundations, with alternating decking boards tapered into a fan-like pattern around the curve. Although the deck's primary purpose is transportation, a low bench in the foreground invites travelers to linger and enjoy the garden._

▼ **_BREEZEWAY WITH A VIEW_** _Tightly integrated into the house, this elegant deck connects two separate interior spaces and offers a lovely spot for dining al fresco or just enjoying the view. An open roof above and wire railing at the rear keep everything light and airy._

▲ **THE CENTER OF THE ACTION**
Stone-clad steps lead to a deck that handily links an outdoor barbecue area above, the family room at right, and the yard below. Cleanly designed cable railings nearly disappear against the wood and stone.

◄ *A **WELCOMING SPACE** Serving several purposes at once, this two-level deck provides a formal entry for the house, pathways to the street and side yard, and a private sitting area. A built-in planter tops the board-and-bat wall that divides the public and private areas of the main deck.*

FRONT-DOOR ALCOVE

This curving deck follows the line of the house façade, leading eyes and feet to the front door. Like an old-fashioned front porch, the deck invites sitting and conversation. Crisply painted railings, posts, and trim create a clean look.

DOORWAY DECK

A broad thoroughfare from the house to the yard is offered by this precisely shaped deck. Built-in benches substitute for railings and encourage people to pause a moment in their comings and goings. Edge-up 2 × 4 decking gives a fine texture to the deck and steps, and permits wider joist spacing underneath.

▲ **PAUSING BY A POND** *This drop-shaped koi-pond deck is at once a pool surround and a garden pathway just a step above the lawn. Low verdigris copper railings and a miniature bridge are all in scale with the small pool.*

▶ **PATHWAY PLATFORMS** *Few decks could be simpler than these low rectangular platforms that act as giant stepping-stones from the main deck into the yard. Easy to build, they provide a flexible solution that works in nearly any setting. For maximum durability, decks such as these should be built of rot-resistant wood set on pressure-treated sleepers.*

► ***ASIAN-INFLUENCED SERENITY***
Zigzagging timber platforms cross a large front-yard koi pool, providing a route to the door as well as a vantage point from which to watch the fish. The heavy timbers and overall simplicity are at one with the pool design.

▼ ***A GARDEN STROLL*** *Broad platforms make a pathway through this verdant garden. Built from cedar with black-stained edges, they dodge in and out of the landscaping rocks in a deceptively casual style, looking almost as if they were thrown into place.*

decks for pools and spas

Decks and water very often go together. A deck is a logical choice around a pool or spa, especially if paving is impractical or undesired; for swimmers, decks are cool underfoot, and modern materials and finishes make them last despite the extra splashing. While the basic idea of enclosing a body of water with convenient decking is simple enough, the projects shown here reveal variations on that theme to suit any situation.

▲ **GEOMETRIC COMPOSITION** *Floating mirrored balls create a one-of-a-kind look for this ornamental pool surrounded by decking. Chairs on an upper platform pick up the metallic motif, while irregularly shaped sections of exposed gravel and plant life within the deck add an organic note.*

▶ **SHELTERED LUXURY** *An octagonal platform within this large deck provides a focal point for a tempting spa. An open overhead design helps set off the spa further and adds dappled shade to moderate the sun.*

◀ **ON THE BOARDWALK** *Weathered to an attractive gray, this classic wood deck echoes the straightforward lines and siding of the house beyond. The broad deck is roomy enough to accommodate loungers alongside the pool as well.*

▼ **WATER ABOVE AND BELOW** *Bathers can enjoy the spa on the more private upper level of this deck, then head downstairs for sun and view. On the spa deck, the diagonal decking pattern leads to the stairs; on the lower deck, it points to the water and an inviting stairway leading there.*

SUITED TO THEIR SURROUNDINGS

Nestled in the corner of a zigzag deck surrounded by trees, the spa at right sits on a low platform—convenient when needed, yet out of the traffic flow. Beautiful railings echo the form of old architectural grillwork. Below, a broad ground-level wood deck makes a great transitional element for a pool-spa combination, helping it to blend into the wooded environs in a spot where concrete or stonework might look harsh.

HIDEAWAY *Sited for maximum privacy at the lowest part of the garden, this secluded spa is reached via layered decks and steps. Edge-up decking, diagonally laid, creates a fine pattern throughout. Matching benches carry the theme.*

PRIVATE ALCOVE *Set in a corner of the yard, this spa deck provides a watery oasis in a naturalistic landscaping plan. Latticework fencing shields bathers from view and also hides the spa equipment. The built-in bench is handy for drying off and taking in the sun.*

delightful details

With some imagination, such seemingly workaday details as railings, stairs, overheads, benches, and even decking can provide the special touch that turns a deck from mundane to memorable. Elements from a deck's surroundings, such as rocks or trees, can also be drawn in effectively to the design. Used with care, more unusual pieces such as artwork or fountains can also create a striking effect.

DECORATIVE VARIATIONS *The routed design along the face of a stepped-up deck level adds an unexpected but welcome decorative touch. A parquet pattern at the center of the upper level and decking that runs in opposite directions add further interest to what could have been a routine two-platform deck.*

GEOLOGY *These two decks incorporate attractive stones: at top, to punctuate a decking corner; at right, to form a natural border for an organically shaped deck. Jigsaw and contour gauge were indispensable to these precisely fitted designs.*

FINE FURNITURE *This deck bumps out to frame a custom-crafted bench in its own alcove and keeps it from intruding on the deck space. Curved laminated railings with band-sawn tops create a masterful woodworking performance.*

TREESIDE SEATING

Instead of interrupting the deck design, this large tree serves as a center of interest, all but surrounded by a built-in perimeter bench that presents the tree as a focal point. Planters provide a graceful transition for each end of the wraparound bench.

▼ **BULL'S-EYE** *The interplay of light and shadow in this creative baluster system is striking in itself, but the bull's-eye circle sets it apart. More than just a whimsical touch, the circle creates a center of interest at the head of the stairs, an effective punctuation mark denoting the end of one thing and the start of another.*

▲ **PLANE GEOMETRY** *A two-level deck steps down the hill at this waterside home, while built-in planters and benches lend a solid, substantial quality to the composition. On the upper level, glass railings allow a good look out at the view. Below, an exuberant sculpture delights in the setting, providing the perfect grace note to the design.*

WATERWORKS *A clever fountain made of copper bowls on white columns provides sonic relief on this tranquil deck. Before returning to the top, the water pools in a unique waterway, or "runnel," that crosses the deck itself, offering yet another variation of the popular pairing of decks and water.*

A SWEEPING CURVE

As a basic rectangle, a deck this long could come across as dull and heavy-handed. Instead, a rhythmic curve in both deck edge and railing adds movement and visual interest to the design.

SIMPLE BEAUTY

Seeming to float above the garden, this low-level deck features subtle details that make it a real standout. A unifying pale finish brings together diagonal decking and a mitered bench that seems to hover just outside the edges of the deck.

A DECK FOR ALL SEASONS *Surrounded by greenery, topped by an elegant overhead with ornamental rafters, and complemented by a flowering bush, the shaded wood deck above looks inviting and open on a summer day. At left, the same deck in winter offers an equally striking scene of exquisite geometric patterns formed by exposed wood and heavy snow— a fine example of a deck that looks as good in winter as in the summer sun.*

AN UNDERSTATED STAIR

Stand-out details are one route to a distinctive design, but sometimes a subtle, classic approach helps fit a deck more effectively into its surroundings. Here, a small but well-crafted railed stair yields center stage to a large rhododendron filled with vibrant flowers.

planning and design

OFFTEN, WHAT MOST SEPARATES professional-quality work from amateurish efforts is the time devoted to planning and design. Among other things, good planning means assessing all of the legal requirements, collecting needed tools, choosing top-quality materials, preparing detailed drawings, and arranging the work to minimize the disruptions to family life created by a major construction project. Good design entails translating a vision into a workable and attractive structure, one that incorporates the comforts and adventures you seek while seamlessly fitting your house and your yard. ■ Before digging any holes or reaching for your hammer, sit down in an easy chair and digest the contents of this chapter. Take plenty of notes, make some rough sketches, and let your mind wander as you work your way through the sometimes conflicting claims of dreams and practicality. Once your ideas come together, proceed with detailed plans.

choosing a location

For many sites, the best location for a new deck may seem obvious; for others, it can be a puzzle. Either way, it is worthwhile to give careful thought to the placement of your deck before proceeding. Sometimes the most obvious-seeming location can create unforeseen problems. Here are some questions to ponder.

Will the deck be accessible from both the house and the yard? If a deck is not in a convenient location, it may go unused.

Will existing windows and doors enhance use of the deck or detract from it? If access to the deck is only through a door from the living room, a bedroom, or a busy part of the kitchen, the traffic could prove disruptive. Casement or awning windows that open outward over a deck could create a safety hazard. And a deck built adjacent to a baby's bedroom or a bathroom could intrude on privacy more than you would like. As a general rule, decks are most convenient to use when they are located off a kitchen or a family room.

What will the weather be like in the location you are considering? This may seem like a silly question, but there really can be differences from one side of the house to another. One side, for example, may be too windy, while another may be too sunny or too shaded. For sun or wind, consider building an overhead or a privacy screen to offset the problem. A deck that wraps around two sides of the house can also offer a choice of microclimates.

Keep in mind that you may want to make some changes to your house to better accommodate the new deck. For example, if your ideal deck location is not near a door, consider installing a new double-wide or sliding glass door to serve the deck. You could also replace a relatively narrow door with a wider one. Likewise, if a sidewalk or driveway intrudes on your deck site, you may want to consider relocating, shortening, or eliminating the obstacle.

Wide patio doors allow easy, convenient access to this deck from the kitchen and dining area. Smaller, more private sections of the deck can be reached through other doors.

PREPARE A SITE PLAN A rough bird's-eye-view drawing of your house and yard can make deck planning much easier. Include property lines; utility lines (overhead and buried); walkways, patios, and driveways; trees, shrubs, and gardens; views you want to save or would like to block; prevailing winds; the effects of sunlight and shading; sheds; septic tanks; and other factors that may affect your decision. You may also want to sketch in doors and windows that could affect, or be affected by, the planned deck. Compromises are often unavoidable. In this example, a deck that takes advantage of good sunlight, privacy from the tree line, and the best view would also require building over the garden and installing a new door.

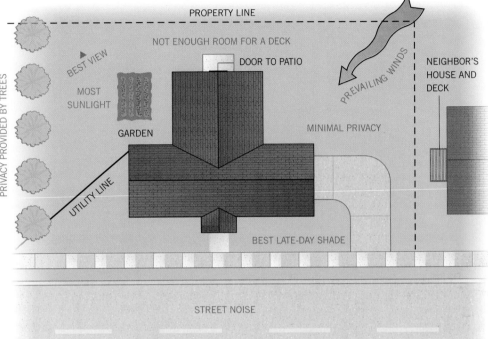

A Rooftop Deck

If you have a flat or nearly flat roof over part of your house, you may be inclined to put a deck on it. Such a choice can be a wise and an affordable option. Sometimes, however, it can become a nightmare. Because the roof must be close to level, a poorly built deck can collect water, causing leaks and serious damage to the house below. To avoid this problem, the roof must be carefully flashed and covered with a waterproof membrane, with a clear path for water to drain. In addition, existing roof rafters are almost certainly inadequate to support the kind of load a deck will impose. To ensure structurally adequate support, the rafters may have to be beefed up substantially, or the roof may have to be reframed. This is the kind of project that only very experienced and knowledgeable do-it-yourselfers should tackle—and even then, only with professional guidance.

determining the style

Decks are often built as a simple rectangle off the back door. With a little imagination, however, you can design your deck so that it takes special advantage of the shape of your house and the size of your yard.

There is really almost no limit to the shape, size, or style that a deck can assume. Let your house serve as the focal point for your deck design, however. An ornate, heavily decorated deck may look great attached to a Gothic Revival house, but downright gaudy on a simple ranch-style house. Likewise, a massive wraparound deck could easily destroy the appeal of a small Cape Cod house, while a tiny deck on a massive house could look silly.

Above: An elevated deck can turn a steep slope into a useful part of the landscape. This thoughtfully designed structure serves as a quiet retreat among the trees. *Right:* Steps and multiple level changes are another way to tie a deck into a slope. Here, trees and boulders, potential obstacles to a deck project, have been incorporated into the design.

DECK VARIETIES

A rectangle near ground level is the easiest type of deck to build, and it is often perfectly sufficient. But to add some flair to a deck, solve a particular problem, or avoid an obstacle, you may want or need to vary the design. Simple adjustments include turning 90-degree corners into 45-degree corners, or adding a bumped-out section to part of the deck. Other common deck types are shown in the illustrations at right.

CONSIDER THE SIZE

A well-designed deck is sized to fit both the house and the yard comfortably. But it is also wise to relate the size of your planned deck to its intended function. Are you looking for a quiet spot to do some reading? Then think small. Do you want a place for outdoor entertaining and dining? Then allow plenty of room for people and furniture.

As a general rule of thumb, allow at least 20 square feet of deck for each person. Following this criteria, a 12-by-20-foot deck, which works out to 240 square feet, could handle up to 12 people at once, although more space would be needed if the deck contained furniture, plants, grills, and other items. Before settling on a final size, consider testing your deck plan with a trial run (see pages 54–55).

< WRAPAROUND DECK

A flat lot is a natural candidate for a wraparound deck, which enlarges the apparent size of the house. A wraparound deck also serves as a kind of outdoor hallway, allowing access from any of the rooms along its course.

MULTILEVEL DECK >

A large lot, especially one with changes in elevation, can often accommodate decks on different levels, linked by steps or a pathway. Such a scheme works well when your outdoor space must serve many purposes, such as sunbathing and barbecuing. Multilevel decks can also avoid blocking views from the house.

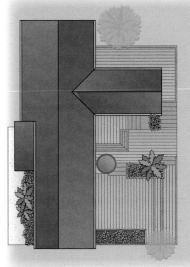

∧ ELEVATED DECK

High decks are commonly built adjacent to upstairs bedrooms; they can be connected with the yard by a stairway, or remain private and secure without stairs. An elevated deck is also a great way to turn a little-used, sloping site into a functional, flat surface.

the parts of a deck

As your ideas for the deck project begin to take shape, you will need to have a basic understanding of the structure of a typical deck. Knowing the name and purpose of each part will also help you in talking with your lumberyard and the local building department, as well as any contractors or architects.

Decks consist of several layers of construction, each with its own components and function. The usual parts of a deck are identified in the illustration below, and are described here in the order in which a deck is typically constructed. There are many variations to this basic deck, which are discussed later in the book.

The ledger joins a deck to the house framing. Concrete piers, often resting on wider footings below ground, provide the deck's solid connection with the ground. Posts establish the height of the deck, tying the piers to one or more beams. Joists attach to the ledger and beams, providing the underlying frame for the decking, which is the surface layer.

If the deck is more than 2 feet above ground, it should be surrounded by a railing, which typically consists of posts, rails, and balusters. Stairs are composed of treads and sometimes risers, attached to stringers, as well as a railing on each side.

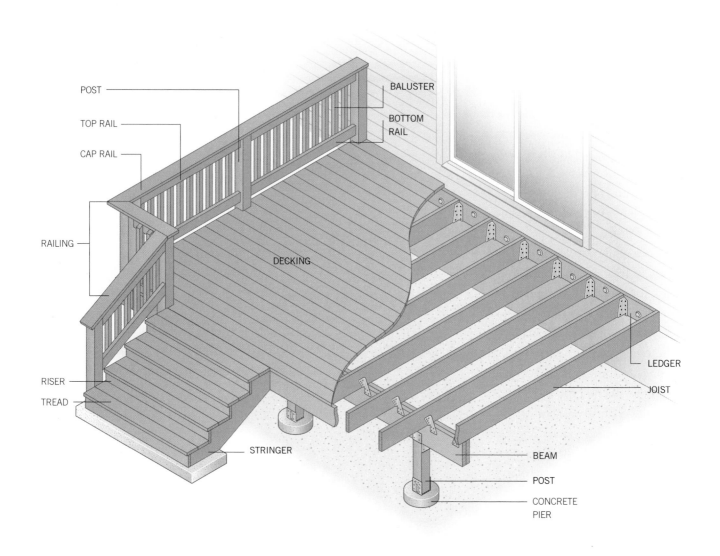

where decks fail

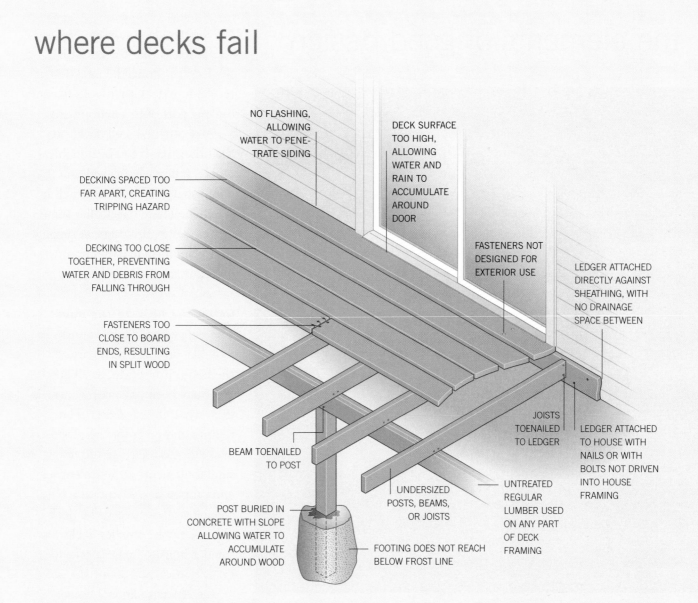

NO FLASHING, ALLOWING WATER TO PENE-TRATE SIDING

DECK SURFACE TOO HIGH, ALLOWING WATER AND RAIN TO ACCUMULATE AROUND DOOR

DECKING SPACED TOO FAR APART, CREATING TRIPPING HAZARD

DECKING TOO CLOSE TOGETHER, PREVENTING WATER AND DEBRIS FROM FALLING THROUGH

FASTENERS NOT DESIGNED FOR EXTERIOR USE

LEDGER ATTACHED DIRECTLY AGAINST SHEATHING, WITH NO DRAINAGE SPACE BETWEEN

FASTENERS TOO CLOSE TO BOARD ENDS, RESULTING IN SPLIT WOOD

JOISTS TOENAILED TO LEDGER

LEDGER ATTACHED TO HOUSE WITH NAILS OR WITH BOLTS NOT DRIVEN INTO HOUSE FRAMING

BEAM TOENAILED TO POST

UNDERSIZED POSTS, BEAMS, OR JOISTS

UNTREATED REGULAR LUMBER USED ON ANY PART OF DECK FRAMING

POST BURIED IN CONCRETE WITH SLOPE ALLOWING WATER TO ACCUMULATE AROUND WOOD

FOOTING DOES NOT REACH BELOW FROST LINE

Decks, like houses, are largely held together by lumber and fasteners. But houses have roofs, sheathing, and siding to protect them from the elements and add support. Decks, on the other hand, are exposed to all kinds of weather. They can be buried in snow one season and baked in the sun the next, and may have to endure heavy foot traffic, deep freezes, and drenching rainfalls. When faced with such conditions,

the materials that go into a deck are prone to deteriorate. Wood rots, fasteners loosen, metal rusts, and foundations may heave.

On many decks, shortcuts or simple errors made in planning or building accelerate the damage. A well-designed and well-constructed deck can survive intact for decades with regular maintenance. A poorly built and maintained deck can begin to deteriorate in just a couple of years.

Following the construction advice offered in this book will help you avoid the typical pitfalls illustrated here, which can cause a deck to fail—sometimes catastrophically. Fine deck building may require that you spend a little more for materials, take a little longer on the construction, and take time to maintain and repair the deck as needed, but the results will be worth it.

the elements of good design

The paradox of design, in most cases, is that the better it is, the less it is noticed. Good design results in a deck that looks like an organic part of its environment.

A poorly designed deck, on the other hand, can be a highly visible, if unpleasant, addition that diminishes the house to which it is joined. These pages offer some proven design tips that can simplify your planning and better ensure a deck that meets expectations.

MATCH THE DECK TO THE HOUSE

The best way to make your deck look like an integrated part of the house is to begin, as all good designers begin, by taking cues from what already exists. The railings and posts for the proposed deck, for example, should mimic similar elements at house entries and on porches. Maintain a reasonable scale between the deck and the house: smaller decks for smaller houses, higher decks for taller houses, and so forth.

On older, traditional houses, wood decks can look somewhat out of place; consider using brick or stone for the support posts. You can also replace a solid wood railing with a more "transparent" type of railing material, or keep the deck low enough to avoid needing a railing.

Above: *With its shape, scale, and choice of materials, this wraparound deck nicely matches the contemporary style of the house.* **Right:** *Since decks were not a feature of traditional houses, sometimes the best choice for an older house is a brick or stone patio like this one. Alternatively, plan a modest deck that spills onto such a patio.*

CONTROL TRAFFIC A new deck can substantially alter the way in which people move in and through your house. Plan the deck to direct foot traffic where you want it. Placing the deck next to the kitchen makes it easier to move food and dishes back and forth. Setting the same deck so that it can be entered only from the living room, on the other hand, could lead to dirty carpets and regular disruption of TV viewing.

Consider the transition from the inside of your house to the outside. Wide French or sliding glass doors make the outdoors look inviting and also make the interior expand psychologically. When existing doors just do not seem to work for the planned deck, consider adding a new one in the ideal location. In the illustration below, the deck is made more useful by wrapping it around the corner of the house and adding a door off the kitchen.

STAY IN LINE A good designer studies the lines of a house, then tries to match the lines of the new deck to them. A house's lines are defined by vertical items such as chimneys, porch columns, and corners, and horizontal elements such as porch railings, eaves, and the alignment of windows and doors. In the illustration above, railing posts line up vertically with support posts, stairs align with the chimney and do not block any windows, and windows and doors are framed by posts, not blocked by them. Also look for ways to align the corners of the deck with corners or bump-outs in the house. Use irregularities in the house façade to justify incorporating angles into your deck design.

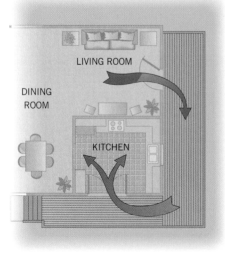

Two doors to this deck allow easy access and efficient foot traffic.

Deck Today; Porch Tomorrow?

While decks satisfy many people's needs, other people grow weary of dodging raindrops or sitting in the sun and swatting mosquitoes. You may want to consider building a deck now that could be turned into a screened porch later, a conversion that will be much easier if it is planned for in advance. Porches with roofs require bigger footings than uncovered decks, for example, so you might want to pour bigger footings now. Also consider how the porch roof will connect with the house. To be sure this kind of advance planning pays off, consult an architect or a structural engineer.

BREAK THE EDGES The edges of exposed boards on a deck will look nicer if you take a little extra time to smooth them over. By doing so, you also make them less likely to develop ugly gashes and threatening splinters. A router equipped with a round-over or a chamfer bit is the quickest way to smooth the front edges of stair treads, dress up the sides of a railing, and add a finishing touch around the perimeter of your decking (see page 70). Sanding, by hand or by machine, is also effective, as is running a plane along the edge of a board to create a slight bevel.

STAGGER THE JOINTS Staggered joints are a cornerstone of good building, whether you're installing sheets of plywood sheathing or constructing a brick wall. Decking, too, is stronger and looks better if you make an effort to prevent butt joints between the ends of the boards from lining up. If possible, use the longest boards available to eliminate or minimize the number of butt joints. If you use the double joist technique for butt joints, plan to use at least two sets of them so that the joints zigzag rather than line up, as shown at right.

ROUNDED

BEVELED

PROVIDE DRAINAGE One thing is certain—your deck will get wet. To keep water from causing problems, use construction techniques that encourage it to drain away as quickly as possible. This advice is most important with a large, flat decking surface. Plan a drainage gap between all rows of deck boards, and plan the framing so that butt joints fall over a gap in the double joists below.

Gaps between boards let water drain through the deck.

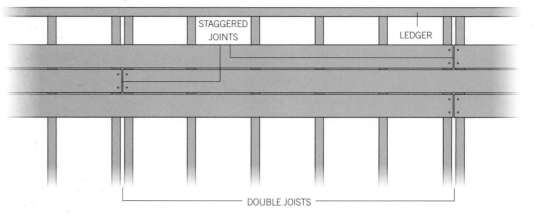

STAGGERED JOINTS

LEDGER

DOUBLE JOISTS

INCORPORATE OVERHANGS

Overhangs, or cantilevers, offer both visual and structural benefits. Joists and decking that extend beyond a beam partially conceal it, and also make the deck somewhat larger without additional foundation work. Deck boards that overhang perimeter joists an inch or so create a satisfying shadow line while allowing fasteners to be installed farther from the board ends, reducing the chance of splitting. Whenever different surfaces meet, see if you can add an overhang to the juncture. See page 57 for recommended limits on joist cantilevers; similar restrictions apply to overhanging a beam beyond a post.

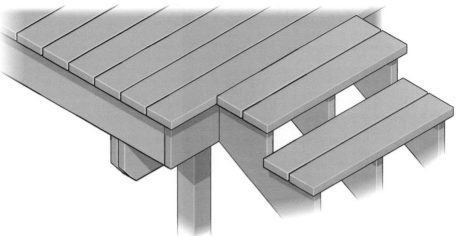

Adding beauty and useful space, decking extends slightly beyond a joist, the joist overhangs a beam, and the beam extends past a post. On the stairs, treads overhang the stringers below.

CONSIDER THE CONSEQUENCES

As you plan your new deck, it is understandable to focus on all the benefits it will bring. But it is also wise to consider some of the consequences of such a large project that may not be so beneficial. Here are some things to think about.

- Decks can bring you closer to great views from the outside, but they can obstruct views from inside the house. You can minimize this effect by creating a multilevel deck or lowering the deck surface a bit.
- A high deck can block sunlight from reaching windows and doors beneath it. Shifting the planned location of the deck or designing it with an opening for the sun are possible remedies.

- Your neighbors may see the deck differently than you, as a noisy construction project (in the short term) that will bring more people and commotion outdoors (in the long term). You may want to discuss your plans with the neighbors before you begin to offset such concerns.

Design often requires compromises. This deck offers a spectacular lake view from outside the house, but blocks some of the scenery from inside the house.

understanding structural framing

A deck must be built to support certain minimum loads. In most areas, building codes specify that a deck should be able to support at least 50 pounds per square foot, which is often divided into 40 pounds of live load (people and movable furniture, for example) plus 10 pounds of dead load (the deck itself, railings, and permanent objects). If you plan to put any unusually heavy items, such as a spa, on your deck, you may need to adjust the deck framing to support the extra load.

SPANS As shown below, a span is the distance bridged by a beam, a joist, or decking between two supports. Spacing is the distance between the centers of adjacent posts, beams, and joists. The two measurements are directly related, since the desired span for any component dictates the spacing

of the pieces that support it. The decking span determines the joist spacing, the joist span determines the ledger-to-beam (or beam-to-beam) spacing, and the beam span determines the post spacing.

Because they determine the strength or weakness of the deck, spans should be calculated carefully. The tables on the facing page give typical dimensions for standard materials. Note, however, that allowable spans for beams, joists, and decking depend on the species, grade, size, and spacing of the individual components.

As you can see, there are many variables to consider when planning the framing for your deck. The number of posts is dependent on the size and spacing of beams, so to minimize the number of postholes you need to

dig, you may want to use larger beams. It is generally easiest and most cost effective to build a deck using only one beam, which can sometimes require that you use larger joists. The spacing between joists can vary depending on which material you choose for decking.

POST SIZES The height of the deck, which helps to determine post size, is yet another measurement that is important in deck framing. Code requirements for assessing post dimensions tend to involve some complicated math. As a general rule, for decks up to 6 feet above ground, 4 × 4s will suffice for posts. For decks more than 6 feet high, you may be required to use 6 × 6s. Larger posts may also be needed if the spacing between beams and between posts reaches the maximum allowable limits. As with all structural lumber, recommended sizes can vary between wood types and grades. Check with your local building department for more details.

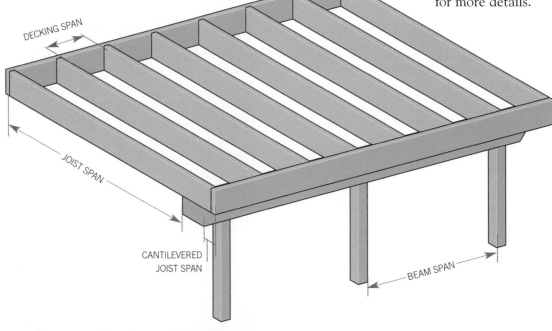

DECKING SPAN

JOIST SPAN

CANTILEVERED JOIST SPAN

BEAM SPAN

SPAN TABLES Span tables are published by several organizations. They can run on for pages, providing allowable spans for a wide range of wood species, grades, sizes, and spacings for a large number of load requirements. The examples given on this page represent only a small number of possible choices, providing information on popular sizes and lumber choices for deck building. Always check with your local building department before making final plans.

TYPICAL BEAM SPANS
Southern pine and Douglas fir, Select Structural grade

| NOMINAL BEAM SIZE | ON-CENTER SPACING BETWEEN BEAMS OR LEDGER TO BEAM | | | | | | |
	6'	7'	8'	9'	10'	11'	12'
4 × 6	6'						
Doubled 2 × 8	7'	7'	6'	6'			
4 × 8	8'	7'	7'	6'	6'	6'	
Doubled 2 × 10	9'	8'	8'	7'	7'	6'	6'
Doubled 2 × 12	10'	10'	9'	8'	8'	7'	7'

TYPICAL JOIST SPANS
Southern pine and Douglas fir, Select Structural grade

| NOMINAL JOIST SIZE | ON-CENTER SPACING BETWEEN JOISTS | | |
	12"	16"	24"
2 × 6	10'3"	9'4"	8'2"
2 × 8	13'6"	12'3"	10'9"
2 × 10	17'3"	15'8"	13'8"

TYPICAL DECKING SPANS

DECKING TYPE	NOMINAL DECKING SIZE	MAXIMUM RECOMMENDED SPAN
Redwood, Western red cedar, Douglas fir	⁵⁄₄ × 4	16"
	⁵⁄₄ × 6	16"
	2 × 4	24"
	2 × 6	24"
Southern pine	⁵⁄₄ × 4	24"
	⁵⁄₄ × 6	24"
	2 × 4	24"
	2 × 6	24"
Composite	2 × 6	Varies by product; typically, 16"–24"

staying safe and legal

Before you go too far in planning your deck, consult with your local building department about any legal requirements and restrictions. In most areas, you will need to file for a building permit and comply with the building code. Also look into local zoning ordinances, which can dictate where—and even if—you can build the deck.

BUILDING CODES Specific code requirements vary from region to region, and even from town to town. They establish minimum requirements for footings, lumber sizes and spans, railings and stairs, deck height, and other aspects of the deck. Keep in mind that these requirements are not always adequate. Building codes are often quite specific about most deck details, but they can be vague or even silent about other construction matters, such as how to connect the ledger to the house. Over the years, many decks built strictly to code have collapsed. The advice given in this book is based on sound construction principles and may well be more detailed and demanding than your local code.

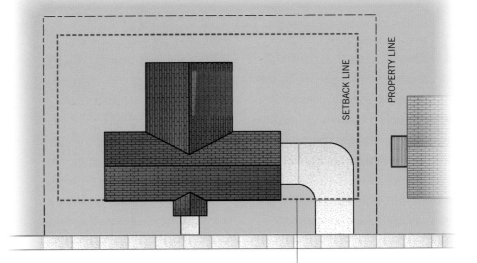

COMMON SETBACK REQUIREMENTS

SETBACK LINE

PROPERTY LINE

NO NEW CONSTRUCTION ALLOWED BEYOND THE SETBACK LINE OR IN THE FRONT YARD

BUILDING PERMITS To obtain a permit, you may have to supply a drawing of your planned deck and pay a fee. Building permits are typically good for no more than one year, so it is wise to obtain the permit just before you begin working and to schedule your work to conclude before the permit expires.

INSPECTIONS To comply with your building permit, you may have to have your deck inspected at specified stages of the project, such as after the footings are poured, after the framing is complete, and again after the deck is finished. Be sure to inquire about the inspection schedule when you obtain your permit.

ZONING ORDINANCES These municipal regulations can affect deck building plans in several ways. Some localities require that you restrict the size of a deck or keep all or parts of the deck a specified distance from adjacent property lines. Common "setback" requirements are indicated in the illustration above right. Historic

districts and subdivisions often have additional restrictions. If your plans conflict with the zoning rules, you can apply for a variance.

HIDDEN OBSTACLES Before you lift a shovel, make sure you know whether you will be encountering any buried pipes or wires. Electrical cables, natural gas pipelines, telecommunications cables, water lines, and drainage pipes can all be hidden below ground. If you are unsure about these potential obstacles, contact your utility companies well in advance. Once you know the location of any buried lines, mark them on your site plan (see page 41).

Watch Out for Rising Taxes

A new deck will almost certainly increase the value of your house, which is a welcome development when it comes time to sell. In the meantime, however, you may find yourself with a higher property tax bill; applying for a building permit can trigger a reassessment of your property, which in turn can result in slightly higher taxes every year. Depending upon where you live, you may be able to avoid this problem by building a deck that is small enough or close enough to the ground (typically less than 30 inches) so that no building permit is required. Also, in some areas, a freestanding deck is not classified as an improvement to the house, and so it will not necessarily result in a tax increase. If you have questions about the tax implications of your planned deck, check with your local department of assessments.

working out a plan

In many cases, most of the decisions about deck size and location are largely predetermined by the house and site. For some homeowners, however, the options are many and the decisions tougher to make. Commonly available deck plans or those for specific projects, such as the ones on pages 197–250, can provide useful ideas, but are likely to require modifications to fit your particular site.

One of the great advantages of building your own deck is that you can take extra time fussing about specific details. The lack of time pressure is particularly evident in the design and planning stages, when you can take as long as you like coming up with a final design that meets all, or at least most, of your expectations. One of the best ways to reach this goal is to "try on" your deck before you begin construction.

DOING A TRIAL RUN

A trial run can be as simple or as complex as you need it to be. If you are most concerned with the "footprint" issues of size and location, use garden hoses or string lines to mark the perimeter of your proposed deck, as shown below. Place some furniture inside the layout, and consider collecting a small group of people to simulate the kind of social gathering you envision for the deck. Expand or shrink the layout as needed.

Are you more concerned about the effect a deck will have on your view from inside the house? Then set up a more elaborate trial run. Use inexpensive plastic fencing and wood or metal fence posts to create a more realistic mock deck. Set the fencing material at the height of your proposed railing, then study the effect from inside the house.

Is your biggest concern how the deck will affect the flow of people into and around the house? Then set up markers along the trial layout to represent railings, stairs, and other elements, and ask people to move through the layout accordingly. Study the effects that different layouts have on congestion and other traffic patterns. This experiment can help you plan ideal locations for stairs and it may also aid in settling the question of whether or not to install a new door.

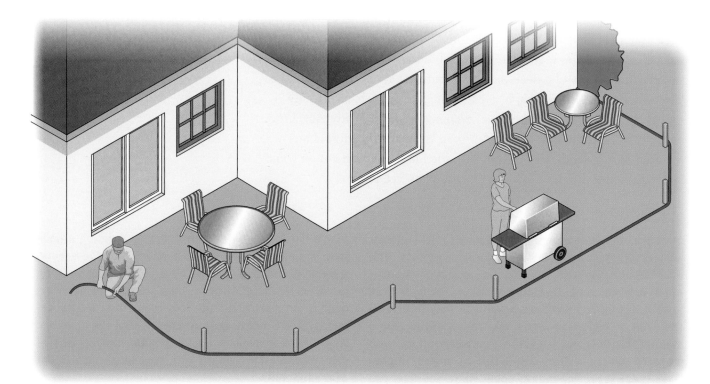

USING YOUR COMPUTER

Computer software can make it easier to try out different options for designing your deck than if you work by hand. One of the advantages of using a computer is that you can make changes quickly. One of the disadvantages, however, is that you may need to spend some time learning how to use the program. Programs are available specifically for deck and landscaping projects, although you may have better luck with an established home-design program intended for do-it-yourselfers. Before investing in a program, read reviews and see if a trial version of the program can be downloaded from a Web site.

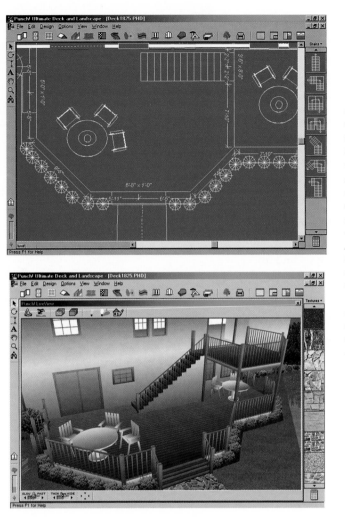

Once you overcome the learning curve, a good software program can speed up the process of designing a deck. Making adjustments is particularly easy. As shown here, you can alter the size, shape, or location in the two-dimensional plan view (top), then immediately see how the new design looks in three dimensions (bottom).

Hiring a Pro There are many ways for you to tackle a deck-building project. You can design and build the deck yourself; design it, then have it built by a contractor; have it designed by a professional and build it yourself; or make any number of intermediate arrangements. If you have a knack for design, there is no reason why you cannot develop a working plan for your deck. Still, you might want to have a landscape architect or a professional designer review your plans.

If you are inexperienced at handling power tools and performing basic carpentry tasks, the decision of whether or not to build the deck yourself can be a tough one. Building a deck can be an ideal project in which to begin accumulating some carpentry tools and skills. But if you are not sure you want to make this commitment, or whether you can handle the hard physical labor, then it may make more sense to talk with some contractors.

There are some deck-building projects for which you should strongly consider seeking professional help, if for no other reason than to review your plans. These include:

HIGH DECKS The higher the deck, the harder it is to build. Positioning posts, beams, and other framing is tougher on high decks. You may also need to add further structural reinforcement.

SITES OVER SAND, MUD, OR WATER Decks perched above water or marshy ground or at lakeside or beach locations require special pilings for support.

STEEP OR UNSTABLE SITES A steep site, especially one where slides may occur, must be checked by a soils engineer. A deck over such a site may require structural engineering and special building department approval.

drawing plans

Once you have determined the best site and size for your deck, it is time to put your ideas on paper and transform them into a workable design. You can generate plans using a computer design program if you have one. But you need only a few basic tools to create useful drawings. Graph paper and an architect's scale rule allow you to make drawings that are to scale, a practice that is highly recommended—and also required by many building departments. Scale drawings help you spot design problems on paper, rather than during construction, and they also make it easier to determine your lumber needs. The most common types of construction drawings are described here.

PLAN VIEWS A plan view shows the deck from above. It gives the scale of the deck in relation to the house and indicates the decking pattern. Since it includes horizontal measurements, a plan view also allows you to visualize how people using the deck will circulate, and to judge the sizes of different areas.

A framing and foundation plan view offers a similar bird's-eye view, but without the decking. It shows the sizes and number of joists, beams, posts, and footings, and the distance between these parts. On relatively basic decks, you can easily combine this plan with a decking plan, as in the illustration at left. More complex decks may require separate drawings.

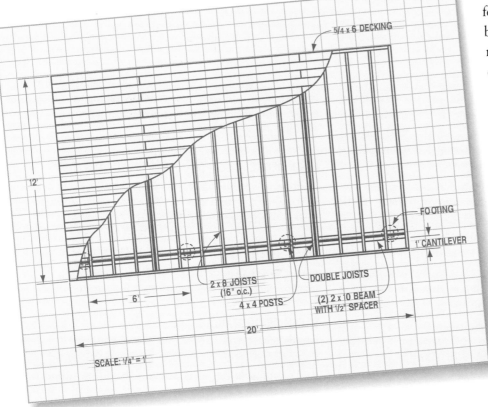

5/4 x 6 DECKING

FOOTING

1' CANTILEVER

2 x 8 JOISTS (16" o.c.)

DOUBLE JOISTS

4 x 4 POSTS

(2) 2 x 10 BEAM WITH 1/2" SPACER

12'

6'

20'

SCALE: 1/4" = 1'

ELEVATIONS An elevation (right) is a side view of the deck that displays vertical dimensions and relationships. An elevation section is a side view of a slice somewhere in the deck.

DETAILS A detail drawing gives you a closeup of a particular feature of the deck—such as stairs, a railing (below), or a bench—whose construction is not apparent in a plan view or an elevation.

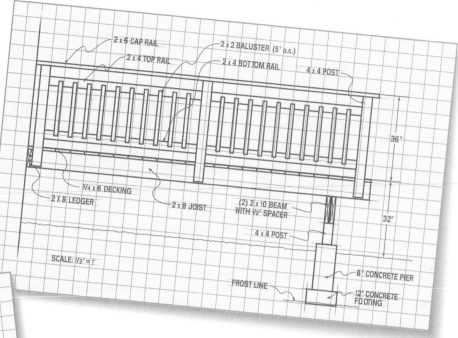

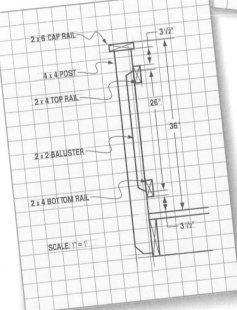

Calculating Joist Overhangs

There are several advantages to designing a deck so that the joists overhang the beam. The overhang, or cantilever, moves the edge away from the beam, creating a more attractive deck. An overhang also allows you to create a larger deck surface than the framing would seem to allow.

But how far can you extend the overhang? From a strictly engineering standpoint, you could safely overhang a joist by up to half of the ledger-to-beam distance. Thus, if a beam was spaced 8 feet from the ledger, the joists could extend up to 4 feet beyond the beam. (Another way of saying this is that up to one-third of the total joist length could extend beyond the beam.) In practice, however, building codes often limit the overhang to 2 feet or less, and from an aesthetic standpoint, a 1- to 1½-foot overhang usually looks best.

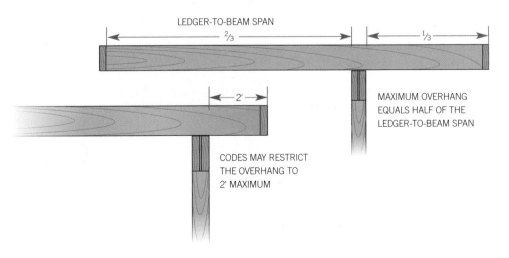

preparing the site

Take care of any drainage problem in the area where you plan to build your deck, and undertake any necessary grading. Now is also the time to take steps to prevent any future weed growth.

DRAINAGE Make sure to check your site for permanent wet spots or standing water. A proper drainage system carries water away from the house and the deck's substructure, especially the footings. A drainage ditch dug in the direction of the runoff is usually the best way to divert water. Direct the water to a dry well or, if available, the municipal storm sewer system. If you have a severe water problem, seek advice from the local building department, a landscape architect, or a professional designer. If a downspout empties near the deck site, reroute it.

GRADING The ground should slope away from your house about 1 inch for every 10 feet. If your lot is improperly graded, or if the ground around the foundation has settled over time, be sure to correct the problem before building your deck.

CONTROLLING WEEDS Most low-level decks prohibit weed growth by blocking sunlight. But you may want to take extra precautions to ensure that weeds will not grow. The best approach is to remove any sod from beneath the deck, then cover the dirt with landscaping fabric. (Do not use plastic sheeting for this job; water will drain through the fabric, while plastic will prevent it from draining.) Cover the fabric with a 2- to 3-inch layer of gravel.

Top: Remove sod under the planned deck along a line marked with flour or spray paint. If you like, the sod can be reused in another part of the yard.
Bottom: Landscaping fabric covered with gravel will keep the area below the deck weed free and well drained.

materials, tools, and techniques

PERHAPS BECAUSE DECKS HAVE *traditionally been composed of wood and nails, there is a tendency to underestimate the need to shop carefully. Often, the choice of materials is the critical factor in determining how long your deck will last and how much care and maintenance it will require through the years. You may also be surprised to learn that top-quality decks today are using less and less wood and more composite products.* ■ *If you do home improvement projects on a regular basis, you may have a nice collection of tools. If you are looking to start or add to a tool collection, however, this chapter offers a primer on what to buy. Whether or not you are new to power tools, you may benefit from some of the tips and techniques on tool use that follow.*

lumber options

If you could keep the wood dry, your deck could last forever. But a deck is exposed to moisture, oxygen, temperature fluctuations, ultraviolet rays, and a host of wood-loving fungi and insects, so you need to choose your lumber carefully. Here is a brief introduction to the choices available.

TREATED LUMBER Wood that has been pressure treated with certain preservatives can survive outdoors for decades longer than untreated wood. The best choice is pressure-treated lumber that has been injected at the factory with water repellent. This lumber will cost more and may have to be special ordered, but it is less likely to split and crack. For many years, the most widely available product was pressure-treated Southern pine containing chromated copper arsenate (CCA). CCA-treated pine is being phased out, however, due to concerns about its arsenic content. Other types of treated wood are available, and new products may emerge to replace CCA-treated lumber.

In some areas, pressure-treated hem-fir has been more common. This lumber-grading category includes hemlock and five types of fir, which are usually treated with ammoniacal copper quaternary (ACQ), and the treatment method results in visible slits in the surface of the wood. The preservative does not penetrate as deeply into the wood as CCA, so it is important to treat any cut ends immediately with water repellent. New formulations of ACQ have been developed to treat Southern pine and Douglas fir. Copper boron azole (CBA) is another product now being used to treat Southern pine and hem-fir. For information on the safe handling of pressure-treated lumber, see page 72.

UNTREATED SOFTWOODS Decks and other outdoor structures were once built with untreated redwood and cedar. But as prices climbed and availability declined, builders turned toward treated wood. Still, in some areas and for some budgets, untreated softwoods are an ideal choice. Redwood has been found to be very stable for outdoor construction projects. Though it is most widely available and affordable in and near California, redwood can be obtained or special ordered elsewhere.

A wide variety of cedars can be used on decks. Both Western red cedar and Alaska cedar are popular choices for decking on the West Coast. Understanding the different grades of untreated softwoods can be a bit confusing, as there are so many of them. But keep in mind that only the heartwood of the tree is resistant to decay and insects, not the outer sapwood. As a general rule, cheaper lumber grades will contain less heartwood.

PRESSURE-TREATED
DOUGLAS FIR

REDWOOD

WESTERN RED CEDAR

Which Material Where?

The smartest way to build a deck is to use different grades and species of wood for different purposes. It makes sense to spend the extra money for top-quality lumber, which will have fewer knots and blemishes, for those parts with the highest visibility. The illustration at right provides guidelines for matching typical materials to their intended function.

RAILS
PRESSURE-TREATED WOOD, CEDAR, REDWOOD, OR COMPOSITE (2×4, 2×6)

BALUSTERS
PRESSURE-TREATED WOOD, CEDAR, REDWOOD, OR COMPOSITE (2×2)

DECKING
PRESSURE-TREATED WOOD, CEDAR, REDWOOD, OR COMPOSITE ($\frac{5}{4} \times 4$, $\frac{5}{4} \times 6$, 2×4, 2×6); TROPICAL HARDWOOD (1×4, $\frac{5}{4} \times 6$)

RAILING POSTS
PRESSURE-TREATED WOOD, CEDAR, OR REDWOOD (4×4)

JOISTS
PRESSURE-TREATED WOOD (2×6, 2×8, 2×10)

RIM JOISTS
PRESSURE-TREATED WOOD (TOP GRADE) (2×6, 2×8, 2×10)

BEAMS
PRESSURE-TREATED WOOD (DOUBLED 2×8, 2×10, 2×12, OR SOLID 4×8, 4×10, 4×12)

POSTS
PRESSURE-TREATED WOOD (4×4, 6×6)

TROPICAL HARDWOODS Several types of tropical hardwoods are available for use as decking. Ipé is a beautiful, durable, rot-resistant wood that does not need to be finished. Cambara and meranti are two other choices. To find suitable products, you may have to do some shopping on the Internet or talk with local wood suppliers.

ALTERNATIVES TO SOLID WOOD Products made from recycled plastic and wood chips are rapidly gaining popularity as decking materials. A large number of such composite products are entering the market. You can find planks that are solid, tongue and groove, or web-like in construction, in a variety of colors. Some composites are intended to mimic the look of real wood, while others make no such attempt. Composites will not splinter or crack like wood; usually can be cut, drilled, and installed like solid wood; and require little maintenance beyond periodic cleaning. Though not suitable for structural members, composite products can be used for railings. Solid vinyl decking and railing products are also increasingly popular. See pages 132–135 for more information on working with composites.

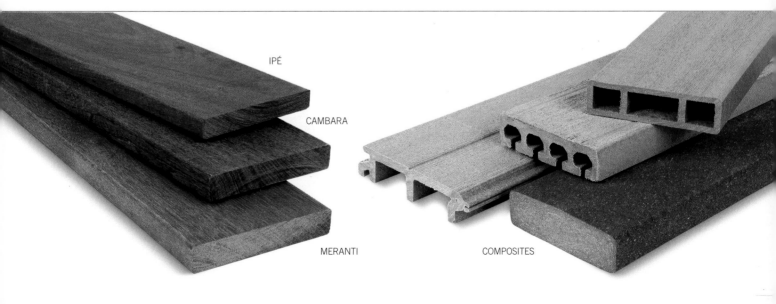

IPÉ

CAMBARA

MERANTI

COMPOSITES

assessing fasteners

Even the best-quality fasteners account for only a small portion of the cost of a new deck, and they are well worth that modest investment. When choosing fasteners, pay close attention to their holding capacity and their corrosion resistance. Fasteners that are too weak for the job or that corrode prematurely can weaken an entire deck.

Stainless-steel screws, nails, and bolts cost considerably more than other fasteners, but they are the most resistant to corrosion. You should certainly choose stainless steel if you are building in an especially wet or salty environment. It is also recommended if you are using redwood or cedar. Hot-dipped (HD) galvanized fasteners are more affordable than stainless steel and are suitable for most decks. Electroplated fasteners are also galvanized, but their treatment differs from hot dipping, and they do not resist corrosion as well. Fasteners that are coated by hot galvanizing (HG) are also inferior to HD galvanized fasteners.

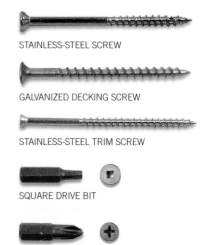

NAILS Nails with smooth shanks have the least amount of holding capacity. As the wood shrinks slightly over time, they will loosen and allow lumber joints to separate. Ring-shank or spiral-groove nails, or screws, hold much better. Other nails serve special functions, such as securing joist hangers or light wood trim.

JOIST HANGER NAIL

COMMON NAIL

RING-SHANK NAIL

SPIRAL-GROOVE NAIL

FINISH NAIL

SCREWS Screws are not available with a hot-dipped galvanized finish, but you should look either for stainless-steel screws or for galvanized screws that have been coated with a weatherproofing resin. Screws with a yellow zinc coating offer less corrosion resistance. If you will be using a lot of screws, look for those that use a square drive bit. They are easier to drive, and the drive bits last longer than standard Phillips drive bits.

STAINLESS-STEEL SCREW

GALVANIZED DECKING SCREW

STAINLESS-STEEL TRIM SCREW

SQUARE DRIVE BIT

PHILLIPS DRIVE BIT

BOLTS Bolts are heavy-duty fasteners intended to carry bigger loads than standard nails and screws. Carriage bolts and lag screws are used to connect ledgers, railing posts, and other critical framing members. Carriage bolts, which require a nut, are usually stronger than lag screws, but cannot be used for very thick connections or if the back side of the fastener is not accessible. Both require pilot holes. Anchor bolts (or J-bolts) are used to secure posts to concrete piers. Use a washer with each type of bolt.

HIDDEN FASTENERS Many people think that the visible heads of fasteners used to secure decking are an ugly presence, especially if they have paid for top-notch decking. In response to that concern, many hidden fasteners are now available. They cost more and take more time to install, but the results can be worth it. See pages 128–131 for more information.

FRAMING CONNECTORS A variety of connectors are made specifically for connecting the various components of a deck; avoid regular, uncoated joist hangers, metal straps, and other connectors, which are not intended for exterior use. Electroplated connectors are fairly easy to find; hot-dipped galvanized and stainless-steel connectors may be harder to locate, but are worth the effort.

ANCHOR BOLT

CARRIAGE BOLT

LAG SCREW

BISCUIT FASTENERS

DECK CLIPS

METAL TRACK FASTENERS

JOIST HANGER

POST BASES

POST CAP

STAIR BRACKET

selecting other materials

Lumber and fasteners are the major materials used in building a deck, but they are not the only ones. If you will be cutting into the siding of your house to install a ledger, you need to pay close attention to selecting materials that can prevent moisture from causing damage. In most cases, you will need concrete to help anchor the deck to the earth. And to protect the deck from premature aging, you should choose a top-quality finish and apply it regularly.

MOISTURE BARRIERS

Several types of moisture barrier can be used for the area where the house and deck framing connect, although your building code may require a specific product. Metal flashing is available in aluminum, galvanized steel, copper, and stainless steel. Preformed aluminum and galvanized flashing are inexpensive and easy to install. The style you are most likely to find is formed to slip behind the siding and over the top of the ledger, but better protection is provided by flashing that runs behind the ledger (see pages 80–84). If you are unable

to find preformed metal flashing suited to that type of installation, you can buy a roll of sheet metal and form one yourself. If you use aluminum flashing, and need to nail it, be sure to use aluminum nails; using galvanized steel nails encourages corrosion.

Another option is a flexible, self-adhering membrane. Although these products offer outstanding protection, they require a little more effort to install than metal flashings that can be slid up behind the siding.

CONCRETE

You will need concrete to form foundation footings and piers, and you may need it to create a landing pad for stairs or a support slab

SELF-ADHERING
BITUMINOUS
MEMBRANE

PREFORMED FLASHING AND
ALUMINUM FLASHING

for a hot tub. If you are building a large deck, with many deep holes to fill, it is probably best to have ready-mixed concrete delivered by truck. Check with local suppliers for costs and minimum order requirements. For smaller decks, you can mix your own concrete. Although dry concrete is a mixture of Portland cement, sand, and gravel, you are usually better off buying bags with the ingredients already combined. Add water as directed on the package. For more information about working with concrete, consult pages 90–91.

For creating concrete piers, inexpensive cylindrical tubes are an excellent choice, and they may be required by your building code. The tubes are available in various diameters and can be cut to the necessary length with a handsaw.

WOOD FINISHES

The essential ingredients for deck longevity include thoughtful design, careful construction, and routine coatings with a good-quality finish. All wood decks perform better with routine finishing. And even if you are using composite decking and railings, you will need to apply a finish to the deck's substructure.

Finishes are available in a variety of colors and formulations (see pages 186–187 for more information). Choose the type of finish you will use when you design the deck. The best time to apply a finish is as soon as possible after the deck is built, so it is a good idea to buy your finish along with other deck materials.

choosing hand tools

You do not need a lot of tools to build a deck. And since all of the tools you do need are standard construction tools, you can be certain that any purchases you make now will be put to use on later home-improvement projects. Basic hand tools are discussed here, while power tools are covered on subsequent pages. One accessory that you will want to have at just about every step of the way is a tool belt.

LAYOUT TOOLS

A tape measure that spans 25 or 30 feet is the best all-purpose choice. If you are building a large deck, you may also want to have a 50- or 100-foot model. A large framing square quickly checks corners for square and is ideal for marking stair stringers. A smaller angle square is handy for marking cut lines on lumber, guiding the base of a circular saw, and marking precise angle cuts. A sliding bevel is indispensable for duplicating angles. Colored mason's line is the best material to use when laying out your deck, as it is strong and easy to see, and a chalk line can be used to quickly mark a long, straight line. For the essential job of keeping your deck lines straight and level, use the tools and techniques on pages 74–75.

EXCAVATION AND CONCRETE TOOLS

If you plan to dig holes by hand, you will need a posthole digger. Even if you are using a power auger, this manual tool will come in handy for removing dirt from the hole. Concrete needs to be mixed in a large mortar tub or a wheelbarrow; a mortar hoe is the best tool for mixing the dry ingredients with water.

FRAMING SQUARE

ANGLE SQUARE

SLIDING BEVEL

CHALK LINE

CHALK LINE

MASON'S LINE

TAPE MEASURE

POSTHOLE DIGGER

MORTAR HOE

MORTAR TUB

CUTTING AND JOINING TOOLS

A curved claw hammer will get lots of use on most projects, including a deck. Sixteen-ounce models are popular, but a heavier hammer will drive nails quicker.

A handsaw is always nice to have around for quick cuts. Wood chisels clean out notches cut in posts, square the corners when removing siding for ledger installation, and can even be used to pry crooked deck boards into place before fastening. A caulking gun is required for sealing joints with caulk. For securing bolts, nuts, and lag screws, you will want to have an adjustable wrench as well as a socket wrench with suitable sockets. Several types of clamps come in handy for a variety of purposes. Tin snips are necessary only if you will be cutting flashing. As you work, a pair of sawhorses allows for easy cutting and can serve as the legs for a temporary workbench (see page 76).

HANDSAW

CURVED CLAW HAMMER

ADJUSTABLE WRENCH

BAR CLAMP

SOCKET WRENCH

SQUEEZE CLAMP

TIN SNIPS

CAULKING GUN

WOOD CHISEL

C-CLAMP

selecting power tools

Unless you are looking for a long, physically demanding project, you will want to have a few power tools available when you build a deck. Along with the hand tools discussed on the previous two pages, you should have a circular saw and a drill when you start building your deck. The other power tools discussed on the following pages, while useful and recommended for deck building (and many other jobs), are not quite as important.

For occasional work around the house, you certainly do not need to buy top-of-the-line professional-grade tools. At the same time, it is best to stay away from low-cost power tools, which are frequently underpowered and may be poorly constructed. Tool manufacturers these days make mid-priced products aimed at experienced and demanding do-it-yourselfers that are usually quite satisfactory. Before you buy, read reviews in consumer and construction-related publications. Seek out advice and recommendations from pros and others with experience in building projects. You may also prefer to rent power tools that you require for only a day or two. See page 72 for additional advice on working safely with power tools.

CIRCULAR SAW

In deck building and most carpentry tasks, no power tool sees more use than a circular saw. If you do not already own one, this might be a good time to buy one. The most common style takes a 7¼-inch blade, which will cut to a depth of about 2½ inches.

Carbide-tipped blades are best for making smooth cuts, and they last much longer than blades with steel tips. A range of blades is available for specific cutting needs. For your deck work, it's best to look for a good all-purpose framing blade.

Circular saws are not difficult to use, but they do demand respect. As with any power tool, be sure to read the owner's manual carefully. If you have never used a circular saw before, buy some inexpensive lumber and practice a variety of cuts before you begin building.

USING A CIRCULAR SAW

Top: With the saw unplugged, adjust the depth of cut so that the blade clears the bottom of the board you plan to cut by about ¼ inch. This adjustment is easiest to make with the blade alongside the board. *Bottom:* If you have trouble making square cuts, use an angle square to guide the saw.

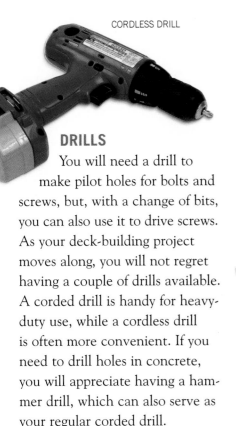

CORDLESS DRILL

DRILLS

You will need a drill to make pilot holes for bolts and screws, but, with a change of bits, you can also use it to drive screws. As your deck-building project moves along, you will not regret having a couple of drills available. A corded drill is handy for heavy-duty use, while a cordless drill is often more convenient. If you need to drill holes in concrete, you will appreciate having a hammer drill, which can also serve as your regular corded drill.

DRILLING PILOT HOLES When driving nails or screws near the ends of boards, you stand a good chance of splitting a board and thus minimizing the strength of the connection. To avoid this, first drill a pilot hole using a drill bit slightly smaller in diameter than the screw or nail, then drive the fastener into place. Drill pilot holes for carriage bolts and lag screws as described below.

HAMMER DRILL

Drill pilot holes before driving nails or screws near board ends.

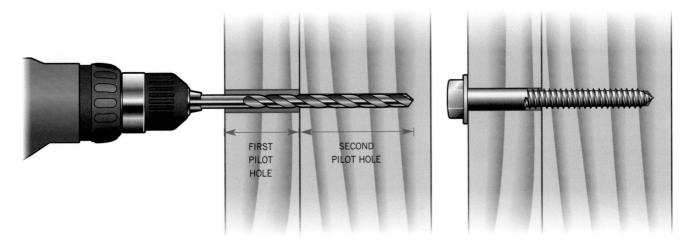

Pilot Holes for Bolts

When installing carriage bolts, first drill a pilot hole all the way through the lumber. Lag screws, which are often used to attach ledgers, require two drilling steps, as shown below. For ½-inch lag screws, first drill a ½-inch-diameter pilot hole into the wood that extends completely through the first board and is at least as deep as the unthreaded shank on the screw. Then drill a hole to the intended depth of the screw, making the hole diameter match the solid core of the threaded part of the screw, about $\frac{5}{16}$ inch. Put a washer on the lag screw. Then, with an adjustable wrench or a socket wrench, turn the lag screw into the hole. Use a screw that penetrates as deeply as possible into the wood without poking out the back side of the second piece of wood.

FIRST PILOT HOLE

SECOND PILOT HOLE

ROUTER

A router is a nearly essential tool for woodworking projects and a handy tool for certain deck-building chores. To create neat, smooth edges on decking, posts, handrails, and stair treads, use a router with a round-over bit that produces a $\frac{3}{8}$- or $\frac{1}{2}$-inch radius. A carbide-tipped bit with a ball-bearing pilot will give the best results. To create 45-degree beveled edges, use a chamfering bit.

SANDERS

If your lumber, especially the ends of the decking, is a little rough, a quick pass with a belt sander will smooth it out. A smaller random-orbit or finish sander (right) can be used to accomplish the router tasks described above. The results will be a bit less uniform than if a router is used.

BELT SANDER

POWER MITER SAW

A power miter saw (less formally known as a "chop saw") can speed up a number of jobs in deck building. Although most of the cuts it can perform can be made with a circular saw, a power miter saw makes them cleaner and straighter. Miters and bevels can be cut quickly and neatly. And for repetitive tasks, such as cutting dozens of balusters to identical lengths, a power miter saw set up with a stop block, as shown in the photo at left, is unbeatable.

RECIPROCATING SAW

A reciprocating saw can cut much thicker pieces of wood than a standard circular saw. If you are installing 6 × 6 posts, you will be able to cut them to length quickly using a reciprocating saw with a long blade. Even 4 × 4 posts can be cut more quickly with a reciprocating saw, since you would need to make two passes (on opposing sides) if you used a circular saw.

Extension Cords

You will need an outdoor extension cord or two to operate power tools outside. Check the owner's manuals for your tools for guidelines on gauges and lengths of extension cord to use. And always make sure that the extension cord is GFCI-protected. If no GFCI outlet is available, use a cord with an in-line GFCI.

working safely

Any construction site is a potential safety concern. You can minimize the dangers by learning how to operate power tools safely, wearing appropriate safety gear, and using your common sense. Keep the area around the deck clean of lumber scraps and other debris. If you are working under a hot sun, drink plenty of water and take frequent breaks. Avoid lifting heavy loads; get a helper if you need one. And if you are feeling tired or sore from spending too much time working on the deck, take a few days off.

HANDLING POWER TOOLS

If you are using a power tool for the first time, read the owner's manual and practice on some scrap lumber. Always keep the tool unplugged when it is not in use for an extended period, or when you are making an adjustment or changing a blade. To guard against deadly shocks, make sure that all power tools are connected to a GFCI-protected outlet. When you leave the work site, put power tools away so that children cannot reach them.

EAR PLUGS: WEAR WHEN USING POWER SAWS, ROUTERS, OR OTHER LOUD TOOLS

SAFETY GOGGLES: WEAR WHEN USING POWER TOOLS, HAMMERING, CHISELING, SANDING, MIXING CONCRETE, OR APPLYING FINISH

DUST MASK: WEAR WHEN CUTTING TREATED WOOD, SANDING, OR MIXING CONCRETE

WORK GLOVES: WEAR WHEN MIXING CONCRETE OR HANDLING TREATED LUMBER—BUT NOT WHEN USING POWER TOOLS

WORKING WITH TREATED WOOD

Some varieties of treated wood contain toxic ingredients, although newer, safer products are becoming increasingly available. When working with any type of treated wood, it is smart to take the following safety precautions:

- Use treated lumber only where its protection is needed.
- Use only treated wood that is visibly clean and free of surface residue.
- Clean up all sawdust and construction debris from the work site.
- Do not burn any lumber scraps. Instead, dispose of them with regular trash.
- When cutting or sanding, wear a dust mask and eye goggles.
- Wear gloves when handling the wood. Wash your hands before eating or drinking.
- Seal the wood with a water-repellent finish at least every two years.

Treated lumber is required by many building codes. A useful strategy for minimizing contact with it is to use it for the posts, ledger, beam, and joists, and to use one of the other options for the decking and railings; see page 61 for ideas.

WORKING OFF THE GROUND

If you are building a deck over a steep slope or outside an upstairs entrance, you must take some extra precautions to ensure a safe work site. In most cases, you can probably get by with a couple of stepladders and a helper or two. To reach higher locations, use extension ladders.

If the job requires that you work above ground for much of the project, or if you need to lift a heavy beam over your head, consider renting some scaffolding. Installed correctly, scaffolding is the easiest and safest way to work off the ground.

LADDER SAFETY Use the right ladder for the job. Match the load capacity of the ladder with the weight you need to put on it, including your own. Place the legs on level ground. Extension ladders and closed stepladders should lean against a solid surface, ideally with both the bottom and top secured (see illustration at left).

Placing boards under one leg of a ladder to make it level is dangerous. A better solution is to dig out a level surface, then place the ladder on a 2 × 10 pad. Do not lean out from a ladder, and do not stand above the second rung from the top on a stepladder, or the fourth rung from the top on an extension ladder.

plumb, level, and square: a carpentry primer

The cardinal rule of carpentry can be summarized as follows: build it plumb, level, and square. The best materials, finest tools, and greatest design cannot overcome a structure that has been put together contrary to this principle, since errors in any one of these attributes can quickly multiply as the project progresses.

"Plumb" means true to a vertical plane. A plumb object takes maximum advantage of gravity, transferring loads directly to the earth. "Level" means true to a horizontal plane (that is, to the horizon). And when a plumb object meets a level object, they form a 90-degree angle, which is the basis of "square."

Fortunately, each of these properties can be checked easily with the techniques described here. By monitoring your deck building for plumb, level, and square at each step, you can ensure that succeeding steps start off on the right foot.

ESTABLISHING PLUMB

When you start installing the posts for your deck, you will need to make sure that each one is plumb. To do so, hold a carpenter's level securely against the post, then move the post until the bubbles are centered in the two end vials. Check and plumb two adjacent sides.

Another tool that can be used is a plumb bob, pictured at left. On a still day, a plumb bob will hang perfectly straight up and down from a piece of string.

FINDING LEVEL

Beams, joists, and decking should all be level. Check them with a carpenter's level placed in the horizontal position. When the bubble is centered in the middle vial, the object is level. When you are using a level to check a long board or post, place the level at several spots along the entire length. If the bubble changes resting spots from one location to another, the lumber is probably bowed and may need to be replaced.

Levels are somewhat delicate tools. To see if yours is accurate, place it on a flat, solid surface that is nearly plumb or level. With the level in position, take a close look at the location of the bubble. Then, without lifting the level, rotate it on its axis 180 degrees, and let it come to rest in the same position on the surface. If the bubble is in the same position as before, the level is accurate.

Sometimes you need to establish a level between a reference point on one surface, such as a ledger, and a point on another, such as a post, without having an installed board between them on which to set a level. There are two methods to accomplish this chore easily and reliably. The first is to set the level at the center of a long, straight board, then move the board up and down until the bubble is centered (opposite, top). This effectively allows you to turn a 2- or 4-foot level into an 8-, 10-, or 12-foot level.

For those times when a carpenter's level will not reach, such as when you are establishing ledger locations on two sides of a house or are determining post heights for a large deck, a water level is indispensable. It operates on the principle that water in a flexible tube will seek the same level on each end. You can make your own using any length of ⅜-inch or 5⁄16-inch clear vinyl tubing. Fill it with water and a little food coloring for visibility. Make sure there are no air bubbles or kinks in the tubing and keep the tubing ends open. Set one end of the tubing so that the water level aligns with your reference mark. Then place the other end of the tubing in the desired location.

Once the water stabilizes, it will be level with the other end. An even simpler approach is to buy a commercial water level that beeps when level has been established in the tube.

CHECKING FOR SQUARE

Most decks are rectangular or made up of several adjoining rectangles. If the corners of the frame are not square, the decking will be harder to install and the results may look odd or worse. There are two methods used by carpenters to check for square, depending on the situation.

To quickly determine if a rectangle is square, measure both diagonals. If they are identical, the corners are square. Be sure in using this method to confirm you are working with a true rectangle; check that parallel sides are exactly the same length.

To check a single corner for square, use the "3-4-5" technique. Measure along one side 3 feet, along a perpendicular side 4 feet, then measure the diagonal formed between these two spots. If it equals 5 feet, the corner is square. This approach can be even more accurate if you use a set of larger numbers that have the same ratio, such as 6-8-10 or 9-12-15.

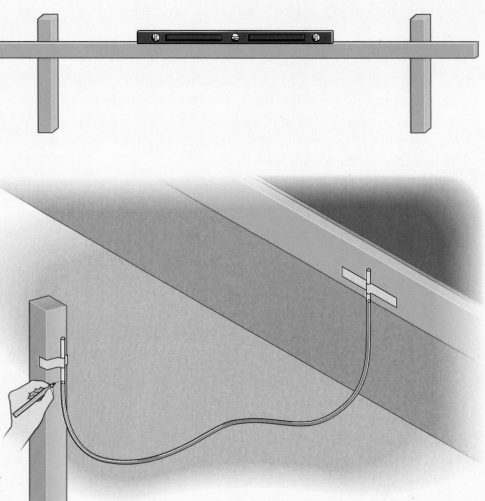

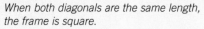

When both diagonals are the same length, the frame is square.

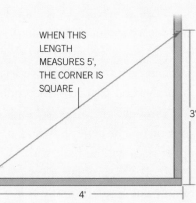

WHEN THIS LENGTH MEASURES 5', THE CORNER IS SQUARE

3'

4'

preparing the work site

A well-organized work site is safer and more efficient than a sloppy, unplanned site. For a deck project, think especially about where you want the lumber to be unloaded. You want it close to the deck site, but not so close as to get in the way when you start building. Keep the lumber neatly stacked. Not only will it take up less room, but the weight of a properly stacked pile will help reduce cupping and warping in the wood. Wood stored outdoors should be covered with a tarp and placed on some scrap 2 × 4s to keep it off the ground.

If you are concerned about theft, keep the lumber stack well lit or store the wood in your garage. Think about where you will store your tools and smaller materials such as fasteners during construction. A garden cart or large wheelbarrow can be used as a temporary, portable toolbox that can be quickly wheeled from the work site to the garage.

If you plan to have ready-mixed concrete delivered, consider where the truck can be parked.

A pair of sawhorses is almost mandatory for measuring, marking, and cutting boards. Another pair can serve as inexpensive legs for a plywood-topped workbench. You can buy sawhorses or build your own. The style shown at upper right can be built with 2 × 4s, 1 × 6s, and fasteners. Simply cut an eight-foot 2 × 4

in half, then fasten the two pieces into an inverted T, as shown. Cut four 1 × 6 legs to the length you prefer (30 to 36 inches is usual). Attach each leg with nails or screws.

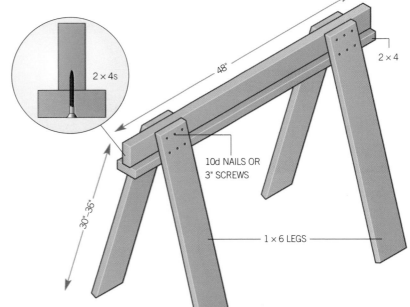

2 × 4s

48"

2 × 4

30"-36"

10d NAILS OR 3" SCREWS

1 × 6 LEGS

foundations

IT IS A WELL-WORN CLICHÉ TO note that the best house, marriage, or business is built on a solid foundation, and decks are no different. A properly prepared foundation is probably the single most important component of a deck. Mistakes above ground can be corrected as needed, but the foundation is buried and will be hard to access once the structure is completed. Before you start, settle any indecision you have about accessories that you may want to incorporate into the deck design, since they could affect the type of foundation you need. Also understand that the work detailed in this chapter can be tough. Even hefty and experienced do-it-yourselfers may balk at the physical effort needed to dig a large number of holes and fill them with concrete. This is the best time in the entire project to round up a helper or two, or to consider spending some extra money to rent labor-saving tools.

understanding foundations

In a deck, as in a house, the foundation anchors the structure against settling, shifting, and wind uplift. It also distributes the weight of the deck and everything on the deck to the earth. But while most house foundations are composed of a masonry wall around the entire perimeter, most deck foundations consist of a series of individual concrete piers and footings.

Building codes govern the size and spacing of foundations and specify how deep into the ground they must go. Typical codes call for 16-inch-square or 18-inch-diameter footings that are 8 inches thick. In cold climates, codes also require that the bottom of the footing be below the frost line. If footings do not extend to this depth, ice can form beneath a footing, pushing up the deck with enough force to weaken the entire structure, a process called "frost heave."

POST ON SOLID CONCRETE PIER

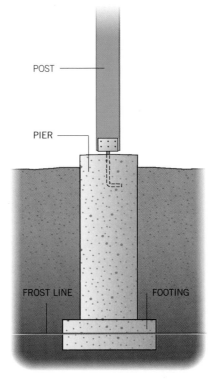

POST

PIER

FROST LINE

FOOTING

POST ON PRECAST PIER

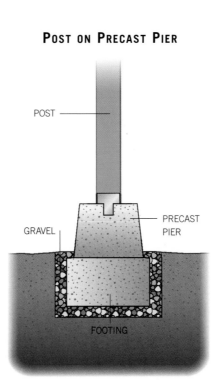

POST

GRAVEL

PRECAST PIER

FOOTING

POST IN CONCRETE FOOTING

POST

GRAVEL OR COMPACTED SOIL

FROST LINE

FOOTING

NAILS EMBED POST IN CONCRETE

Decks are usually constructed with posts anchored on solid piers that extend down to the footings. Codes also typically allow the option of embedding the posts in the footings. In warm climates, deck posts can sometimes be set into precast concrete piers set in shallow footings.

SUPPORTING THE LOAD

From an engineer's perspective, there are two kinds of weight, or load, on a deck. As noted on page 50, the "dead load" is the weight of the structure itself, along with all of its permanent components, such as railings, overheads, and built-in benches. The "live load" consists of variable factors, such as people, portable furniture, and snow. The typical code require-ment for decks is that they be able to support a dead load of 10 pounds per square foot and a live load of 40 pounds per square foot, for a total maximum load of 50 pounds per square foot.

These load requirements apply to decks that will be used in normal conditions and are built on undisturbed soil. If you want to include any particularly heavy features in your deck, such as a spa or a large planter, or if the soil is loose or composed of a lot of clay, discuss your plans with the local building department or a construction professional.

Typical decks must be able to support 50 pounds per square foot (large arrow). Here, small curved arrows show how the load is carried through joists, beam, and posts from the deck to the earth. Additional load is carried through the ledger to the house and its foundation.

Freestanding Decks

An alternative to the ledger-mounted decks that are shown on the following pages is a freestanding deck, one that is not connected to the house at all. Instead of being bolted to a ledger, the part of the deck alongside the house rests on an extra row of posts and an additional beam. This approach eliminates the need to cut into the siding on the house, which is one of the trickier jobs in deck building. Because they require extra posts, however, free-standing decks generally require extra work. And because the additional posts need to be within a couple of feet of the house itself, the footings often must be dug very deep to reach undisturbed soil. Freestanding decks also often require additional bracing.

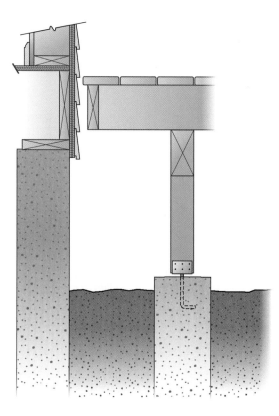

attaching ledgers

The ledger is a board that is bolted to the house to support one end of the deck joists. It is a bit of a hybrid—part foundation, part framing—and installing it is usually the first construction task in deck building. With the ledger firmly and properly in place, it will be easier to lay out the rest of the foundation. Procedures for installing a ledger vary, depending upon the type of siding on your house. Common installation methods for most types of siding are covered on pages 81–84.

LOCATING THE LEDGER To keep snow and water away, the finished surface of the deck should be lower than the interior floor of any room leading onto it. To avoid creating a tripping hazard, the deck can be located an inch or less below the interior floor. Where snow is a concern, or for other design reasons, locate the deck surface 4 to 8 inches below the interior floor. This distance will produce a safe, clearly visible step from the deck up to the house. Your local building code may offer more specific guidelines on this issue.

When determining the height at which to install the ledger, you need to take into account both the drop from the interior floor and the thickness of the decking material you plan to install.

SIZING THE LEDGER As a general rule, you should use the same size of board for the ledger as you plan to use for the joists. You can use a larger board, however, if it allows for a better connection to the house framing. Calculate the length as 3 inches less than the width of the deck framing. This leaves room for the end joists to overlap, and thus hide, the ledger ends. Also, reduce the length of the ledger as needed to allow the decking to overhang the framing.

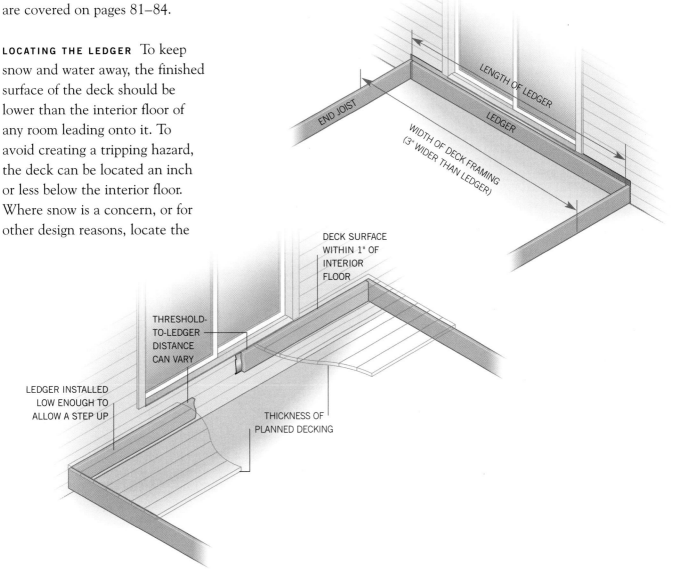

END JOIST

LENGTH OF LEDGER

LEDGER

WIDTH OF DECK FRAMING
(3" WIDER THAN LEDGER)

DECK SURFACE
WITHIN 1" OF
INTERIOR
FLOOR

THRESHOLD-
TO-LEDGER
DISTANCE
CAN VARY

LEDGER INSTALLED
LOW ENOUGH TO
ALLOW A STEP UP

THICKNESS OF
PLANNED DECKING

MAKING THE CONNECTION

Some types of siding should be cut away to make room for the ledger. Relatively flat siding, however, can remain intact. Regardless of the type of siding, the strongest ledger connection relies on bolts that run through the ledger and the house sheathing and rim joist, with nuts and washers attached in the basement or crawl space. When access to the other side of the fasteners is not feasible, you can use lag screws instead. Sometimes it is necessary to use both types of fasteners, as shown in the illustration.

Ledgers should never be merely nailed to the house, and they must always connect to the house framing or foundation—never just the sheathing, which cannot support a deck.

The size and spacing of the bolts should be spelled out in your building code. If they are not, use ½-inch bolts every 14 inches on decks with joist spans of up to 10 feet; every 10 inches for joist spans of up to 14 feet; and every 8 inches for longer spans. Avoid installing bolts that will interfere with joists and joist hangers (see page 108). Drill pilot holes as shown on page 69 to install carriage bolts or lag screws.

DRAINAGE AND MOISTURE It is a good idea to leave a space behind the ledger to allow for drainage. This is easily accomplished by placing three or four washers (galvanized or stainless steel) on each bolt, as shown below. Alternatively, wood spacers can be cut out of pressure-treated plywood and placed behind the ledger, as shown at bottom. As added protection against moisture infiltration, squirt some caulk into the holes before inserting bolts or lag screws. For many installations, you will also need to add flashing, as described on pages 82–84.

NONSTANDARD JOISTS If the floors in your house are framed with something other than solid wood, such as wood I-joists or another kind of manufactured joist system, you will probably need to take extra steps to secure the ledger. Discuss your options with the building department or a construction professional.

TYING THE DECK TO THE HOUSE

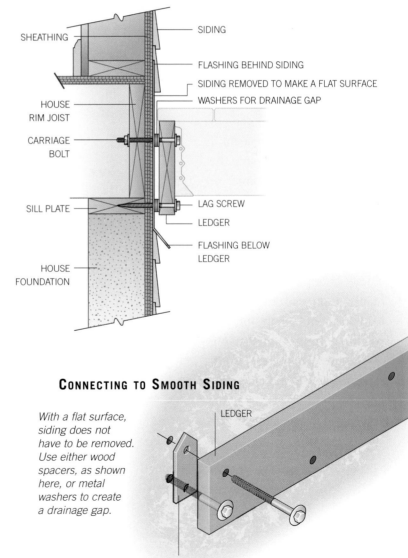

SHEATHING
SIDING
FLASHING BEHIND SIDING
SIDING REMOVED TO MAKE A FLAT SURFACE
WASHERS FOR DRAINAGE GAP
HOUSE RIM JOIST
CARRIAGE BOLT
SILL PLATE
LAG SCREW
LEDGER
FLASHING BELOW LEDGER
HOUSE FOUNDATION

CONNECTING TO SMOOTH SIDING

With a flat surface, siding does not have to be removed. Use either wood spacers, as shown here, or metal washers to create a drainage gap.

LEDGER

WOOD SPACER

REMOVING SIDING

If your house has clapboard, beveled wood, metal, or vinyl siding, you will need to remove some siding to accommodate the ledger. Also cut away siding 1½ inches to each side of the ledger to allow for the end joists of the deck. Plan to remove enough siding so that flashing can be tucked behind the siding above the ledger and overhang the siding below the ledger, as shown on page 81. Although metal flashing is often installed to cover the top edge of the ledger, a better technique is to extend it below the ledger.

If you will be using self-adhesive membrane instead, prepare for it by removing the entire row of siding above the ledger. After you apply the membrane, reattach the siding.

If your house was built before 1978, there is a good chance that paint on the siding may contain lead. Inhaling lead dust can be harmful, so if you are cutting painted siding of that vintage, wear a HEPA-rated respirator and clean up any paint chips or other debris you create immediately.

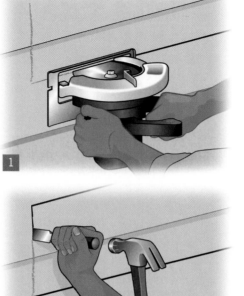

1 Cut the Siding
Carefully mark lines for the cuts on the siding. Make sure to check for level and to allow room for the end joists. Adjust the blade of your circular saw so that it cuts just to the depth of the siding and not into the sheathing underneath. Do not let the blade cut beyond the layout lines. If you are cutting vinyl siding, you can also use a sharp utility knife.

2 Finish with a Chisel
Use a chisel to finish each cut and make clean corners. You may find it easier to make the vertical cuts with the chisel alone.

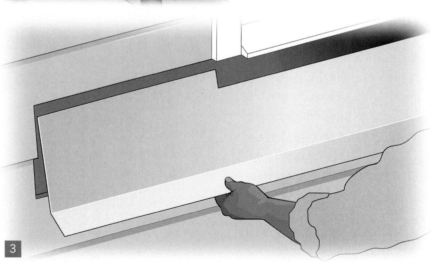

3 Add Flashing
Slide metal flashing beneath the siding. You may need to temporarily remove some siding nails first. Cut the flashing to fit around the door threshold, as shown. Apply caulk to the joint between the threshold and flashing.

ATTACHING LEDGERS TO MASONRY WALLS

Ledgers can also be attached to solid concrete or solid masonry walls. For walls of concrete block, fill the hollow cores with grout; if that is not possible, consult a professional. For solid concrete and grout-filled concrete block, use ½-inch galvanized expansion or wedge anchors. For other types of masonry walls, epoxy anchors are best.

1 Prepare the Wall and Ledger
Outline the ledger location on the wall. Drill holes in the ledger for the bolts, taking into account the planned joist locations. Set the ledger against the wall, using 2 × 4s to hold it in place. Mark bolt hole locations on the wall with a nail.

2 Drill the Bolt Holes
Using a hammer drill and masonry bit, drill holes to the depth necessary for the bolts.

3 Attach the Ledger
Remove debris from the drilled holes with a shop vacuum. Prop the ledger back in place and insert an expansion bolt equipped with a washer in each hole. Tighten the bolts with a socket wrench. Apply a bead of silicone caulk to the joint between the wall and the ledger.

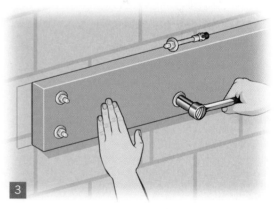

Using Epoxy Anchors

For a wall that requires epoxy anchors, place a glass vial of epoxy into each hole. Quickly insert a threaded rod into the hole. Let the epoxy harden, then slip the ledger over the rods, add washers, and attach the ledger with nuts.

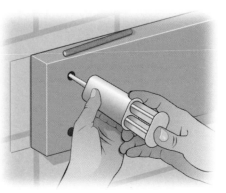

ATTACHING LEDGERS TO STUCCO WALLS

The procedure for attaching a ledger to a stucco wall is similar to that for a masonry wall. The big difference is that you need to make a secure connection to wood framing behind the stucco. Once you have located the rim joist in the house, follow the first two steps on page 83, but then use carriage bolts or lag screws (see page 81) instead of expansion bolts or epoxy anchors.

Because you are connecting the ledger to wood framing, plan to add flashing. Special preformed flashing is available for use on stucco walls. It has an extra lip on the top that can be inserted in a saw kerf. If you cannot find this product, use pliers to form a ¼-inch lip on regular flashing. Install the flashing as shown in Step 2.

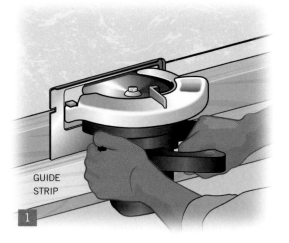

GUIDE STRIP

1

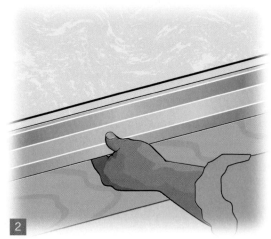

2

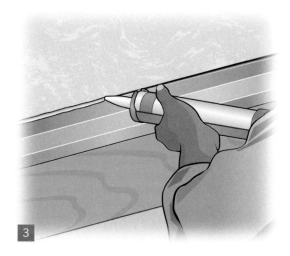

3

1 Cut a Kerf
After the ledger has been bolted into place, attach a temporary cutting guide on the ledger and put a masonry blade into your circular saw. Cut a kerf—a slot the width of your saw blade—³⁄₈ inch deep into the stucco.

2 Add Flashing
Squeeze silicone caulk into the kerf, and insert the flashing.

3 Caulk the Edge
With the flashing seated firmly in the kerf and along the ledger, add a bead of caulk along the top edge of the flashing.

preparing the layout

With the ledger installed and the site prepared (see page 58), you can begin to lay out your deck. A layout involves establishing the edges of the proposed deck framing with string lines, then using the string lines to locate the planned foundation holes. The work is not physically challenging, but it is critically important. An accurate layout is much easier to accomplish if you have a helper.

BUILDING BATTERBOARDS Batterboards are temporary attachment points for string lines. They are usually made with 1 × 4s or 2 × 4s, but you can use any scrap lumber available. Each batterboard consists of a crosspiece mounted on two stakes, which are cut with pointed bottoms and can be driven into the ground. To make the string lines level, the top of the crosspiece must be level with the top of the ledger. If you are building on a flat site, you can usually use 3-foot-long stakes. On a sloping site, however, the stakes will have to be longer. For a basic rectangular deck, you will need two pairs of batterboards. Typical construction details are shown in the illustration at lower left.

REFERENCING A HIGH DECK If you are building an elevated deck, it would not be fruitful to attach string lines to the ledger itself. Instead, attach a plumb bob to each outside edge of the ledger and drop it to near ground level. Set up batterboards so that the front edges of the crosspieces are plumb with the front face of the ledger. (In some cases, you can attach the crosspieces directly to the house.) To account for the end joists that will be attached to the ledger later, measure $1\frac{1}{2}$ inches outside the plumb bob on each side and make a mark. Drive a nail or screw at each mark to attach the layout string lines, which will represent the framed sides of the deck.

BATTERBOARD

CROSSPIECE

STAKE

REFERENCING A HIGH LEDGER

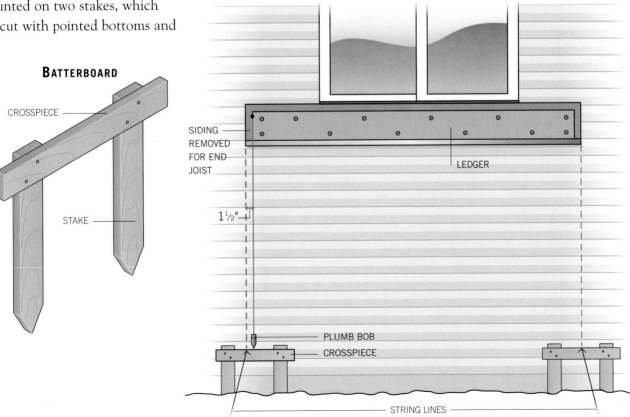

SIDING REMOVED FOR END JOIST

LEDGER

$1\frac{1}{2}$"

PLUMB BOB

CROSSPIECE

STRING LINES

laying out the site

Position the batterboards a few feet beyond the edges of the planned deck, drive a screw or nail into the ends of the ledger, and tie a length of string to each screw or nail 1½ inches from the ledger. The other ends of the string lines will be tied to screws or nails driven into the tops of the crosspieces after the lines are positioned. String lines can be used to mark the perimeter of the deck framing on all sides, or the positions of all foundation holes, or, as in the drawing at right, a combination of both. The goal is to position the string lines so that they are perfectly square, then to determine hole locations on the ground using a plumb bob. After the holes have been dug and the footings and piers poured, string lines can also be used to check the alignment of the posts and to position the beam properly.

Use the same approach when you are building a deck that is not just a rectangle. If you are building a deck that wraps around a corner of the house, run a single corner string line out from one of the ledgers, as shown. This creates two rectangles, each of which can be checked for square.

If you want to create a deck with mitered corners, begin by establishing a standard rectangular layout. Then measure back from the outside string line an equal distance on both sides and run another string line. Even more complicated decks can be laid out in similar fashion. Try to break the deck down into a series of rectangles, each of which can be checked easily for square.

LAYING OUT A RECTANGULAR DECK

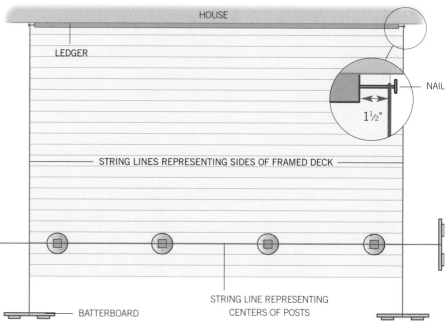

HOUSE

LEDGER

NAIL

1½"

STRING LINES REPRESENTING SIDES OF FRAMED DECK

BATTERBOARD

STRING LINE REPRESENTING CENTERS OF POSTS

LAYING OUT A WRAPAROUND DECK

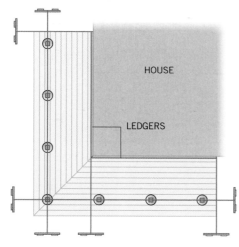

HOUSE

LEDGERS

LAYING OUT A DECK WITH MITERED CORNERS

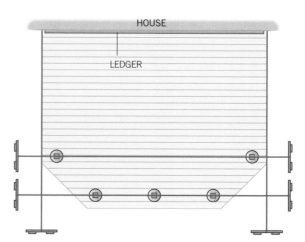

HOUSE

LEDGER

1 Run String Lines

For a rectangular deck, measure 1½ inches out from the ends of the ledger (to allow for the end joists) and run string lines to represent the sides of the deck framing. Set up another string line parallel to the house to represent the center line of the posts, piers, and footings. Check that the outside string line is the same distance from the ledger on both ends, then set the other two lines as close to square as possible.

2 Check for Square

With a helper, carefully measure the diagonals within the string lines. Adjust the strings as needed until the two measurements are identical. Drive screws into the tops of the crosspieces where the string lines meet them and tie the strings around the screws.

3 Locate Foundation Holes

With the string lines squared, measure in from the side strings to find the center of the outside footing holes. The exact distance will depend on your plans, including how far you plan to have the beam overhang the posts. Drop a plumb bob from the correct location, then have your helper drive a small stake into the ground. Continue measuring along the string line to find the other hole locations.

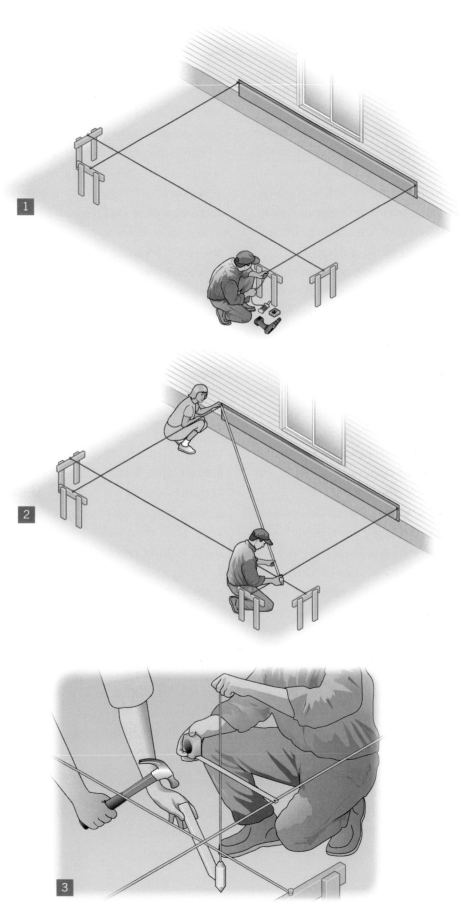

digging holes

Depending on the size of your deck and where you live, hole digging can range from quick and easy to down and dirty. Small rectangular decks can be built with three or four footings, while larger and more complex decks may need dozens. Decks built in warm climates may require footings no more than a foot deep, while in cold climates footings may have to reach a depth of four or five feet to get beneath the frost line. Your local building department should be able to tell you how deep footings must be. If you talk to experienced builders in your area, however, you may find that they pour footings even deeper, just to stay on the safe side.

Even when you use a power auger, digging holes is hard work. If you have a lot of deep holes to dig and are not looking for a tough physical workout, consider hiring someone to do the digging. Contractors who build fences and playgrounds often have powerful augers that can dig holes quickly and cleanly, and for a relatively modest cost.

Your building code may also specify the minimum width for footings and piers. If you are using cardboard tubes to form concrete piers, the method this book recommends, the width of the piers also depends on the size of the tubes. Dig a hole just wide enough for the tube to fit. If you are using 4 × 4 posts to support your deck, 8-inch-wide tubes are usually sufficient. For 6 × 6 posts, use 10- or 12-inch-wide tubes. If you plan to bury the posts in concrete (see page 78), you will have to dig wider holes to account for the space taken up by the posts.

Before you start digging, remove the string lines used to establish the layout. Unless they interfere with subsequent work, however, leave the batterboards in place. Later, you can reattach string lines to check the alignment of your deck frame.

You may not be required to create a flared footing, and in certain types of soil you do not need a footing that is any wider than the pier itself. In most cases, however, you will have to dig the bottom of the hole wider than the top.

Plan ahead for how to deal with the dirt you remove; you will need some later to backfill the holes. Pile the dirt away from the holes, preferably on a plastic tarp or in a wheelbarrow for easy cleanup.

MANUAL DIGGING

A garden spade may be the only tool you need to dig shallow holes, but to dig deeper than a foot you will want to use a posthole digger. A clamshell digger like that shown at right is effective in most types of soil. First remove the sod with a spade, then grasp the digger with the handles held together. Stab the digger into the ground and spread the handles apart. Carefully lift out the dirt. If you encounter large rocks or need to loosen hard soil, use a breaker bar, also called a digging bar. Cut tree roots with a pruning saw.

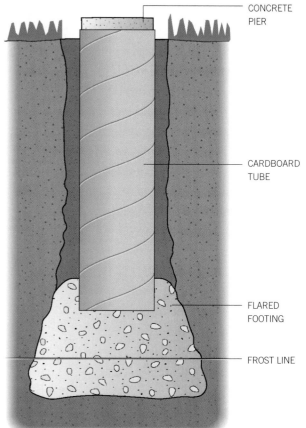

CONCRETE PIER

CARDBOARD TUBE

FLARED FOOTING

FROST LINE

an engine mounted on top of the auger; in this case, the operator stands on a small platform at the rear of the device. This tool must be anchored to the ground with chains and spikes. Be sure to get thorough instructions for any rental tool before you try to operate it. Alternatively, you may prefer to hire someone with an auger mounted on a truck, tractor, or skid-steer loader (bottom photo).

POWER HOLE DIGGERS

Power augers can remove dirt much faster than manual diggers. But that does not mean that they make the job easy. Check local rental stores to see what kinds of tools they carry, and choose an auger bit that matches the width of hole you want to dig. Make sure to wear ear and eye protection when working with a power auger of any type. Two-person power augers like the one at upper right are quite common. They are best used by two relatively strong people who can maintain a firm grip on the handles at all times.

If you are working alone, a flexible-shaft auger is a good choice. It has an engine separated from the auger, rather than sitting on top of it, which makes it lighter and easier to handle. You may need a trailer hitch to tow one of these tools home. A more powerful one-person auger features

working with concrete

One of the major decisions you need to make early on is whether or not to mix your own concrete. The choice is largely dependent on the number and depth of piers and footings you need, as well as your budget and available time. If you are not sure how to proceed, consider mixing the concrete yourself for one pier and footing, then decide if you can handle the effort for the others. Concrete can irritate your eyes, lungs, and skin, so it's best to wear gloves, long sleeves and long pants, a dust mask, and eye protection when you work with it.

Keep in mind that as soon as you add water to the dry mix, the clock starts ticking. Have tools, materials, and helpers in place ahead of time, and mix concrete in batches small enough to finish your work before the concrete starts hardening (about 90 minutes in cool weather, 45 minutes—or less—in warm weather). If you use a power mixer, read the instructions before you turn it on.

MIXING BY HAND

Concrete is a mix of Portland cement, sand, gravel, and water. Fortunately, you can buy pre-mixed bags of the dry ingredients and add your own water. One 80-pound bag should yield about 0.6 cubic feet of mixed concrete. You will need a plastic mortar tub or wheelbarrow, a mortar hoe (a shovel or garden hoe can also be used), and a source of water. A mortar tub is sturdier and less expensive; a wheelbarrow is easier to move around the site. When you mix concrete, measure out the amount of water specified on the bag, but pour in only about 90 percent of it at first, then add small amounts as described below. Avoid adding too much water. If the mixture becomes runny, with small pools of water forming on the surface, you will need to add another full bag of dry ingredients and more water.

Empty a full bag of dry, premixed concrete into your mortar tub. If you try to use only a partial bag, you may not pour out the properly balanced mixture of ingredients. Mix the dry ingredients together, then pour about 90 percent of the suggested amount of water into a small crater in the middle. Pull dry ingredients into the water with the hoe, and mix carefully.

As you mix the concrete, add small amounts of water at a time, and mix each addition in thoroughly before adding more. When you can form a small pile of concrete that holds its shape, the mixture is ready to use. Be careful not to add too much water; if you do, the mix will look wet, with pools forming on the surface. Adding a partial bag of dry mix to fix the problem is not recommended, because the proportion of ingredients may not be right.

POWER MIXING

A rented electric or gas-powered mixer can be used with premixed concrete, but you may find it more economical (if a bit more complicated) to mix your own dry ingredients. Use a shovel to mix one part Portland cement, two parts sand, and three parts coarse gravel, then slowly add water until you achieve the right consistency. Turn off the power whenever you check the mixture. Some power mixers can be emptied right into the hole.

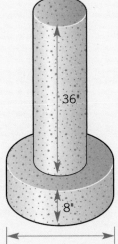

CONCRETE DELIVERY

If you need a large amount of concrete, your best option is to have it delivered in a commercial truck. Concrete is ordered in cubic yards (a cubic yard equals 27 cubic feet), so you will have to calculate how much you need very carefully before ordering. Tell the supplier you are using the concrete for deck footings. When the truck arrives, you should have a couple of helpers ready to go to work immediately. You will probably need to unload concrete into wheelbarrows, which need to be emptied quickly into holes and refilled. If you keep the truck waiting, you may incur extra charges and the concrete may harden.

Left: With a power mixer you can reduce physical exertion. You can also save money by buying dry ingredients separately and mixing them yourself, but be sure to measure the relative proportions carefully.

Above: If you order ready-mixed concrete from a supplier, be ready to go to work as soon as the truck arrives. Plan to have helpers and extra wheelbarrows available. Some companies will also pour the concrete for you for an additional fee.

PIER
$(4" \times 4") \times 36" \times 3.14 =$
1,808.64 CUBIC INCHES

FOOTING
$(8" \times 8") \times 8" \times 3.14 =$
1,607.68 CUBIC INCHES

TOTAL FOR PIER AND FOOTING
$1,808.64 + 1,607.68 =$
3,416.32 CUBIC INCHES
3,416.32 CUBIC INCHES ÷
1,728 = 1.98 CUBIC FEET

8" DIAMETER (4" RADIUS)

36"

8"

16" DIAMETER (8" RADIUS)

Estimating Concrete Needs

When ordering or mixing concrete, you should know how much you need, and that requires some work with a calculator. For estimating purposes, figure the size of a flared footing as though it were an equivalently sized cylinder. To determine the amount of concrete in each footing and pier (or for any cylinder), first use the following formula: radius^2 × inches of depth × 3.14 = cubic inches. Then convert cubic inches to cubic feet as described below.

In the example, the pier contains 1,808.64 cubic inches and the footing another 1,607.68 cubic inches, for a total of 3,416.32. Divide this total by the number of cubic inches in one cubic foot (1,728) to reach the total of 1.98 cubic feet for each pier and footing combination (all figures here are rounded to no more than two decimal places). Multiply that figure by the number of footings for the deck to find the total amount of concrete required.

preparing footings and piers

Footings and piers are designed to support the weight of a deck through all types of weather and stress. The following steps demonstrate the use of waxed cardboard tubes for making concrete piers. These tubes may be required by your building code, especially if the local soils are sandy or loose. But they are convenient and practical in all circumstances. They create smooth-sided piers that resist uplift caused by frost; make it easier to estimate how much concrete you will need; and hold moisture in the curing concrete longer, resulting in stronger piers.

This is a good time to double-check your building code and permit. Under some codes, you may be required to have the footings inspected before making the piers, or you may need to add several inches of gravel to the bottom of each footing before adding concrete. Be sure to have sufficient rebar cut to length, as well as anchor bolts or post bases on hand, as they must be added to the concrete while it is still wet (see pages 95–96).

1 Pour the Footings

Sometimes the footings and piers can be poured simultaneously, in which case you can skip this step. But if your footings need to be inspected you should begin here. As described on pages 78–79, the hole for the footings should be below the frost line, as large as required by code (typically 16 inches in diameter and 8 inches deep for 8-inch-wide piers), and flared. Shovel or pour concrete into the hole until it reaches the top of the flared section. Take care not to disturb dirt on the sides of the hole.

2 Cut the Tubes

Cardboard form tubes are sold in lengths up to 12 feet. In most cases, you will need to cut them to the length you require. (The length will vary depending on whether you are seating the tube into a wet footing or pouring the footing and pier at the same time; see Step 3.) Tubes can be cut with a handsaw, but the job will go quicker if you use a reciprocating saw. Make square cuts and cut the tubes long enough so they all extend the same distance—at least 2 inches—above the ground. Measure and cut tubes for each hole individually, as hole depths are likely to vary by a few inches.

3A

3B

3 Set the Tubes in Place

Set the tubes in their respective holes. If you have already poured footings and the concrete is still wet, push the tubes an inch or two into the footings. Use a level to ensure that the tubes are plumb in the holes and level at the top. Begin backfilling by shoveling dirt into the hole around the outside of the tube. When 6 to 8 inches of dirt have been placed in the hole, tamp the dirt with a piece of wood. The dirt needs to be firm, but do not pound so hard that you damage the tube. Continue with this routine until the hole is filled, checking the tube's position periodically with a level.

If you are pouring footings and piers simultaneously, you need to lift the tubes so that the bottom of each is even with the top of the flared footing section; the tubes can be suspended with braces, as shown in the lower picture. Once a tube is level and plumb, drive two screws through each brace into the side of the tube. Do not backfill around suspended tubes.

If the batterboards are still in place and you would like to be sure that the tubes are centered and aligned properly, put the string lines back in place. Drop a plumb bob from the line at each of the planned hole locations, and adjust each tube so that the plumb bob is centered.

Setting Posts in Concrete

Decks are most often built with posts set on top of solid concrete piers, a technique that allows you to use shorter posts, keeps the wood out of the ground, provides for easy repair in the event a post is damaged, and offers a greater margin of error. There are occasions, however, when it makes sense to set the post itself in the ground in concrete. Done correctly, this approach produces a more rigid frame, which may be necessary for a freestanding or an elevated deck, and required where earthquakes are common. The post can be set in a hole that is partially filled with concrete, then topped off with soil or gravel (see page 78), or, for even greater stability, the hole can be filled to the top with concrete. For best results, use a treated post and set the uncut end in the ground. The earth itself can serve as the form for concrete, or you can set the post in a large cardboard tube. The posts must be carefully plumbed, aligned, and braced (as shown here) before you pour any concrete.

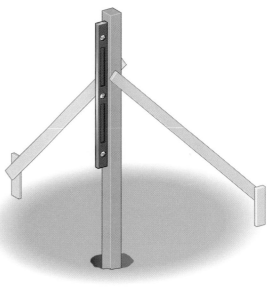

4 Pour the Concrete

If you mixed your own concrete, shovel it into the bottom of the hole. Use a fairly narrow shovel or garden spade so that you can fit the end of the shovel into the tube. A helper can tip a wheelbarrow close enough to the hole that you can scoop concrete directly into the tube. Fill the bottom 2 feet of the tube with concrete and work the concrete as shown in Step 5 before continuing to fill the tube. If you are having concrete delivered, ask the company if they offer the option of having the concrete pumped directly into the holes through a hose. Though you will probably pay more for this service, the work will progress much faster and with little physical exertion. Otherwise, have a couple of helpers on hand, along with multiple wheelbarrows, and be prepared to pour concrete without interruption until all the tubes are filled. Fill 2 feet of a tube at a time before working the concrete as shown in Step 5.

5 Work the Concrete

After filling a tube with about 2 feet of concrete, use a piece of wood to stir and agitate the mix to remove any air pockets. Work the stick up and down, then add more concrete and agitate again, continuing until the tube is just slightly overfilled.

6 Add the Rebar

As soon as a tube has been filled with concrete, add some reinforcement in the form of rebar. Check your local code for requirements, but as a general rule plan to use two pieces of #4 rebar for each pier and footing combination. Cut the rebar so that it will rest 2 to 3 inches below the surface of the pier when the base touches the bottom of the footing. Push the rods into the wet mix, spaced about 2 inches from the cardboard tube so that they will not interfere with the anchor bolt or post base (Step 8).

7 Smooth the Surface

With the tube still just slightly overfilled with concrete, use a short 2 × 4 to level and smooth the surface. Move the 2 × 4 from side to side in a sawing motion. Fill any low spots with additional concrete. (For clarity, the tubes here and in Step 8 are shown without bracing; the same two steps apply for braced tubes, and the bracing should be left in place for both steps.)

8 Set the Anchor Bolts

With the concrete smooth but still wet, insert an anchor bolt into each pier; the bolt will later be used to secure a post base. Alternatively, you can use one-piece post bases if they are required or if you prefer (see page 96). With either approach, the important point to keep in mind is that your goal is to have posts aligned perfectly so that they can support a very inflexible beam. Although the bases that attach to anchor bolts allow for some small adjustments, you should still set the bolts as carefully as possible. If your batterboards are still in place, set up the string lines again to help guide you. Otherwise, use a board long enough to span from one pier to the next to help with alignment and spacing. Insert the bent end of the anchor bolt into the concrete. Allow 1 inch of the threaded end to rest above the surface, and make certain that the bolt is perfectly plumb.

Project continues next page >

Working with Rebar "Rebar," the abbreviated name for reinforcing bar, is a special steel rod that substantially increases the strength of concrete. With its ribbed surface, the rebar bonds with concrete to reduce the chances for settling and cracking. Rebar is designated by a numbering system that identifies its diameter; #4 rebar is four-eighths (or one-half) of an inch thick. Rebar is very strong and hard to cut with hand tools. The best tool for the job is a metal-cutting blade in a reciprocating saw. Clamp the bar to a workbench or a piece of lumber. Use caution. A freshly cut piece of steel can be very hot, so let it cool before you touch it.

9 Let It Cure

With all the anchor bolts or one-piece post bases in place, it is time to take a break. Let the concrete cure for at least two days before you start setting posts. The concrete should stay damp while curing. Keep it covered with plastic sheeting if the air is very dry. Although you may be in a hurry to keep working, concrete should be allowed to cure slowly. For suspended tubes, leave the braces on until the concrete is cured, then backfill as described in Step 3. Once the concrete is cured, remove the exposed portion of the cardboard tubing, as shown.

Choosing Post Bases

Your building code may specify the type of post base to use for your deck. A one-piece base with fins, like that in the illustration at right, offers the strongest connection and may be required. With one-piece post bases, take extra care to ensure that they are aligned before the concrete cures, since they cannot be adjusted later. If the posts do not line up, the beam will not be properly supported. If you have a choice, however, you might find adjustable post bases to be more forgiving. With the latter, you insert only anchor bolts into the wet concrete, as shown in Step 8. Once the concrete has cured, the rest of the hardware can be added (see page 100). If your anchor bolts are a little bit out of alignment with each other, adjustable bases allow you to shift the hardware enough so that all of the posts can be lined up.

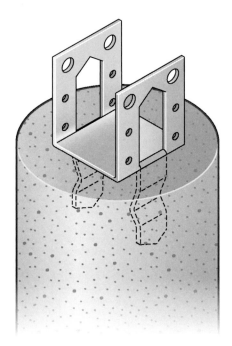

framing

AS THIS CHAPTER OPENS, YOUR WORK SITE HAS *little more to show for itself than a group of disconnected concrete piers sticking out of the ground. By the time the chapter concludes, however, you will be able to admire the fully framed skeleton of a new deck.* ■ *A deck frame is composed primarily of three components: posts, beams, and joists. This chapter will show you how to prepare and install each of these parts for a typical deck, as well as how to tackle more advanced techniques such as framing around the corner of your house and building openings in the deck. A special feature highlights the process of building a deck at ground level.* ■ *Much of the framing will be out of sight once the deck is complete, which is another way of saying that it will be hard to fix any errors you make. So while looks may not count for much when framing, quality certainly does. Take a little extra time to build a frame for your deck that will last.*

setting posts

Posts give decks most of their elevation. If you are building a high deck, you will need long posts. If, however, you are building a very low deck, you may not need any posts at all (see pages 114–115).

Most decks are built with 4 × 4 posts, but 4 × 6s and 6 × 6s are often used as well, and even larger posts are sometimes required. Some people think that 4 × 4s look too weak and skinny on a high deck, even when they are structurally sound. Feel free to use larger posts than are required if you prefer a bulkier appearance. Post size is also related to how far the beam spans from one post to the next (see pages 50–51).

Posts must be plumb, well secured, and cut to the right length. They are rarely the same length on a deck, however, since piers are usually not perfectly level with each other. So it is best to avoid cutting posts to their anticipated length before setting them in place. To determine the length of each post, use one of two methods. The first, which may be easiest with short posts, is to set the post in the post base, check it for plumb, and mark the desired post height using a level or a water level. Remove the post, cut it to length with a power miter saw, and then attach it to the post base.

Posts are a prominent visual feature of many decks. With good planning, they can be transformed from merely functional components into decorative design features.

The more typical approach, which is presented in numbered steps on pages 100–101, is to put all the posts in position, brace them so that they are plumb, attach them to the post bases, and then mark and cut them in place.

If you are using pressure-treated posts, it is best to place the uncut ends into the post bases. But it is even more important that the bottom surface of every post be flat and square. Use a small square to check the ends of each post. If neither end is square, cut just enough off the bottom to make it square, then coat the cut surface with a water-repellent preservative before setting it in place.

FRAMING OPTIONS

The most common means of joining posts to beams is to have the beam rest directly on top of the posts, to which it is secured by special connectors. This is also the strongest connection, and usually the easiest construction technique.

Decks are sometimes built with posts that extend above the deck surface to serve double duty as railing posts. This requires that notches be cut carefully into the posts to fit the beam. This approach is feasible only when using posts that are at least 6 × 6.

Avoid building your deck with the beams bolted to the sides of extended posts (box, right), even though your building code may not explicitly bar this approach. It is not a recommended practice, since the entire connection relies on fasteners to support the load.

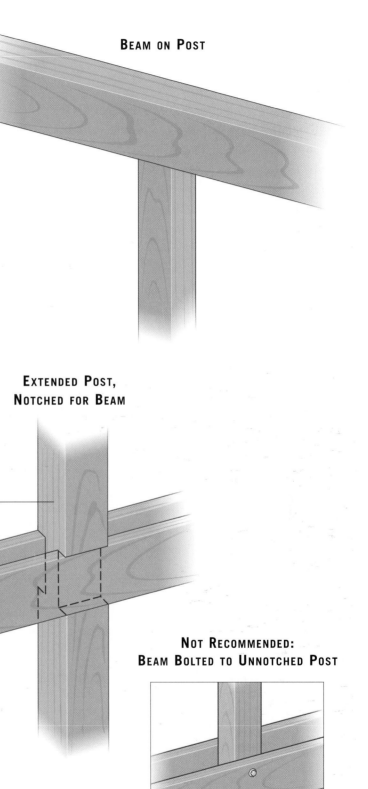

BEAM ON POST

EXTENDED POST, NOTCHED FOR BEAM

6 × 6 POST (MINIMUM)

NOT RECOMMENDED: BEAM BOLTED TO UNNOTCHED POST

1 Brace the Posts

If you are using adjustable post bases, first attach the hardware to the anchor bolts. (Fixed one-piece bases will already be in place.) Set a post in each post base. Drive one nail through the base and into the post just far enough to hold the post in place; you may have to remove and reposition the nail later. Plumb the post by checking it on adjacent sides with a carpenter's level. If you are working alone, it may be easier to attach a post level (inset) to the post to leave both hands free to continue working. With the post plumb, attach temporary braces to two adjacent sides. Use 1 × 4s for braces, securing them with screws to stakes in the ground and with clamps to the posts.

POST LEVEL

2 Attach the Posts

With all the posts plumbed and aligned (see below), drive nails through the post bases into the posts. Use only the nails recommended by the manufacturer of the post bases you are using. If you are using adjustable bases, be sure that the nuts on the anchor bolts are tightened snugly, but not so tightly that you strip the threads.

If your batterboards are still set up, you can run a string line to help align the posts. Since this string line relates to the sides of the posts, rather than their centers, reposition the string on each crosspiece by one-half the thickness of the post.

Stay in Line

If the batterboards have been removed, you could set a couple of them back in place quickly. Just be certain that the string line is perfectly parallel with the ledger, so that it's the same distance from the ledger on both sides.

BATTERBOARD   STRING LINE

3 Find the Post Height

The first step in determining post height is to mark each post at the spot that is level with the top of the ledger. Place a carpenter's level on the straightest 2 × 4 you can find. Set one end of the 2 × 4 on top of the ledger, then adjust the other side along the post until it is level. Mark the post at the bottom of the 2 × 4. If the posts are too far from the ledger for this method, use a water level as shown on page 75.

4 Mark the Cut Line

With the height of the top of the ledger now marked on each post, you need to determine where to cut the posts. Place a short piece of joist stock under the mark on one post, then mark the post again. If the joists will attach on top of (rather than beside) the beam, set a piece of beam stock under this line, and again mark the bottom. This final line is the height at which you need to cut the post. (Of course, you can also measure down the post with a tape measure rather than lumber, but using the latter is a bit more foolproof.) You can repeat this process at each post, but it might be quicker to transfer the cut line from post to post using a 2 × 4 and a level.

5 Cut the Post

Use a square to transfer the cut line to all four sides of each post. Set the blade of your circular saw to cut as deeply as possible. For a 4 × 4 post you will need to cut the post twice, on opposite sides. For a 6 × 6 post, cut along the line on all four sides, then finish the cut with a reciprocating saw or handsaw.

installing beams

The beam, or girder, is the structural member that spans from post to post. Modest-sized decks typically are built with a single beam, but larger decks may require two or more. There are several ways to make and mount a beam. Regardless of the style of beam you use, you can be sure that it will be heavy. Plan to have a helper or two available when you need to lift a beam into place.

POST-TO-BEAM CONNECTIONS The strongest and most secure way to install a beam is directly on top of the posts. In most cases, the easiest way to connect the beam to the posts is with galvanized post caps. Post caps are available to fit most typical post-and-beam configurations, even where the beam is narrower than the post. The top three illustrations at right show some of the more common connections.

Beams and posts can also be fastened together with wood cleats made from framing lumber, which must be bolted to both members. Although the cleat method requires a bit more work, some people prefer the look of wood to less attractive metal caps, especially when the connection will be fairly visible.

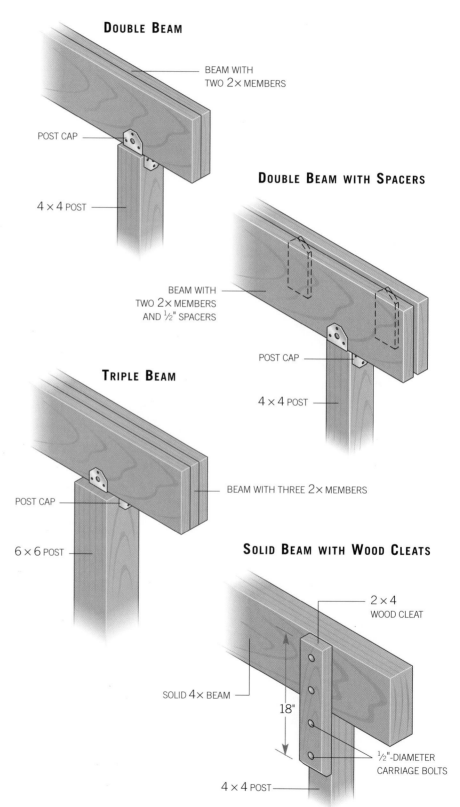

DOUBLE BEAM

BEAM WITH
TWO 2× MEMBERS

POST CAP

4 × 4 POST

DOUBLE BEAM WITH SPACERS

BEAM WITH
TWO 2× MEMBERS
AND ½" SPACERS

POST CAP

4 × 4 POST

TRIPLE BEAM

POST CAP

6 × 6 POST

BEAM WITH THREE 2× MEMBERS

SOLID BEAM WITH WOOD CLEATS

2 × 4
WOOD CLEAT

SOLID 4× BEAM

18"

½"-DIAMETER
CARRIAGE BOLTS

4 × 4 POST

CONSTRUCTING A BUILT-UP BEAM

When the design calls for placing a beam made of two 2× boards over 4 × 4 posts, a very common arrangement, many deck builders like to construct the beam with ½-inch spacers between the boards. This produces a beam that fits perfectly on top of the post, since 2× lumber is 1½ inches thick. Additionally, the spacers allow water to drain through the boards, which prolongs the life of the beam. Use pressure-treated plywood for the spacers. Note, however, that if your plans call for a single 4× beam, which would be 3½ inches thick, this built-up beam will not be sufficient. Structurally, it amounts only to a 3-inch-thick beam.

You can also make a built-up beam without spacers. Attach boards to each other with 10d nails driven through both sides at least every 16 inches. Apply a bead of silicone caulk to the joint between the boards to keep any moisture from penetrating.

PLAN THE JOINTS When buying stock to use as beams, plan to have each joint fall directly on the center of a post. The adjoining sections of the beam should be cut as squarely as possible to provide maximum bearing on the post. With built-up beams, stagger the joints between boards, still making sure that each joint falls on the center of a post.

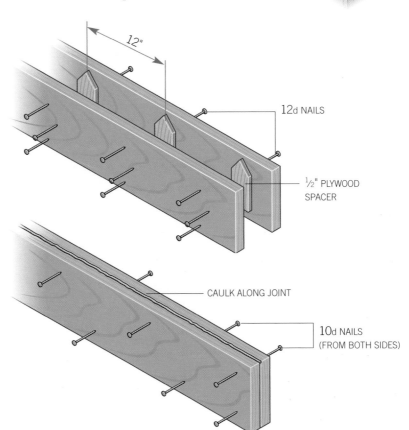

BEAM

JOINT

POST

12"

12d NAILS

½" PLYWOOD SPACER

CAULK ALONG JOINT

10d NAILS
(FROM BOTH SIDES)

Crown Side Up Lumber that is used for beams and joists nearly always has a visible crown, or arch, as shown below. Install both beams and joists with the crown facing up. That way, once the deck load begins pressing down on the crown, it will level itself out. In constructing a built-up beam, make sure the crown on both boards faces the same way (see Step 1, page 104).

SETTING UP THE BEAM

1 Find the Crown
Locate and mark the crown for the beam. You can usually spot the crown by sighting down the edges of the board. Alternatively, set the board on edge on a flat surface, such as a concrete driveway or garage floor. You might want to mark the board with an arrow clearly indicating the crown. Always install the board crown side up. When building a built-up beam, sight down each board, mark for the crown, and attach the boards with both crowns up.

2 Assemble the Beam
It is smart to build a beam that is a bit longer than needed. That way you can shift the joists slightly to square up the frame if necessary. Once that is done, the beam can be cut to finished length. Assemble a built-up beam on a pair of sawhorses. Attach spacers to one board every 12 inches, then set the other board on top and drive three 12d nails at each spacer location. Flip the two boards over and repeat the nailing pattern. Stagger joints between boards, and secure each joint with a spacer and nails.

3 Set the Beam in Place

If possible, position or reattach string lines representing the sides of the deck (see page 86). Align the beam with the string lines at each end. If you made the beam a bit longer than needed, overlap the string an equal distance on each end. Lifting a typical deck beam overhead may require three or more relatively strong workers. The safest way to install a high beam is to use scaffolding (see page 73), which will also make joist installation much easier. If you are concerned about a heavy beam tipping over as you try to set it in place, temporarily attach 2 × 4s to a couple of posts so that the 2 × 4s stick up by 8 to 10 inches. Set post caps on the other posts and fasten them to the posts with a single nail each. Remember to install the beam with the crown side up.

4 Attach the Beam to the Posts

With the beam safely in place, add post caps to any additional posts that need them. Check the beam's alignment with the string lines. You can also check the alignment by measuring the diagonals; provided that the beam is equally spaced from the ledger on both sides, the beam will be properly positioned when the diagonals are identical. Once you are confident that the beam is squared up with the ledger, attach the post caps to the posts and the beam with nails as recommended by the post cap manufacturer.

bracing

Bracing is a way to stiffen and strengthen a deck's substructure with diagonal boards. Bracing is required on some decks, so check your local building code for specific guidelines. Even if it is not mandated, as a general rule it is wise to add bracing to decks with 4 × 4 posts more than 4 feet high and 6 × 6 posts more than 8 feet high. Freestanding decks over 3 feet high also should be braced.

POST-TO-BEAM BRACING

The most common type of bracing is called Y bracing. The simplest form of Y bracing, and the style that many codes demand, has one 2 × 4 on each side of the post and beam (top, right). Carriage bolts are used to secure the connections. Cut the ends of the 2 × 4s plumb, as shown, so that water and dirt will not have a place to accumulate. A single 2 × 4 brace can also be used on the sides of the deck to tie posts to joists, once the latter are installed.

Many people prefer the look of solid 4 × 4 braces (right), which can be used with solid beams. The ends must be cut at 45-degree angles, and lag screws secure the braces to the bottom of the beam and the side of the post.

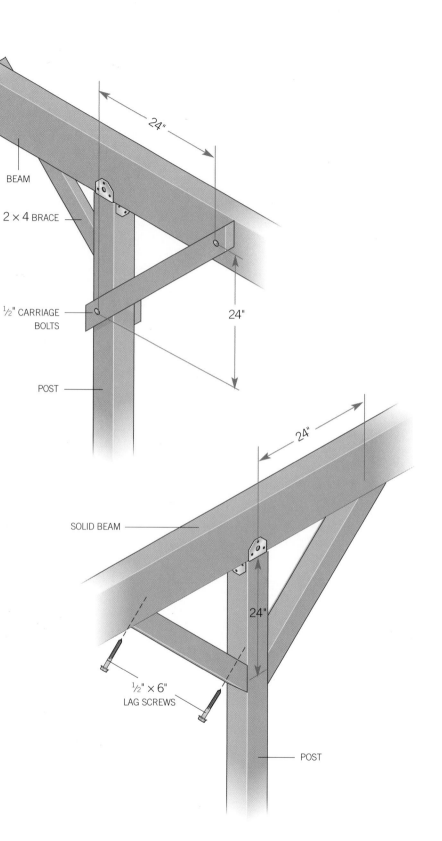

BEAM

2 × 4 BRACE

½" CARRIAGE BOLTS

POST

24"

24"

SOLID BEAM

½" × 6" LAG SCREWS

24"

24"

POST

POST-TO-POST BRACING

Post-to-post bracing is often necessary for decks with high posts (such as those built over a steep slope); for decks with long spans between beams; or along the sides of decks where post-to-joist bracing is not feasible. You can normally use 2 × 4s for braces up to 8 feet long. Make longer braces from 2 × 6s. Use $\frac{1}{2}$-inch carriage bolts at all connections. X-shaped bracing also requires blocking between the crossing braces.

Local codes may stipulate the type of post-to-post bracing you can use. If not, choose the style that looks best to you.

PARALLEL BRACES

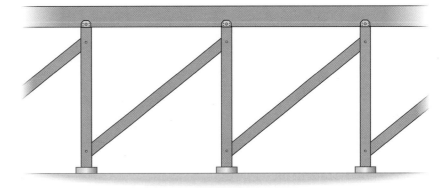

BRACES ALTERNATING SIDES AND DIRECTIONS

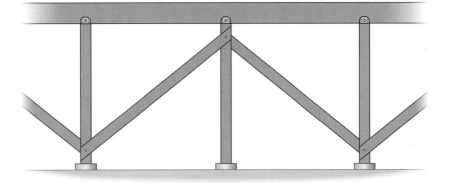

V-SHAPED BRACES

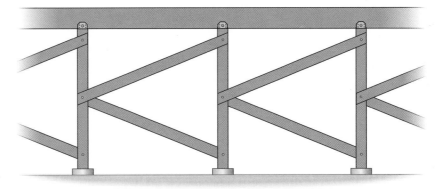

X-SHAPED BRACES

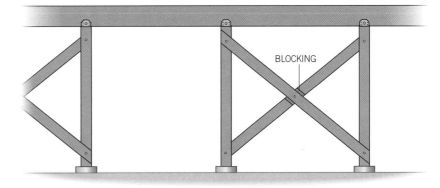

BLOCKING

hanging joists

Joists are the structural members that support the decking. The size of the joists, as well as their span and spacing, should be determined in the planning stage. Joist spacing is commonly given as "on center" (o.c.), which means the spacing is measured from the center of one joist to the center of the next one. The most common joist spacings are 12, 16, and 24 inches on center. The illustration at upper right provides an example of how a plan drawing would indicate that joists should be installed 16 inches on center. Note that the distance from the end joist to the first intermediary joist is often less than 16 inches on center, to allow decking boards to reach or overhang the outside edge of the end joist.

Joists are attached at one end to the ledger with joist hangers. At the other end, they typically overhang the beam for a foot or two and are attached to it with toenails or metal fasteners known as hurricane or seismic ties. In some deck designs, joists are installed at the same level as beams, and are attached to both the ledger and the beam with joist hangers.

Choose joist stock carefully. Look for the straightest boards available, and always install them with the crown side up (see page 103). Although you may have to square the ends where they meet the ledger, individual joists do

not need to be cut to length at this stage; cut them only after all the joists are installed. If your design calls for double joists (see page 48), do not disrupt the regular on-center spacing. Instead, as shown in the illustration above, treat the center of the gap between the double joists as a single joist center.

JOIST HANGERS Joist hangers are available to fit almost any size joist imaginable. Always use joist hangers that are made specifically for the size joists you are using, and attach them with the type and quantity of fasteners specified by the manufacturer.

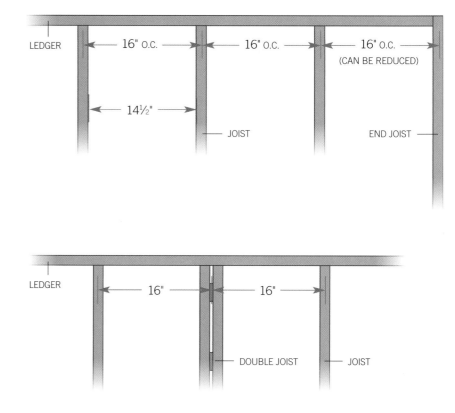

1½" joist hanger

3½" joist hanger

PUTTING THE JOISTS IN PLACE

1 Attach the End Joists
Begin your joist installation with the end joists. As discussed on page 80, it is best to design your deck and ledger so that these joists cover the ends of the ledger. The joists should be attached on both sides. On the outside, drill three pilot holes through the joist and into the ledger to prevent splitting, then fasten with 16d nails. Attach reinforcing angle brackets to the inside corners.

2 Trim the Beam
Square up the end joists at the ledger and at the beam, either by using string lines or by measuring the diagonals. The end of the beam should be flush with the outer edges of the joists. If you need to cut the beam, use a square to mark the vertical cut line, then make the cut with a circular saw or reciprocating saw. Trim the bottom corner at an angle for a nicer look.

3 Lay Out the Ledger
Before installing the intermediary joists, measure and mark the ledger for the location of each joist. Begin the layout from the edge of the deck. Hook a tape measure over the outside face of an end joist, then mark along the top of the ledger according to the planned on-center spacing. If your joists are to be installed 16 inches on center, mark the ledger every 16 inches. You can reduce (but not extend) the spacing to the end joists if it better suits the length of the decking boards you are buying. Then take a framing square and make a vertical line on the ledger at each mark, as shown. This line represents the edge of a joist, so you need to mark an X alongside it to indicate where to place the joist.

4 Lay Out the Rim Joist

The rim joist (also called a header joist) covers the ends of the other joists. Laying out the rim joist is an optional step, but it does come in handy when you need to check to see that the joists are square. On a basic rectangular deck, the rim joist is the same length as the width of the deck. Use the straightest board you can find and cut it to length. Hook your tape measure over an edge, and mark the joist spacing along the inside face. Mark vertical lines and Xs, as in Step 3.

5 Attach Joist Hangers

To create a flat surface for your decking, the tops of all the joists must be level with the top of the ledger, and the only way you can achieve that is to install joist hangers in just the right position. Carpenters sometimes use a short piece of joist stock as a guide, but using the jig shown here is easier and more accurate (see below for instructions on making one). Align the 2 × 4 in the jig with the layout line on the ledger, then tap the two 10d nails on top into the ledger just enough to hold the jig in place. Slide a joist hanger onto the 2 × 4, fasten one side to the ledger, then fasten the other side.

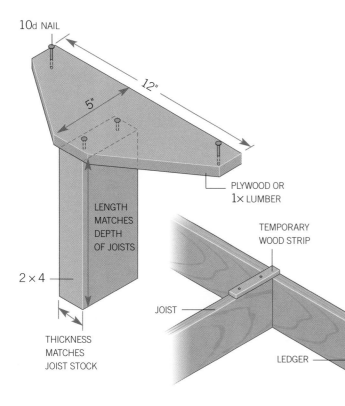

10d NAIL

12"

5"

PLYWOOD OR 1× LUMBER

LENGTH MATCHES DEPTH OF JOISTS

2 × 4

THICKNESS MATCHES JOIST STOCK

TEMPORARY WOOD STRIP

JOIST

LEDGER

Simplifying Joist Installation

Installing joist hangers and joists is another job in which three hands are much better than two. If you do not have a helper available, you will almost certainly want to use a jig. To make the jig shown in Step 5, cut a 2 × 4 to the exact depth of the joists, and fasten it to a 12-by-5-inch piece of plywood or 1× lumber cut as shown. Since 2× lumber can vary slightly in thickness, make sure the 2 × 4 is exactly as thick as the joist stock.

Another trick for installing joist hangers is to attach a wood strip to the top of the joist with just enough of an overhang so that it rests on the ledger. Set the joist in place, then attach the joist hanger (this will be easier if you have a helper holding the joist steady). Remove the wood strip.

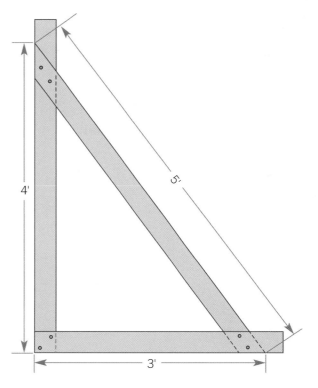

6 Attach Joists to the Ledger

Set the joist into the joist hanger. Use a homemade wood square (see sidebar below) or a framing square to ensure that the joists are perpendicular to the ledger. After you have installed a few joists, you can also use the laid-out rim joist to check for square, if you chose to mark it up in Step 4. Bear in mind that no matter how accurately you install joist hangers, you will still be faced with joists that are a bit larger or smaller than others. If you wind up with a joist that sits too high in its hanger, trim a bit off the bottom with a chisel. Similarly, if a joist is too low, shim the bottom. When you are satisfied with the fit, drive nails through the joist hanger into the joist on both sides.

7 Attach the Joists to the Beam

With the joists attached to the ledger, it is time to attach them to the beam. You should do this only after you are sure the joists are square. An easy way to check the alignment is to lay the rim joist on top of the joists, with the layout marks on the rim joist lined up with the joists. Building codes often permit you to fasten the joist to the beam with three 8d or 10d nails driven at an angle (that is, toenailed). For added strength, use seismic or hurricane ties, as shown here, or rafter ties.

Project continues next page >

Keeping Things Straight

Joists should be perpendicular to the ledger and also parallel to each other. One simple way to get each joist quickly squared up is to make an oversized framing square, which is really nothing more than a physical expression of the "3-4-5" principle explained on page 75. Make the square out of 1 × 4s, paying attention to the dimensions noted in the illustration. When you install a joist, set the 3-foot-long side against the ledger, and use the 4-foot-long edge to align the joist.

8 Lay Out the Joist Ends

To cut the joists to length, first measure out from the ledger along each end joist and mark the desired length. Snap a chalk line between these marks across the tops of the joists. Use a square and a pencil to transfer the chalk marks to the face of each joist. Note that even if you are not planning to cut the joists, it is still wise to snap a chalk line and see that the joists line up properly; if they do not, trim those that are too long.

9 Trim the Joists

Cut each joist to length with a circular saw. Cut carefully so that the ends are straight and plumb.

10 Attach the Rim Joist

Aligning the top of the rim joist with the tops of the other joists can be tricky. To make the process easier, tack pieces of scrap lumber to the bottoms of a couple of joists to give the rim joist a place to rest while you work. If you laid out the rim joist as suggested in Step 4, it will be easier to keep it properly aligned with the joists. Have a helper apply pressure to align the joists, then drive three 12d nails through the face of the rim joist and into each of the joist ends, working from one end to the other. To avoid splitting the ends of the rim joist, drill pilot holes before driving the nails into the end joists. After nailing the rim joist to the end joists, attach angle brackets to the inside, as you did at the ledger. Alternatively, to keep the face of the rim joist free of visible nail heads, you can attach the intermediary joists with joist hangers instead.

SPECIAL CIRCUMSTANCES

Depending on your deck design and local codes, you may need to use the specialized installation methods shown below. Aligning twisted joists also calls for special techniques.

DIFFICULT BOARDS When you cannot align a joist by hand, use a pipe clamp. In the photograph, the clamp is pulling a joist into vertical alignment, but you can also use a clamp to force the tops of joists into horizontal alignment or to pull a joist closer to the rim joist. In the latter case, attach one end of the clamp to a nail driven into the top of the joist and the other end to the face of the rim joist.

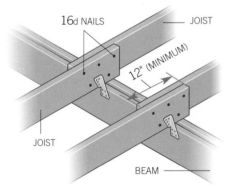

OVERLAPPING JOISTS Larger decks typically require more than one beam, and this, in turn, generally means you will need to use two joists to span the distance from the ledger to the rim joist. The best way to handle this transition is to have the joists overlap each other at the middle beam, as shown at left. Allow at least 12 inches of overlap, and secure the joists to each other with 16d nails. Note that this approach will result in the ledger and rim joist having different layouts. Rather than mirroring each other, as in the example on page 110, the joists at the rim will be offset by 1½ inches from the joists at the ledger.

BLOCKING Some building codes require the use of blocking (also called bracing) between the joists. Blocking can strengthen floors that have deep joists with spans of 10 feet or more. Check your building code for specific requirements. Blocking should be cut from joist stock. Snap a chalk line across the tops of joists, then install blocking on alternating sides of the line. Toenail the blocking with three 12d nails at each connection.

Blocking is staggered between joists to facilitate nailing.

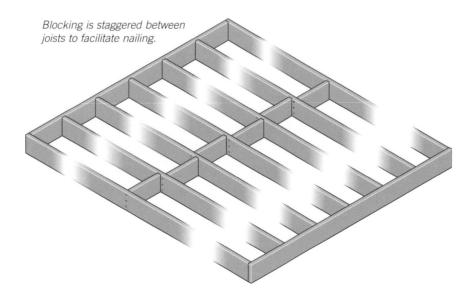

building a ground-level deck

ow decks are sometimes a choice and other times a necessity. If the floor of your house is close to the ground, if you need to keep a deck low to avoid an overhead obstacle, or if you just want to create a dry, flat, freestanding surface away from the house, the techniques on these two pages should offer a solution. A ground-level deck can also serve as the lowest part of a multilevel deck.

Bear in mind that you can usually lower the height of a deck by using smaller joists and beams, a change that requires you to reduce the beam span (by pouring more footings and piers) and reduce the joist spacing (by using more joists). Another strategy is to install joists on the same level as the beam, as shown below, by using joist hangers to attach the joists to the side, not the top, of the beam.

BEAM-TO-PIER FRAMING

One of the simplest ways to create a strong, secure deck at ground level is to build a normal deck, but without posts. The beams can be attached directly to the concrete piers using post bases sized for the beams (right).

For a low deck that is not attached to the house, plan to install two rows of piers (more for a larger deck) with identical beams installed along each row. Make the beams with double

2× members, with the inside board offset on each end by 1½ inches to create room and a nailing surface for the end joist. Attach joists with joist hangers on the inside faces of each beam. The illustration below shows a plan for a freestanding deck with very short beam and joist spans, requiring an intermediary beam, and 12-inch on-center joist spacing. This deck frame could be built with 2 × 6s, keeping it very close to the ground.

Beam-to-pier framing can also be used for decks attached to the house. Adjust the size of the beam or the height of the piers to align the frame with the ledger on the house.

LEDGER

JOIST   BEAM

JOIST HANGERS

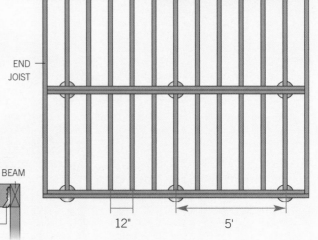

CONCRETE PIER   BEAM

END JOIST

12"   5'

A FLOATING DECK

The small platform deck shown below right in plan view requires no footings. The foundation is provided by two 4 × 6 timbers, which are partially buried in the ground. You may want to remove any sod from beneath the deck.

Dig parallel trenches about 6 inches deep for the timbers, then add about 4 inches of sand to each trench. Set the timbers on the sand (below). Then level the timbers by adding or removing sand. The timbers should be squared up, with both ends equally distant from each other. Mark a joist layout on each timber. Install the joists with two 12d toenails driven through each side into the beam. Trim the joist ends, if necessary, and attach the rim joists. Install 2 × 6 decking with 3-inch decking screws, spacing the boards with a 16d nail for drainage.

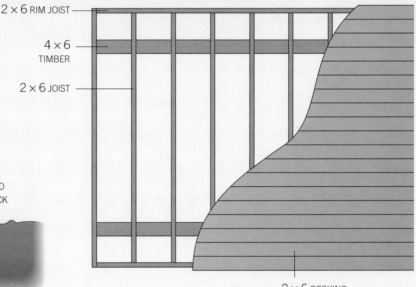

2 × 6 RIM JOIST

4 × 6 TIMBER

2 × 6 JOIST

2 × 6 DECKING

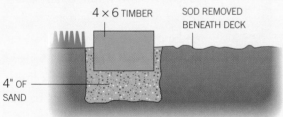

4 × 6 TIMBER

SOD REMOVED BENEATH DECK

4" OF SAND

Avoiding Short Posts

Decks built close to the ground often require very short posts. But posts under 10 inches in length, with nails securing fasteners at the top and bottom, are prone to splitting. You can usually design your way around short posts by increasing the beam size or raising the height of concrete piers. Either technique requires that the piers be level with each other, so make sure the tops of cardboard tubes are level before pouring any concrete.

Avoid using very short posts (1) by increasing the size of the beam (2) or installing higher concrete piers (3).

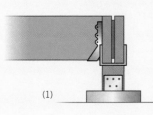

(1)

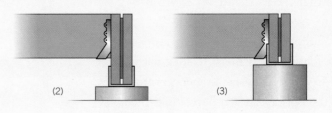

(2)   (3)

special framing techniques

Single-level rectangular decks are the easiest and quickest to build. But it does not necessarily take much extra effort to add some variety to this basic design. And some decks almost demand to be built with multiple levels, around a corner, or without damaging the health of a favorite tree. The remaining pages of this chapter show you how to handle these and other commonly encountered framing dilemmas. If you want to explore the more complex matter of incorporating curves into your deck, see pages 180–184.

CUTTING CORNERS

Angled corners are an easy way to avoid a boxy-looking deck. Although you can use any number of angles, it is smart to stick with 45-degree angles. To incorporate the options shown here, build the

deck as though it were a normal rectangle, then cut the framing to allow for the angle.

The short 45-degree corner shown below requires only two cuts in the framing. Set your circular saw at a $22\frac{1}{2}$-degree angle and cut the rim and end joists as close to plumb as you can. Cut a short filler piece with a $22\frac{1}{2}$-degree angle on each end and attach it with nails.

A larger angled corner requires cutting several joists. You can increase the size of the corner by maximizing the distance that the joists overhang the beam (check your building code for restrictions). In the example at lower left, the end and rim joists are cut at $22\frac{1}{2}$-degree angles, with a filler piece cut to fit and nailed in place. The two intermediary joists are cut at 45-degree angles and can be attached to the filler piece with skewed 45-degree joist hangers (inset, above). Snap a chalk line across the tops of the joists to guide your cutting.

For an even longer angled corner, you would need to install an angled beam to provide the necessary support.

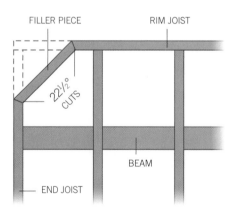

FILLER PIECE   RIM JOIST

$22\frac{1}{2}$ CUTS

BEAM

END JOIST

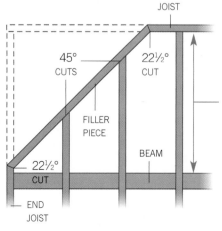

RIM JOIST

45° CUTS $22\frac{1}{2}$° CUT

FILLER PIECE

$22\frac{1}{2}$° CUT

BEAM

END JOIST

LONG JOIST CANTILEVER (ALLOWS FOR A LONG ANGLED CORNER)

TURNING CORNERS

Wrapping a deck around the corner of a house offers many benefits, usually with minimal added effort. It can allow you to take advantage of different views or micro-climates, create a private area, or make it possible to reach a deck from more than one door to the house.

One of the first decisions you need to make with a wraparound deck is how you want to install the decking. The two styles shown at near right can be framed the same way. Both have decking that runs entirely in the same direction, one across the joists and the other at a diagonal. Both have three parallel beams, although the diagonal design includes a short diagonal beam that allows for an optional angled corner.

The deck at upper right is perhaps the simplest to build. It is essentially two conventionally framed rectangular decks that meet at the corner of the house, but with one ledger extended under the decking. The mitered decking pattern requires more time and effort, but produces what many will find to be a more attractive deck.

PARALLEL DECKING

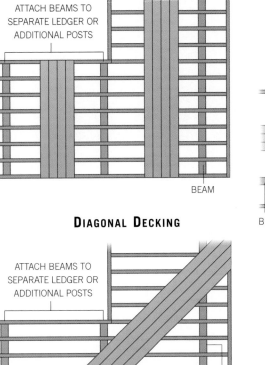

ATTACH BEAMS TO SEPARATE LEDGER OR ADDITIONAL POSTS

BEAM

PERPENDICULAR DECKING

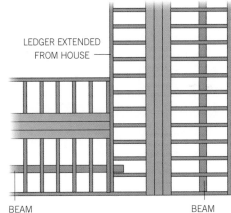

LEDGER EXTENDED FROM HOUSE

BEAM

BEAM

DIAGONAL DECKING

ATTACH BEAMS TO SEPARATE LEDGER OR ADDITIONAL POSTS

BEAMS

MITERED DECKING

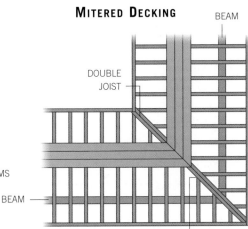

BEAM

DOUBLE JOIST

BEAM

45° CUTS

LEVEL CHANGES

Level changes can dramatically boost the visual appeal of a deck. While separate decks, built at separate levels, can be constructed next to each other, the most efficient and cost-effective approach is to use the same foundation to support adjacent levels. The transition between levels, no matter how wide it is, constitutes a step and should be designed to provide a safe and code-approved rise.

SHARED BEAM A relatively easy technique utilizes one beam to support two levels. The rim joist for the upper level falls directly over the lower rim joist, and the two are joined with tie plates. This style of level change can also be built by attaching the lower joists to the side of the beam with joist hangers and securing the upper joists to the top of the beam. With 2 × 6 or 2 × 8 joists, the shared-beam technique creates a comfortable step between levels.

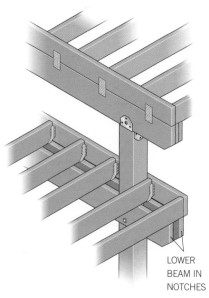

SHARED POSTS

SHARED BEAM

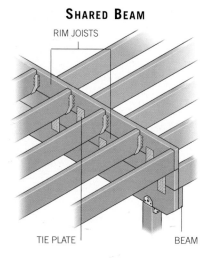

RIM JOISTS

TIE PLATE   BEAM

SHARED POSTS A technique using shared posts is preferred if you want to create a greater difference in height between two levels, which must then be joined with stairs. Plan to use 6 × 6 posts, which must be notched on two sides to accept the lower beam. The upper beam rests on top of the posts, with joists overlapping, as shown above, or hung from the side of the beam.

LOWER BEAM IN NOTCHES

STACKED DECK One way to create a small raised area is simply to construct a separate deck frame and set it on top of the regular frame. Use tie plates to hold the top frame in place, and attach short joist sections to the joists on both sides of the upper level to provide nailing surfaces for the decking. Although it is not particularly cost-effective for large sections of the deck, this technique is a handy way to create a step up to the house.

STACKED DECK

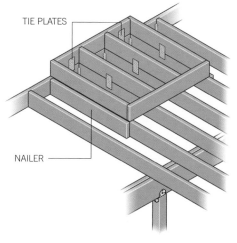

TIE PLATES

NAILER

SIMPLE OPENINGS

Sometimes it is necessary to build a deck around a large object, such as a tree. Small openings can be framed quite easily. First, install double joists on both sides of the object. Then attach header joists, using two pieces of joist stock, between the joists on the other two sides of the opening. Outside the opening, attach joist sections to each header, maintaining your regular on-center spacing. Cut and install the decking so that it overhangs the framing by about 1 inch on all four sides. Use joist hangers (3 inches wide for double joists and 1½ inches wide for single joists) at all connections.

ROUND OPENING

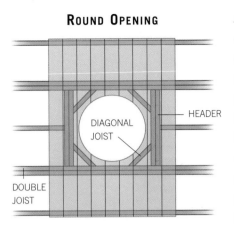

RECTANGULAR OPENING

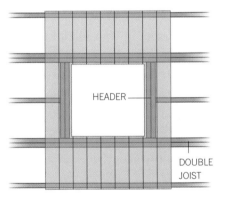

If you would rather create a round opening to better match a tree trunk, start by framing the opening as described. Then cut and install four diagonal joist sections, as shown above. Install the decking so that it covers as much of the opening as possible, then mark and cut the circle.

If you are building around a young tree, take extra care to allow plenty of room for the trunk to expand.

ACCESS PANEL If your deck will cover a water faucet or electrical outlet, you may need to build a small access panel. Attach 2 × 4 cleats to facing joists, 3½ inches from the top of each joist. Build a frame with 2 × 4s, with the frame width about ½ inch less than the distance between joists. Cut and attach decking, then drill two finger holes.

ACCESS PANEL

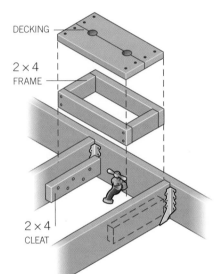

framing for a hot tub

While a standard deck should be able to support the weight of a small children's wading pool, a larger hot tub or spa requires added support. This support is generally provided in one of two ways, as described below. Choose your tub or spa before you begin building, and be sure to follow the manufacturer's instructions. Keep in mind that you will need to have some plumbing and electrical work done, and you may want to give some extra thought to privacy and shading when you design the deck.

FRAMING AROUND THE TUB On a low deck, it is usually best to rest the hot tub or spa on a concrete pad. Check with the manufacturer and with your local building department for specifications on the size of pad required, and plan to pour the concrete before you begin framing the deck. When a spa or a tub is installed with this

approach, the deck frame surrounds the tub or spa, but provides no additional support. The top of the tub or spa can be above the surface of the deck, or be level with it. If you prefer the latter style, plan the height of the deck very carefully. The framing is similar to that needed around a tree (see page 119), except that a larger opening is needed, as shown below.

HOT TUB OR SPA ON CONCRETE PAD

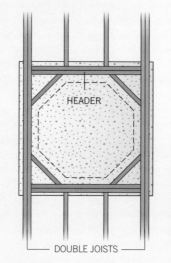

HEADER

DOUBLE JOISTS

FRAMING BENEATH THE TUB If you prefer to set the hot tub or spa on top of the deck surface, you will need to substantially increase the framing beneath it. The frame must be able to support the weight of the tub or spa filled with water and people. Check with the manufacturer or a structural engineer for more detailed recommendations. The framing plan below provides an idea of the additional support that will be needed. Once the decking has been installed, you can construct an elevated platform to surround the tub or spa; make sure to allow for that weight, too, in your planning.

HOT TUB OR SPA ON DECK

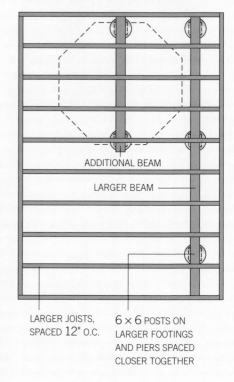

ADDITIONAL BEAM

LARGER BEAM

LARGER JOISTS, SPACED 12" O.C.

6 × 6 POSTS ON LARGER FOOTINGS AND PIERS SPACED CLOSER TOGETHER

decking

YOU WILL LOOK AT THE DECK SURFACE EVERY time you step out onto your deck, so you want to make it as attractive as possible. That entails making a smart choice in the decking you buy and taking the time to ensure a neat installation. The deck surface must also withstand a lot of abuse—from feet, furniture, and the elements—so it needs to be tightly and securely fastened to the framing, and maintained and repaired as needed. ■ This chapter provides you with the information you need to arrange and install decking that will live up to its dual responsibilities of visual appeal and durability. In addition to looking at the traditional option of wood decking installed with screws or nails, this chapter takes a close look at the newer and promising choices of composite decking and hidden fasteners.

choosing a pattern

Y ou can install decking in a wide variety of patterns. Most decking variations require adjustments in the framing, however, so you need to decide early in the design stage exactly how you want your deck surface to look.

SIMPLE PATTERNS

Installing boards that are all parallel to each other is the easiest approach. Most decks are constructed with decking that runs parallel to the house, as shown in the first illustration below and throughout this book. There are good reasons for this predominance: this style is the easiest to design, the quickest to install, and, to some minds, the best looking.

A slight variation on this theme is to alternate different widths of decking (such as 2 × 6s and 2 × 4s). Running the decking perpendicular to the house looks like a minor modification, but it actually requires the entire frame except the ledger to be rotated. This can be an advantage when you want to use short decking boards and avoid butt joints, or when you expect to shovel a lot of snow.

Diagonal decking can be installed over conventional framing, but it requires that you measure the joist spacing (that is, the decking span) along the diagonal run of the decking. This usually means that joists must be spaced a little closer together, or that you need to use thicker decking. Since each board length differs, and both ends must be cut at an angle, diagonal decking takes more time to install.

PARALLEL TO THE HOUSE

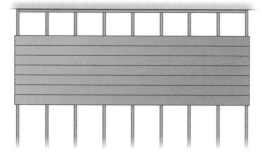

PERPENDICULAR TO THE HOUSE

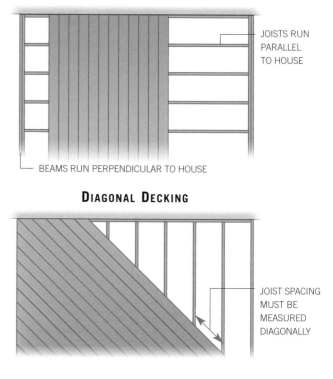

JOISTS RUN PARALLEL TO HOUSE

BEAMS RUN PERPENDICULAR TO HOUSE

PARALLEL TO THE HOUSE, ALTERNATING WIDTHS

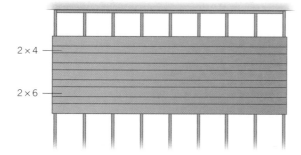

2 × 4

2 × 6

DIAGONAL DECKING

JOIST SPACING MUST BE MEASURED DIAGONALLY

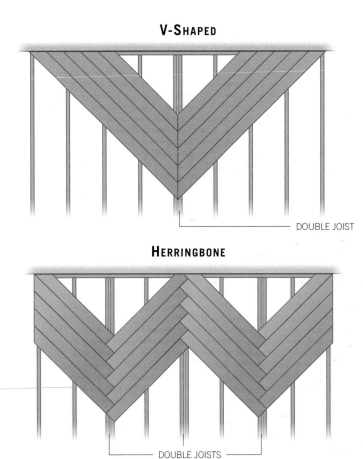

V-SHAPED

DOUBLE JOIST

HERRINGBONE

DOUBLE JOISTS

COMPLEX PATTERNS

Tastes vary, of course. If yours runs contrary to the straight and narrow, and you do not mind the extra effort, by all means choose a more compelling pattern, such as one of those shown here.

Complex decking patterns require very careful planning, and the details will vary from one deck to another. Regardless of the design, however, two principles must always be observed: the ends of every piece of decking must be supported by framing, and no piece of decking should exceed its allowable span. You may want to seek professional design assistance if you want to create one of these decking patterns.

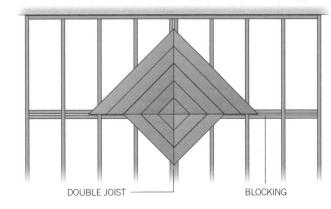

DIAMOND

DOUBLE JOIST — BLOCKING

MITERED BORDER

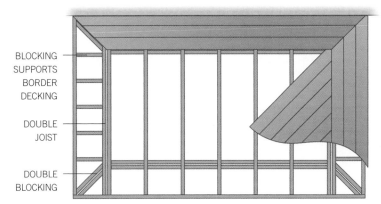

BLOCKING
SUPPORTS
BORDER
DECKING

DOUBLE
JOIST

DOUBLE
BLOCKING

laying out decking

The more complicated your decking pattern, the more time you need to spend on the layout. But even a simple deck will benefit from a careful layout, which usually boils down to getting the first board installed as perfectly as possible.

PLAN THE FIRST BOARD

With most decking patterns, the first installed board becomes a reference for the rest of the boards. If it is not perfectly aligned, the rest of the pattern will suffer accordingly.

On each side of the deck, measure out from the house the width of a decking board plus an additional 1/4 inch. Mark the location on each end joist. Snap a chalk line between the two marks. Use the straightest board you can find for this first row, and install it so the outer edge is aligned with the chalk line.

If you are installing diagonal decking, check the distance from the house to the end of the deck. Measure an equal distance along the rim joist and make a mark. Snap a chalk line between that mark and the outside corner of the end joist at the house, and install the first row of decking aligned with the chalk line.

GETTING STARTED: DECKING PARALLEL TO HOUSE

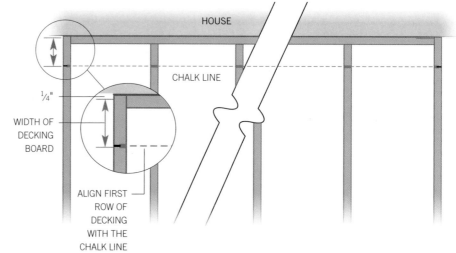

GETTING STARTED: DIAGONAL DECKING

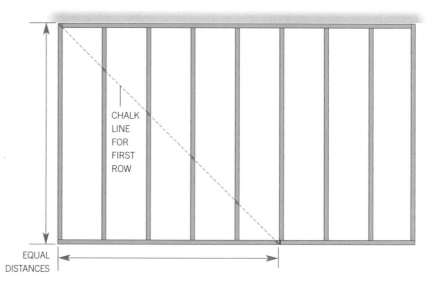

PLAN THE EDGING

This is the time to think about how you want the edges of the deck to look. The most common approach is to leave the board ends exposed, overhanging the perimeter joists by an inch or so. This is also the easiest technique, allowing you to install slightly oversized boards, then go back and cut them to length at one time.

If you do not like the look of all that end grain on the edges, however, you should consider installing a fascia board. This requires that you trim the decking flush with the joist faces. The fascia will look best if it matches the decking as closely as possible. Use 2× boards for the fascia, choosing a width that can span from the top of the decking to a bit below the joist. Miter the corners for the neatest appearance.

If you are not bothered by the exposed decking edges, but want

to dress up the highly visible joists around the perimeter, attach a fascia board beneath the decking. You can use a 1× board for this purpose, since the top of the board will not be stepped on. Install the decking so that it will overhang the fascia by about an inch on all sides.

FASCIA FLUSH WITH DECKING

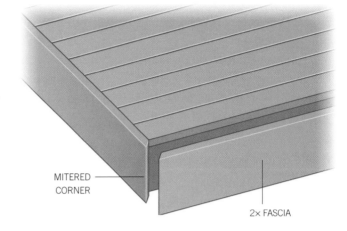

MITERED CORNER
2× FASCIA

FASCIA BELOW DECKING

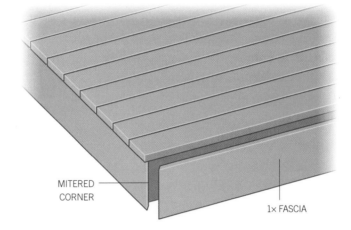

MITERED CORNER
1× FASCIA

If you are installing wood decking, you will need to decide which side of the board should face up. When you examine the end of a piece of lumber, you can see that the grain has a specific orientation, depending on how the log from which it came was cut. Most often you will see the grain forming a ringed pattern. As the rings move out from the center, they approach what was the outside, or bark side, of the tree.

Traditional wisdom dictated that the wood should be oriented consistently according to the grain, with most advising "bark side up."

Best Side Up

BARK SIDE UP
BARK SIDE DOWN

Wood usually forms a slight cup or hollow side-to-side over time. By installing wood so the cup forms underneath, water runs off. If the cup forms in the other direction, water collects.

Research has shown that there are small advantages to following the "bark side up" rule for dried lumber. But these advantages are usually not significant enough to overcome the advantages of installing the best-looking side up. The best defense against excessive cupping is to attach the decking with screws and apply a water-repellent finish regularly.

fastening the boards

The quickest and the least expensive way to fasten decking boards is to nail them on. Be sure to use ring-shank or spiral-groove nails, which hold much better than common nails. For the tightest connection, it is hard to beat decking screws. The one shortcoming that both fasteners share is that they are visible on the deck surface. If you would rather not have to see screw or nail heads on your deck, consider using the hidden fastener systems described on pages 128–129.

Be sure to match the fastener you use with the decking you are installing. Galvanized fasteners work fine on pressure-treated lumber, while stainless steel is a better choice with redwood, Western red cedar, and tropical hardwoods. Composite decking can usually be installed with galvanized fasteners, but it is smart to check with the manufacturer. Stainless steel should also be used near salt water. In terms of fastener lengths, use 3-inch screws or 12d nails for 2×4 or 2×6 decking, and $2\frac{1}{2}$-inch screws or 10d nails for $\frac{5}{4} \times 4$ or $\frac{5}{4} \times 6$ decking.

The job will go quicker if you scatter boards for 10 to 15 rows of decking across the joists first. That way you will not have far to reach for a new board as you work. This is particularly important if you have to deal with butt joints; arrange the decking so that the joints are staggered before you start driving fasteners.

SPACING THE BOARDS

Gaps between decking boards are necessary to allow water to drain, but should not be so large that small objects fall through or toes get caught. A $\frac{1}{8}$-inch gap is ideal, but since wood decking often shrinks after it has been installed, this shrinkage must be taken into account during installation.

Determining how much your decking is likely to shrink can be a little difficult. Boards that are wet and heavy will likely shrink the most. These boards can usually be installed tight against each other; over the course of a year or so they will shrink enough to create a satisfactory gap. Dry, kiln-dried boards may not shrink much at all, however, and so should be installed with a $\frac{1}{8}$-inch gap. An 8d common nail makes a useful spacer, although an inexpensive deck-spacing tool might be a bit handier.

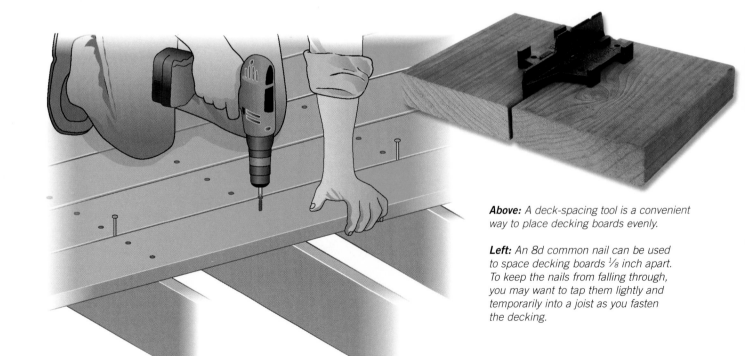

Above: A deck-spacing tool is a convenient way to place decking boards evenly.

Left: An 8d common nail can be used to space decking boards $\frac{1}{8}$ inch apart. To keep the nails from falling through, you may want to tap them lightly and temporarily into a joist as you fasten the decking.

ATTACHING THE BOARDS

Fasteners need to be driven through the decking at each joist location. Butt joints, where board ends meet, must be centered over joists (or, preferably, double joists). When driving screws or nails at board ends, drill pilot holes first to avoid splitting the wood (see page 69). Install screws or nails 1 inch from each edge of the decking, and try to keep the pattern as straight as possible along each joist.

DRIVING SCREWS Screws are best driven with a drill-driver with variable speed and an adjustable clutch. A corded drill is best, but a good-quality cordless drill (with an extra battery so that you do not have to wait for recharging) can work just fine. If your drill has a clutch, you can set it so that the head of the screw is driven flush with the deck surface, no more and no less. Since clutches can sometimes slip on encountering harder sections of wood, you may prefer to buy an attachment (left) that will allow you to adjust the screw depth.

DRIVING NAILS Drive nails as straight as possible into the board. Try to avoid mis-hits, so as not to create a line of hammer-induced indentations on the decking. Drive nails flush with the top of the decking.

PLANNING THE LAST ROW As you approach the last several rows of decking, give some thought to the width of the last row. If full-sized boards are not going to fit perfectly, plan to rip small amounts off boards in the final three or four rows, rather than leave yourself with a single, narrow row at the edge of your deck.

Right: A single, narrow row of boards makes for an unattractive deck edge. A better, less conspicuous approach is to rip small amounts from several rows of decking.

using hidden fasteners

Decking has been traditionally installed with fasteners that are driven through the tops of the boards, as described on pages 126–127. At best, the visible fastener heads detract at least a little from the appearance of a deck surface. At worst, poorly driven fasteners can pop loose, cause splits and stains in decking boards, and allow water to penetrate and damage the wood. Fastener heads may also protrude over time as the decking shrinks, requiring that they be reseated.

If you would rather not accept such compromises, consider one of the hidden fastener systems described here and on pages 130–131. The fasteners are attached to either the edges or the bottoms of the decking boards. Although these systems differ in expense and installation, you can be assured that any of

them will cost more and require more time and effort than the traditional method.

The following survey is intended to acquaint you with the major products that are available (see page 252 for a list of suppliers) and to offer an idea of how they work. If you decide to use a hidden fastener system, check with the manufacturer for more detailed instructions. Make sure

that the system you choose is compatible with the type of decking you use. Excessive shrinkage of the decking can weaken the bonds of many hidden fastener systems, so it is wise to use decking that is as dry as possible.

DECK CLIPS

Deck clips are attached to the edges of decking boards. Most manufacturers instruct you to toenail the first row of decking to the joists before you begin using clips on subsequent rows. One advantage of clips is that, because of their location, they provide a uniform gap between boards.

The clip, as shown below, has no connection with the joists at all. After the first board is in place, the clips are installed on the edge of the next decking board, positioned 2 inches from each joist. The decking board is then installed by slipping the clips under the previously installed board. Then the outside edge of the board is toenailed to the joists.

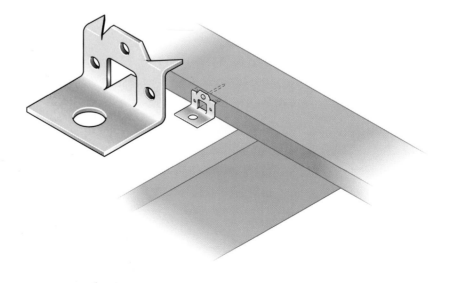

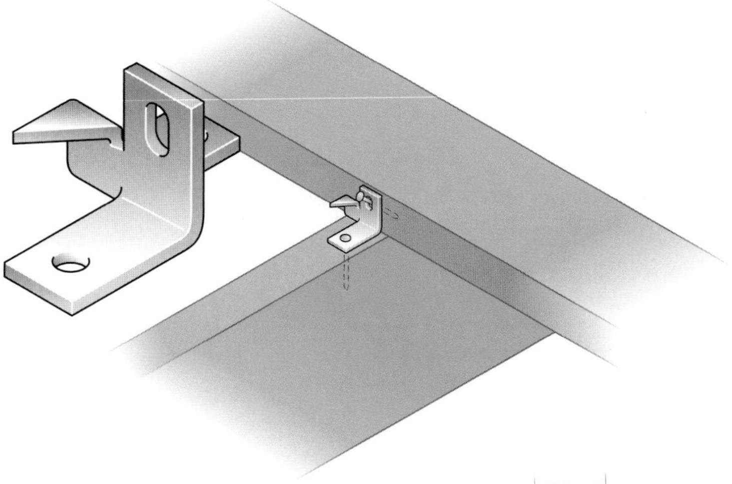

The deck clip below requires a special installation tool to drive the sharp prong into the previously installed decking board. The clip is then nailed to the side of the joist. The next board must be tapped into place against the installed clips before attaching the next row of clips. These clips also keep the decking from resting directly on the joists.

To install the clip shown above, you drive a nail at an angle through the hole in the vertical neck of the clip, and on through the decking and into the joist. Another nail ties the clip directly to the joist. The next board must be forced into the sharp prong on the clip, and then attached with another clip on the other side. The bases of the clips hold the decking board off the joist, which encourages drying. Since you cannot install side-by-side clips at a single joist location, these clips are best used for a deck in which butt joints fall over double joists.

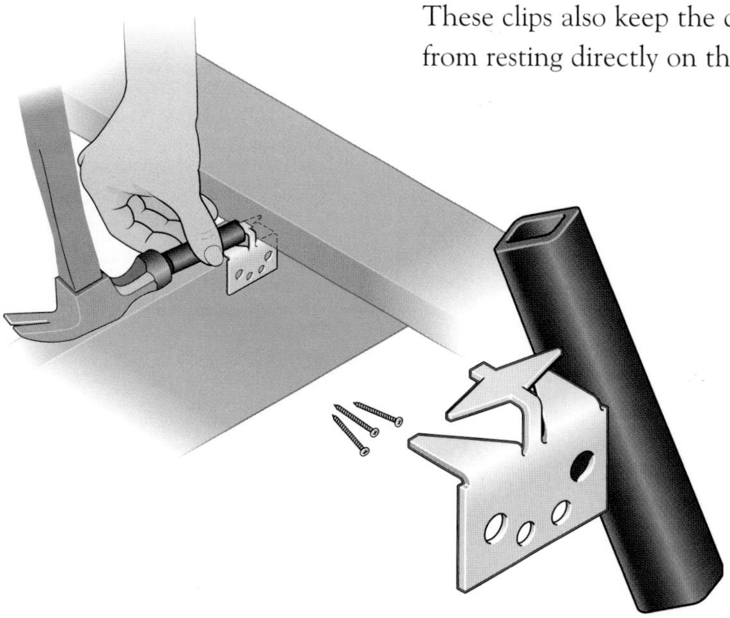

METAL BRACKET FASTENERS

Installation of a metal bracket system is labor intensive (be prepared to drive lots of screws), but the connection it produces is strong and secure. Brackets are available in both galvanized and stainless steel, with screws to accommodate either 2× or ⁵⁄₄ decking. As shown below, the brackets are first installed at the sides of the joists, and then attached to the decking with screws driven upward. If you can't work from beneath the deck, this second step will be somewhat awkward, although still doable.

The shiny surface of the brackets may produce glare from between boards on sunny days. To prevent this, you can spray-paint the brackets a flat black before installing them. The top flange on the bracket holds the decking above the joist, which helps keep the connection dry.

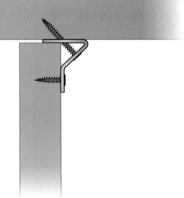

1 Attach to the Joists
Fasten brackets along the full length of each joist on alternating sides of the joist. Use tin snips to cut pieces to length, if necessary.

2 Connect to the Decking
Decking must be fastened to the brackets with screws driven from below. This is much easier to accomplish if you can work from below the deck.

BISCUIT FASTENERS

Still another innovative hidden fastener system features polypropylene biscuits and stainless-steel screws. Installation requires cutting slots into both sides of the decking boards at each joist location, a task for which you will need a biscuit joiner or a router equipped with a slot-cutting bit. Slide the biscuits into the slots, and fasten them to the joists with screws.

Unlike most other hidden fasteners, the biscuit system places the decking directly on top of the joists. To strengthen the connection and minimize the chance of squeaks, place a bead of construction adhesive across the tops of joists before installing the decking (see sidebar below).

The biscuits are thin enough to use with 1× decking, which makes this system particularly useful when installing tropical hardwood decking. With hard lumber, be sure to drill pilot holes before driving screws.

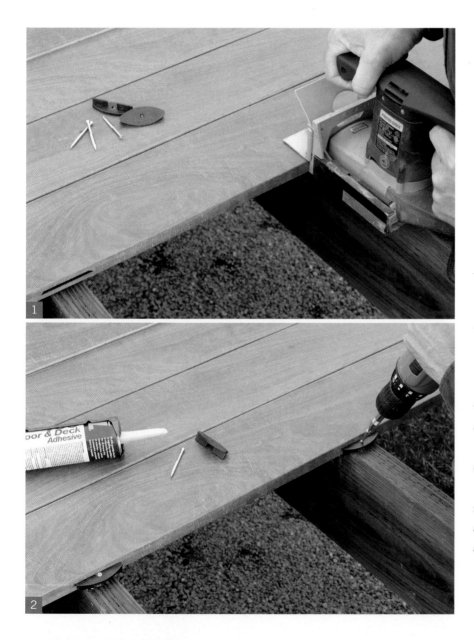

1 Cut the Slots
Set the decking board across the joists. With a biscuit joiner (as shown) or a router equipped with a slot-cutting bit, cut slots centered over each joist on both sides of the board.

2 Install the Board
Apply a thin bead of adhesive to the tops of the joists, then slide the decking board into place against the previously installed board with the slots on that side fitting over the previously installed biscuits. Install biscuits in the slots on the exposed side of the board and drive screws through the biscuits and into the joists.

Gluing a Deck?

Adhesive is used with decking in different situations. With the biscuit fastening system described above, it may be used to prevent squeaks from occurring when foot traffic causes the decking to rub against the joists. If you take this extra step, be sure to use an exterior-grade flooring adhesive, which is applied with a caulking gun. Some professionals have also had success using only an adhesive to fasten high-priced and dimensionally stable tropical hardwood decking to the joists. For that approach, use a fast-curing, exterior-grade polyurethane adhesive, but check with the decking manufacturer first.

composite decking

Wood decks are primarily built to promote leisure and comfort, but they can require a fair bit of upkeep to keep them looking good. Composite decking has been gaining in popularity in recent years because it significantly reduces the maintenance that a deck needs from year to year. New products are being introduced all the time, though many of them are not available in all areas or carried by all stores. If you are curious about composite decking, plan to visit as many stores as possible and do some research on the specific products available to you.

The most common type of composite decking is made of wood fibers mixed with plastic, which is then formed into planks up to 20 feet in length. Solid planking is available in 2× and ⁵⁄₄ sizes. Some products are made to resemble real wood, at least from a distance, while others offer a range of colors. Some manufacturers have begun offering composite lumber that can be used for railings and fascia boards, giving you the opportunity to construct the most visible portions of a deck out of the same material. You may also be able to use composite lumber for stair treads and risers.

Composite lumber is generally not as strong as wood, which is why it is not used for structural framing. The strength of composite decking varies from product to product, however. Follow the manufacturer's instructions for design and installation. Decking made with recycled polyethylene (PE) may require shorter spans than products made with polyvinyl chloride (PVC), which itself may not be able to span quite as much as some solid wood decking. Each product is made from a unique mix of materials, and some may fade more than others.

With a growing variety of products available and an expanding list of happy consumers, composite decking is rapidly becoming the material of choice for those seeking a low-maintenance deck. Because of its flexibility, it is also well suited to use in curved decks and even matching benches such as those shown here.

CUTTING AND DRILLING

A nice feature of composite decking is that, although the product itself is new, you do not need to acquire new tools and skills to work with it. Composites can be cut and shaped just like solid wood.

Use regular carpentry tools to cut, drill, and shape composite lumber. Fine-toothed, carbide-tipped blades work best.

STAINING AND PAINTING

Unlike wood, composite decking does not have to be coated with a protective finish. If you are not satisfied with the color choices available, however, or if you would like your deck to match the color of your house, most products can be stained or painted. Keep in mind that if you do apply a finish, you will have to recoat the surface regularly. Some manufacturers suggest oil-based paints and stains for their products, while others recommend latex finishes.

Cutting or drilling composite lumber may produce a sharp burr, which can be quickly eliminated with a rasp or sandpaper.

Composite lumber does not have to be coated with a protective finish, but for decorative purposes you can apply stain or paint, as suggested by the manufacturer.

Vinyl Decking Vinyl decking is another low-maintenance option, although one that offers a particularly nontraditional-looking deck. Installation differs as well. In general, first an aluminum or vinyl track is installed across the joists, and then top pieces are snapped into place. One of several available products is shown here.

FASTENING

Most composite decking can be attached with standard deck screws or nails. Some manufacturers suggest that you drill pilot holes before driving screws, others do not.

SOLID DECKING Solid composite decking is the composite product most similar to solid wood and can be fastened accordingly. Hidden fastener systems can also be used with some products, but check with both the fastener and composite manufacturers for compatibility. Some solid composite boards may have a slight cup, which should be installed facing up to allow water to run off.

WEBBED DECKING Webbed, or hollow-core, composite decking is available in both rectangular and tongue-and-groove profiles. Because of the products' design, manufacturers specify exactly where fasteners must be driven in each board. Some products are made with a surface groove to accommodate fasteners. You can buy matching caps to enclose board ends, or you can install fascia boards (see page 125).

Attach composite decking with screws or nails, as recommended by the manufacturer. Some products tend to flare up a bit when the screw head enters the decking. If that happens, drive the screw about ⅛ inch beneath the surface, then hit the raised section with a hammer. In addition to leveling the surface, this step will hide the screw.

With webbed decking, fastener placement can be particularly important. This 2 × 6 product requires that screws be driven only through the outer cores, not the center one.

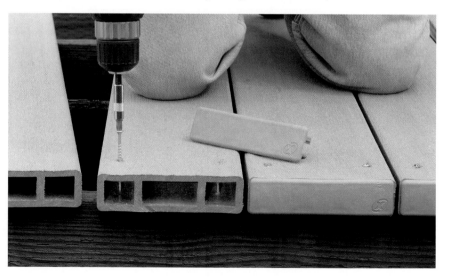

TONGUE-AND-GROOVE DECKING

Tongue-and-groove composite decking is installed much like hardwood flooring in your house. Fasteners are driven through the grooves, which are then covered with the tongues of subsequent boards. This type of decking is installed beginning at the outside edge of the deck, working toward the house. You'll need to add fascia boards on the three exposed edges to hide the decking edges.

1 Install the Starter Strip
The starter strip is attached at the far end of the deck, with screws driven into the rim joist. The strip must be straight and parallel with the side of the house.

2 Attach the Decking
Slide the tongue of each new board into the groove of the installed board (or, to begin with, the starter strip). The decking is designed to create a 1/4-inch gap between boards. Drive screws through the tongue of the board and into the joist.

3 Install the Last Row
If a full board fits comfortably in the row next to the house, drive screws vertically through the groove section. Otherwise, rip the board to fit and attach it to a 1-inch-square block of wood. As for any decking, allow a 1/4-inch gap between the decking and the house. Attach fascia boards to cover the edges of the decking.

working with decking

For the most part, installing the decking is a relatively easy and straightforward part of deck construction. If your decking boards are all straight, your deck frame is a perfect rectangle, and a railing is not needed, you may have little need for the rest of this chapter. But most deck builders are going to have to deal with unruly boards and obstacles that require special care.

FORCING BOARDS

If you are installing wood decking, chances are very good that many of your boards will be bowed, some more than others. (One of the advantages of composite decking is that you are not likely to face this problem.) To maintain a consistent gap between the decking boards, that means some will require a bit of persuading to get them into alignment. Moderately bowed boards can usually be pulled into line with one hand while driving a screw or nail with the other. More difficult boards may require one of the techniques shown here. Whichever method you use, remember to place a spacer between the boards before pulling the problem board into place.

A flat pry bar or utility chisel can be used to straighten most boards. Knock the sharp end into the joist at an angle, as shown, then pull the board toward you. Hold the pressure on the board until the fasteners are installed. If you are working alone, start the fasteners before pulling the board in.

When prying by hand fails to move the board far enough, a pipe clamp is a good alternative. Hook one end against a pry bar stuck between two boards and the other end over the edge of the problem board. Tighten the clamp until the board is properly aligned. Fasten the board, then remove the clamp.

If you are building a large deck and have a plentiful supply of bowed boards, it might be worth investing in a specialized tool. This one hooks over the joists, then pulls the board into line quickly and with little effort.

NOTCHING BOARDS

Most decks have obstructions that require decking to be notched. These include posts for railings or overheads or legs for built-in seating. Many of these supports need to be installed before you finish the decking. The photos here show you how to make clean, accurate cuts and provide ample support for the decking that remains. These methods can be used on solid decking, whether wood or composite. For other decking materials, check with the manufacturer before cutting notches.

1 Mark for the Cut
To mark an accurate cut line in a board that needs to fit around a post, set the decking in place against the post. With an angle square or combination square, mark the post location on the decking.

2 Make the Cut
Cut the notch with a jigsaw. Cut a little to the outside of the marks so that the notch is not too tight.

3 Add Support
You always need to support cut ends of decking. When notching to fit around a post or another obstacle, attach cleats to serve as supports, then drive fasteners through the decking and into the cleats.

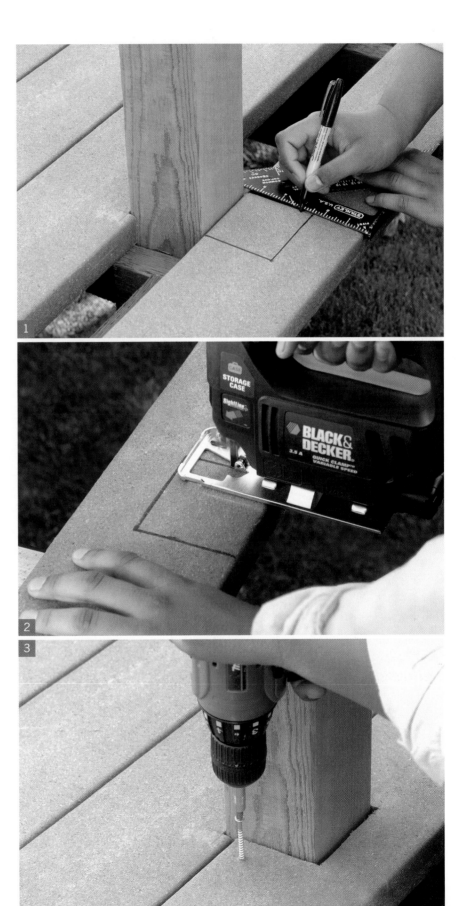

TRIMMING BOARDS

It is much more efficient to cut the decking to length after it has been installed. Measure and mark the end boards for any over-hang you have planned (typically 1 inch), then snap a chalk line to guide your cut. If you are concerned about being able to make a straight cut, tack a 1 × 4 to the deck surface to guide your saw. Follow the same method for any decking material.

1 Trim the Ends
Carefully follow the chalk line to cut the decking to its final length. You can finish cutting near the house with a handsaw or jigsaw.

2 Smooth the Cut
Clean up the edges with a power sander, or use medium-grit sandpaper wrapped around a block of wood.

Handling the Leftovers If you wind up with a pile of short pieces of cut-off decking, you need to dispose of these leftovers properly. Pressure-treated wood and composite or vinyl decking should never be burned. In most areas, you can dispose of unneeded scraps with normal household waste. Larger pieces of decking, however, can be used to build small planters or tables for use on the deck or around the yard.

stairs

YOU MAY REQUIRE STAIRS TO GET FROM THE YARD TO THE deck, from the deck into the house, or from one deck level to another. When they are needed, stairs can also add a welcoming, visually appealing element to a well-designed deck. But by their very nature, stairs can be dangerous, and they are a primary site of household accidents. Deck stairs may not have the glamour and character of a fine interior stairway, but they do pose the same risks and require the same level of care regarding safety. ■ This chapter provides the basic information you need to design and build attractive, functional, and safe stairs for your deck. Ramps can make your deck even more accessible, but their construction can vary because of local code differences and the variations from deck to deck. See pages 232–235 for plans for a deck project incorporating ramps. Before designing your own, be sure to consult your local building department.

understanding codes and safety

Unless your deck is set on the ground, it will most likely need some type of stairs. There are a number of different ways to build stairs, but in most places they must conform to strict requirements. And, although basic stair building is not especially difficult, building stairs that are safe and legal does require careful attention to detail.

STAIR CODE REQUIREMENTS

As parts of a house go, stairs are dangerous places because of the risk of tripping and falling. That is why their construction is so often tightly regulated. Specific requirements vary from place to place, however, so be sure to check your local code. Some building codes are more flexible for exterior stairs than for those inside the house; some are not.

The vertical distance from one stair tread to the next is called the rise. Codes usually specify a maximum rise of 8 inches or so, but a rise of 6 to $7\frac{1}{2}$ inches is generally more desirable. The rise must be consistent from one step to the next, with a differential of no more than $\frac{3}{8}$ inch.

The tread depth (or run) is measured from the face of one riser to the face of the next (or from tread nosing to tread nosing). Codes may require a 9-inch minimum for the run, but 11 to 12 inches is better. Within the measurements allowed by code, choose a rise and run that work well together. In general, steps with a shorter rise are more comfortable with a deeper run; those with a taller rise are better with a shorter run. A good rule of thumb is that the tread depth plus the rise should equal 17 to $17\frac{1}{2}$ inches.

Stairs are usually required to be at least 36 inches wide. Up to this width, you should be able to use only two stringers, while wider stairs will require an intermediary stringer. Regardless of code requirements, however, many builders always use at least three stringers for stairs between 30 and 48 inches in width. The middle stringer adds strength and stiffness to the stairs, and requires only a little extra work.

COMMON STAIR CODE REQUIREMENTS

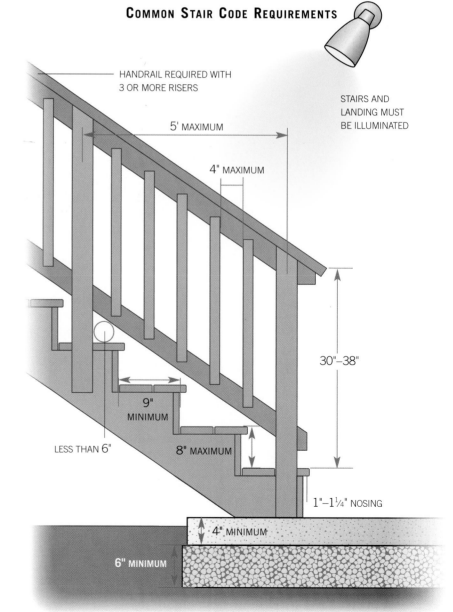

HANDRAIL REQUIRED WITH 3 OR MORE RISERS

STAIRS AND LANDING MUST BE ILLUMINATED

5' MAXIMUM

4" MAXIMUM

30"–38"

9" MINIMUM

LESS THAN 6"

8" MAXIMUM

1"–1$\frac{1}{4}$" NOSING

4" MINIMUM

6" MINIMUM

Stairs with three or more steps should have a railing on at least one side. The railing must be located 30 to 38 inches above the nosing on each tread. Railing posts must be spaced no more than 5 feet apart, and balusters must be spaced no more than 4 inches apart. Deck stairs are frequently built without risers, but codes often require them, and many people think stairs also look much better with risers.

To help keep children or pets from falling through, the triangular area formed by the tread, riser, and railing must not be large enough to permit a 6-inch ball to pass through. The stringers should be attached to a concrete pad, and the stairs and landing may have to be illuminated.

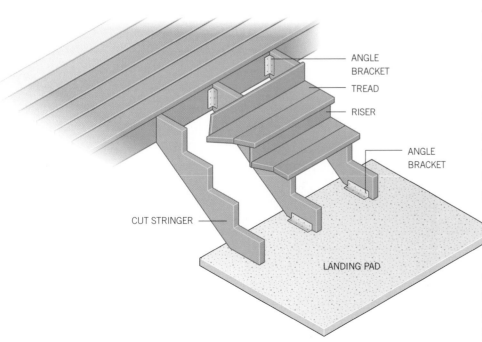

STAIR COMPONENTS

The basic framing components of stairs are stringers, also called carriages. Typically made out of 2×10s or 2×12s, stringers are often cut to create level surfaces for treads and plumb surfaces for risers. Stringers can also be solid boards with brackets attached for the treads (see page 150). Stringers can be attached to the deck framing and the landing pad with angle brackets.

The treads and the risers are related components. Treads are the part you walk on. Risers, if any, fill the vertical gaps between treads.

assessing styles

Stairs are primarily functional elements, but they can also have a large impact on the visual appeal of a deck. They can be prominent and grand, or minimal and understated. Sometimes the site and deck style dictate the type of stairs you need; at other times you have a great deal of latitude in the design. Either way, stairs can be a major component of your deck's appearance, so take some time to find a style that suits you.

One of the most visible parts of a stairway is the railing. Whether you are required to include a railing or just want to have one, be sure to include the railing in your overall design (see pages 164–165). Likewise, lighting the stairs and the landing is an important safety consideration, even if it is not explicitly required. See pages 178–179 for more on lighting.

STRINGER OPTIONS

Much of the variation in stair styles boils down to how you handle the stringers. The easiest stairs to construct use solid stringers with metal brackets supporting the treads, and no risers. This style is best used on short, narrow stairs or where risers are not required.

Cut stringers involve more effort, but they result in stronger, more attractive stairs. They also provide a solid vertical surface for attaching risers. If you want to build stairs with cut stringers, but prefer the profile of solid stringers, you can add a decorative trim board, as shown at right.

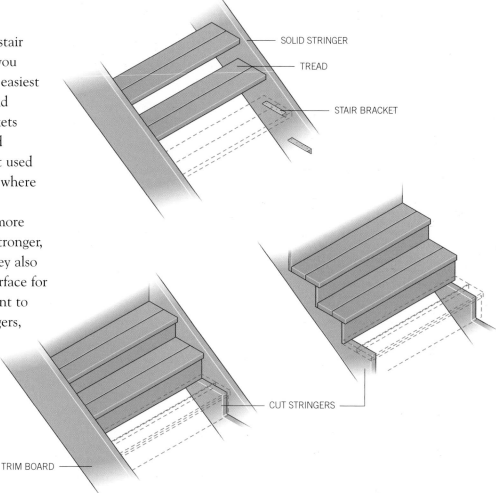

LANDING CHOICES

The landing is a very important consideration for any stairway, since it provides a firm surface for the first step up or the last one down. On decks, the landing also serves as support for the stringers. The best type of landing is a concrete pad. With careful planning it is possible to pour the pad while you are working on the footings and piers, but it is safer to wait until the decking is installed.

The bottoms of the stringers are usually attached to the landing pad with angle brackets. Alternatively, the stringers can be cut to fit over a 2 × 4 kickboard

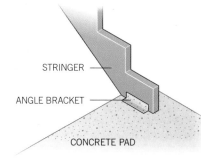

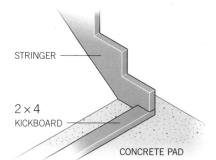

fastened to the pad. For short stairs, you may be satisfied with a landing of compacted gravel; attach two 2 × 4s across the bottoms of the stringers to distribute the load.

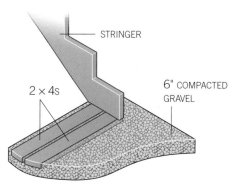

finding stair dimensions

Regardless of how you plan to build your stairs, you must first calculate the overall dimensions. In the terminology of stair building, the rise is the vertical distance or height, and the run is the horizontal distance.

FIND THE RISE The total rise is the vertical distance the stairs must travel from the landing to the deck surface. The measurement should be taken directly over the landing pad, not off the end of the deck. Use a level or 2 × 4 to extend the deck surface over the pad, then measure the total rise from the pad.

CALCULATING THE TOTAL RISE

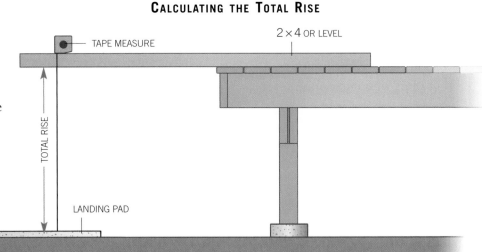

TAPE MEASURE

2 × 4 OR LEVEL

TOTAL RISE

LANDING PAD

The next step is to calculate the unit rise (the vertical distance from one tread to the next), as illustrated by the diagrams at right. Let's assume that the total rise is 32 inches. Divide that figure by 7, which is an ideal unit rise. The result, rounded to the nearest whole number, is the ideal number of risers (5 in this example). Now divide the total rise (32) by the number of risers (5), to determine the actual unit rise (6.4 inches). You might find a rise of less than 6½ inches to be too short, in which case you could reduce the number of risers to 4, resulting in a unit rise of 8 inches (far right).

FIGURING THE UNIT RISE

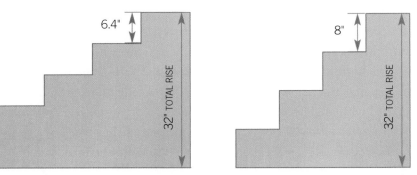

6.4"

32" TOTAL RISE

8"

32" TOTAL RISE

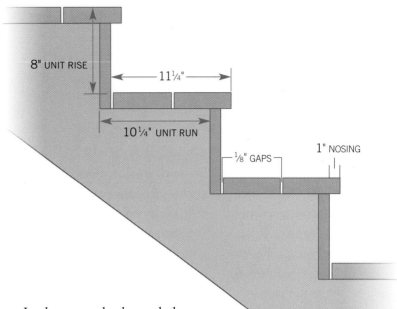

DETERMINE THE RUN With deck stairs, unlike interior stairs, you are usually not pressed for space, so you can plan for a convenient and comfortable tread depth. The illustration shows treads made with two 2 × 6s, allowing ⅛-inch gaps between boards and a 1-inch nosing. While this produces a depth of 11¼ inches from the nosing to the riser, the actual unit run, which is the dimension needed to lay out stringers, is 10¼ inches.

CHOOSE THE LUMBER SIZE Short deck stairs can often be made with 2 × 10 stringers, although many builders routinely use 2 × 12s. The critical determination is the minimal width left in the board after the notches have been cut. If this width would be less than 4 inches (see illustration, page 146), you should use wider boards for the stringers.

To determine the length of boards you will need for the stringers, use your framing square and a tape measure, and assume that 1 inch on either represents 1 foot. On many squares, one edge of the square is graduated in twelfths of an inch to facilitate this calculation. Figure the total rise and total run in terms of feet and inches, then mark the total run on the long side of the square and the total rise on the short side. Determine the distance between the marks with a tape measure to determine the minimum length of the boards you will need.

In the example shown below, the total run is 52½ inches (5 treads × 10½ inches each), or 4 feet 4½ inches, and so the tape measure is placed at the 4 feet 4½ inch mark on the left side of the square. The total rise is 43½ inches (6 risers at 7¼ inches each), or 3 feet 7½ inches, and so the tape is set at that mark on the right side. The total distance between these two marks is about 5⅝ inches. That measurement means you need a board at least 5 feet 8 inches long for each stringer. To be safe, buy one 12- or 14-foot board to make into two stringers for this stair.

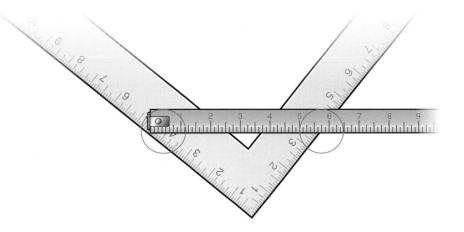

building the stairs

For safe stairs, stringers are the key. They must be strong, accurate, and well secured at the top and bottom. To cut good stringers, you need a framing square and a pair of stair gauges, which you should be able to find at a well-stocked home improvement store or lumberyard. As with all stairs, the top and bottom landing surfaces must be finished before you establish the final dimensions. That way, you can get an accurate measurement of the total rise, which is the only way to calculate accurate stair dimensions.

Stringer layout is quick and easy once you understand the basic principles. First you must establish the rise and run (see pages 144–145). Use the long, wide blade on the framing square for the run and the short, narrow blade for the rise. Attach the stair gauges to the outside edges of the square at the appropriate dimensions.

LAYING OUT SOLID STRINGERS

To mark solid stringers, set the corner of the square flat on the stringer along the crown side of the stringer and with the stair gauges against the edge. Mark the outside edges of the square. Slide the square down so that it aligns with the previous mark and lay out the next step, until all the steps are laid out.

To create the plumb cut line at the top, extend the riser line to the bottom of the stringer. If the stringers will be installed beneath overhanging decking, add the overhang amount to the length of the stringer.

Shorten the bottom of the stringer by the thickness of one tread. Set a piece of tread stock (typically a 2 × 6) along the bottom cut-off line and draw another line. Cut the stringer along this line and the plumb cut line. Lay out the second stringer the same way.

MAKING CUT STRINGERS

Deck stairs built with cut stringers are strong, and they may be easier to build than you imagine. Stairs with cut stringers are usually designed so that the top tread is on the same level as the deck surface, rather than one step down. The advantage of this method is that it is easier to attach the stringers to the deck, since they will be resting against a rim joist or an end joist. But this approach also results in a longer run for the stairs, which may not be possible if you are squeezed for space. If you need to build stairs with the first tread resting below the deck surface, you will probably need to use a hangerboard, as discussed on page 149. In terms of stringer layout, the first approach calls for an equal number of risers and treads; the second, using a hangerboard, will result in one more riser than tread on the stairs.

Begin by establishing the unit rise and unit run, then set the stair gauges on the framing square. Set the board for the first stringer across a pair of sawhorses. If there are any splits in the end of the board, cut the board to eliminate them. Then proceed as shown in the numbered steps.

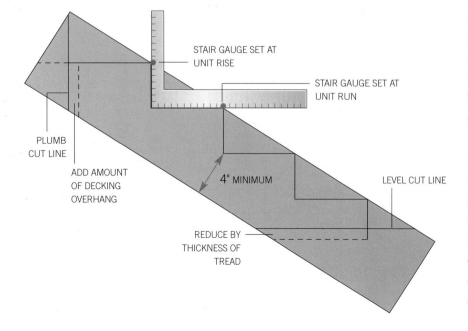

STAIR GAUGE SET AT UNIT RISE

STAIR GAUGE SET AT UNIT RUN

PLUMB CUT LINE

ADD AMOUNT OF DECKING OVERHANG

4" MINIMUM

LEVEL CUT LINE

REDUCE BY THICKNESS OF TREAD

1 Mark the Stringer

The object here is to lay out and cut one stringer, then use that stringer as a template to mark the others. Place the framing square along the crown side of the stringer with the corner resting on the board, as shown, and the stair gauges flush against the edge. Mark along the outside of the square. Slide the framing square along the board until it aligns perfectly with the previous mark, then mark again. Continue until you have marked the stringer for all riser and tread cuts.

2 Establish the Top and Bottom Cut Lines

When you have finished laying out the stringer for risers and treads, extend the line for the plumb cut at the top. (Adjust for overhanging decking as described on page 146 for solid stringers.) You also need to shorten the bottom of the stringer by the thickness of one tread. Set a piece of the tread stock along the bottom line and draw another line across the stringer. The stringer should be cut off at this line.

3 Cut the Stringer

After taking care to get the layout right, do not rush through the job of cutting. Clamp the stringer to your sawhorses. With a circular saw, cut the top of the stringer along the plumb cut line and the bottom along the level cut line. Then set the stringer in its intended position against the deck. Check that the tread lines are level and that the riser height is identical on the top and bottom steps. If you detect a problem, go back and check your measurements and calculations. If the stringer looks good, clamp it back onto the sawhorses and continue cutting. Run the saw blade only up to the spot where the tread and riser lines meet. Cutting beyond this line with a circular saw will weaken the stringer.

4 Finish the Cuts

With a jigsaw or a handsaw, finish cutting along the layout lines. Once all cuts have been made, set the stringer in place along the deck and check the fit one more time. The stringer should rest flat on the landing pad and against the deck joist, with the tread cuts level and the riser cuts plumb.

5 Mark the Other Stringers

If you are satisfied with the fit of the first cut stringer, clamp it on top of another piece of stringer stock, making sure that the bottom edges are perfectly aligned. Mark the bottom piece by tracing along the cuts with a pencil. Use the first stringer as a template to lay out any additional stringers.

Framing for a Landing

If you have to build stairs to a high deck, you may need to add a landing midway up. Building codes often limit the total span of stringers to 16 feet, so you may have no choice in the matter. Stairs with a landing also look better than stairs with long, straight stringers, and adding a landing allows you to change directions with the stairs.

Designing stairs with a landing is not much more complicated than designing straight stairs. Determine the total rise, then calculate a suitable rise and run for each step. The landing should be supported by four posts resting on individual concrete footings and piers. Build it so that the finished surface rests at the height of one of the planned treads. Then cut and install the stringers for the upper and lower sections of the stairs, as shown in the illustration. Be sure to plan the size of the landing to allow for a section to support the upper stringers. That is, if you want a finished landing surface that is 3 feet square, and the bases of the stringers take up 1 foot, you should build a landing that is 3 feet by 4 feet.

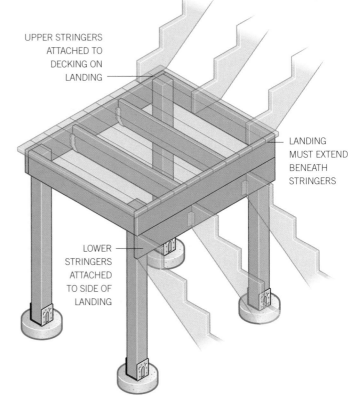

UPPER STRINGERS ATTACHED TO DECKING ON LANDING

LANDING MUST EXTEND BENEATH STRINGERS

LOWER STRINGERS ATTACHED TO SIDE OF LANDING

ATTACHING STRINGERS TO THE DECK

Stringers should be installed straight and square against the deck and properly spaced apart from each other. You may want to make a layout on the joist as a guide. If you are planning to cut treads to a specific width, move the outside stringers in just enough to allow the treads to overhang the sides.

Set each stringer against the deck so that its top is flush with the top of the joist. Then use angle brackets to attach the stringers to the joist.

Metal angle brackets are the best connectors for attaching stringers to the deck. Place the brackets at the insides of the stringers, where they will not be visible once the treads have been installed.

Attaching to a Hangerboard

When you want or need to set the first tread a step down from the deck, you will probably discover that the stringer does not rest against much of the joist. In that case, add a hangerboard, which is a carpentry term for an extra board to provide a solid nailing surface for stringers.

In most cases you should be able to use a 2 × 4 or a 2 × 6 for the hangerboard; the only guideline is that it must be big enough for the stringer to rest on it. The hangerboard does not have to be too conspicuous; just cut the board long enough to accommodate the outside stringers. Attach 2 × 4 cleats to the inside of the rim joist or the end joist at each stringer location, as shown at top right. Then fasten the hangerboard to the cleats as shown at lower right. Now you can attach the stringers as you would to an outside joist.

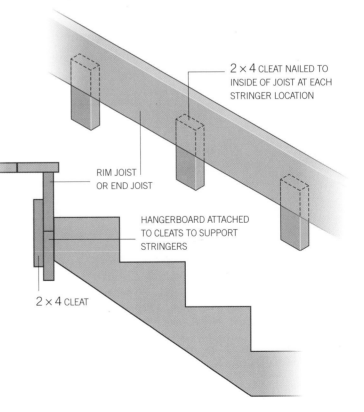

2 × 4 CLEAT NAILED TO INSIDE OF JOIST AT EACH STRINGER LOCATION

RIM JOIST OR END JOIST

HANGERBOARD ATTACHED TO CLEATS TO SUPPORT STRINGERS

2 × 4 CLEAT

ATTACHING STRINGERS TO THE LANDING

With the stringers attached to the deck, check that the bottoms are evenly spaced. Use a framing square to make sure that each stringer is square with the joist at the top. Attach a temporary brace to the fronts of the stringers to hold them in place while you secure the bottoms of the stringers.

The easiest way to attach stringers to a concrete pad is with angle brackets. The brackets can be secured to the stringers with screws, but you will need self-tapping concrete screws for the connection with the pad. These screws require that you first drill pilot holes; check with the manufacturer for the recommended size of masonry bit. Keep the angle brackets on the insides of the joists, where they will be concealed.

INSTALLING RISERS AND TREADS

If you are installing risers as well as treads, cut the risers to size. Risers should be installed flush with the stringers, and the bottom riser needs to be cut narrower than the others by the thickness of a tread. Attach risers with screws or nails driven into each stringer. Now cut the treads to length, allowing for a 1-inch overhang on each side. For drainage, leave a gap of about ⅛ inch between the riser and the tread and, if you are using two boards for each tread, a comparable gap between the boards. Allow the treads to overhang the risers by at least 1 inch. Secure the treads with screws or nails driven into each stringer.

Attach the risers first, then the treads. Drive screws or nails through the treads into the stringers, using nails to maintain a drainage gap between boards.

USING STAIR BRACKETS When building stairs that rely on metal brackets to support the treads, you need to lay out both end stringers as discussed on page 146. Instead of cutting the stringers, however, install brackets along the layout lines. Be sure to choose brackets that are sized for the tread material you are using and attach them with fasteners recommended by the manufacturer. Note that you can use solid stringers and brackets only on the two sides. If you require additional stringers to support the treads, they will have to be cut.

Top: Stringers must be installed carefully. Measure the spacing between the stringers at both top and bottom, and check that they are square with the rim joist. Bottom: Special concrete screws are used to attach the angle bracket at the bottom of each stringer to the landing pad.

STAIR BRACKET

railings

FROM MOST VANTAGE POINTS, A DECK'S RAILING is its most visible feature. While you may feel justifiably proud of the top-quality decking you bought and installed, it is the railing that will create the first impression of your deck for neighbors and passersby. Yet, while railings are a significant visual component, they exist for the purest of functions— they keep people from falling off the deck. ■ The need to build railings that can perform their safety duty necessarily restricts the design options that are available, but it certainly does not eliminate them. This chapter focuses on designing and building safe railings that will complement your deck while standing up to the bumps and bruises that are bound to come their way.

understanding codes and safety

Local building codes regarding deck railings (also called guardrails) range from extremely lenient to tightly restrictive. If yours tends toward the former, do not take that as an excuse to cut corners. Railings perform an important function on decks by ensuring that they can be used safely by people of all ages and sizes.

A railing may not be required unless your deck surface is 30 inches or more above ground. But 30 inches is a long way to fall, and more safety-conscious codes lower the requirement to 24 or even 15 inches. If you are concerned about the well-being of children who might use your deck, keep in mind that there is no reason why you cannot put a railing on any deck, no matter how close to the ground it is.

Railings are often designed to withstand a force of 200 pounds pushing down on them or against them. Imagine the stress caused

COMMON CODE REQUIREMENTS FOR RAILINGS

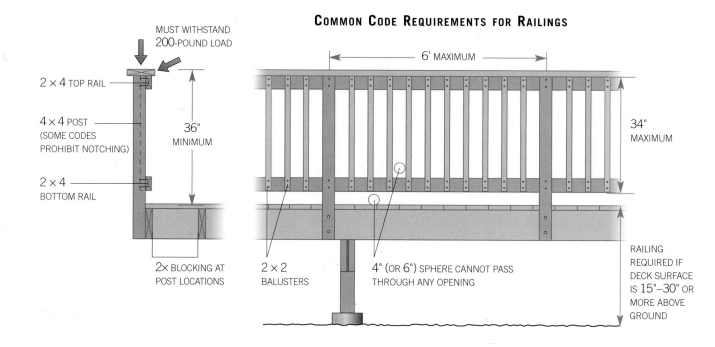

MUST WITHSTAND 200-POUND LOAD

2 × 4 TOP RAIL

4 × 4 POST (SOME CODES PROHIBIT NOTCHING)

2 × 4 BOTTOM RAIL

36" MINIMUM

2× BLOCKING AT POST LOCATIONS

2 × 2 BALUSTERS

4" (OR 6") SPHERE CANNOT PASS THROUGH ANY OPENING

6' MAXIMUM

34" MAXIMUM

RAILING REQUIRED IF DECK SURFACE IS 15"–30" OR MORE ABOVE GROUND

by someone sitting on or leaning against the railing, and you will understand the need for such considerations.

The minimum height of a railing is usually 36 inches, but some people prefer a higher railing. Maximum railing height is often limited by restrictions that limit the span of 2×2 balusters to 34 inches, but adding a middle rail will allow you to use longer balusters and thus create a higher railing.

Spacing between all components of the railing should not be large enough to allow a 4-inch sphere to pass through (some codes say 6 inches). The 4-inch limitation is meant to eliminate the chance of a child's head getting stuck and is well worth obeying.

Some codes stipulate the sizes of fasteners that can be used at different locations. The instructions in this chapter specify fasteners that will help to maintain the ability to withstand a 200-pound

load. In some jurisdictions you are not permitted to notch railing posts to fit against the outside joists, although notched posts are often used; techniques for both solid and notched posts are discussed on pages 156–159.

Deck railings usually rely upon vertical members, and for good reason. If you build a railing with horizontal members (such as in the illustration at right), which is perfectly legal in many areas, it is almost inevitable that children will want to start climbing the railing. This condition is potentially less safe than no railing at all.

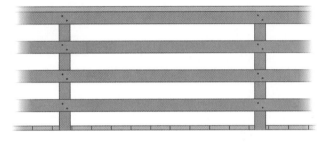

Horizontal rails create a ladder for children to climb, a fact that makes them impermissible under some local codes.

Railing design begins with safety, but from that point it can branch off into many directions. With a great view like the one off the deck on the facing page, an unobtrusive metal railing seems the perfect choice. At right, the formidable structure surrounding the deck appears to be an extension of the house itself.

railing styles

Deck railings are generally made up of posts, rails, and balusters. But there are many potential variations on this basic theme, and some of the common ones are shown on this and the facing page.

One decision you must make in planning for railings is what material or materials you will use. Then you need to consider how your building code will limit your choices. Even where code issues are not relevant, it is still necessary to assess the trade-offs between safety and aesthetics. A railing on a low deck that is not likely to be used by children could call for a very different design choice than one on a high deck that is attached to a house where there are young children.

The components of wood railings are usually readily available. You can even find decorative balusters, if that suits your fancy. Availability of the products on the facing page is likely to be more hit or miss. You may need to visit a variety of stores and do some research online to see what is available to you.

WOOD RAILINGS

Wood railings are the traditional choice for wood decks. They are affordable, easy to build, and time-tested. Perhaps the most typical style of wood railing is shown in the diagram on page 152. Other varieties are shown here.

Balusters can be attached directly to the rim or end joist, as shown below at left. This kind of railing is particularly easy to build and it uses a minimal amount of lumber, but it also requires that the decking be installed without any overhang. The absence of a gap between the decking and a bottom rail also makes it harder to sweep off debris.

Railings are also often built with flat cap rails covering the post tops (below, right). Another, less rustic look can be created with railing sections installed between posts (see page 162), with the post tops decorated by caps or with designs cut into them.

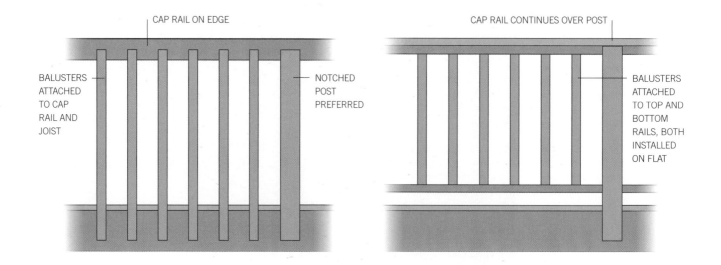

CAP RAIL ON EDGE

BALUSTERS ATTACHED TO CAP RAIL AND JOIST

NOTCHED POST PREFERRED

CAP RAIL CONTINUES OVER POST

BALUSTERS ATTACHED TO TOP AND BOTTOM RAILS, BOTH INSTALLED ON FLAT

COMPOSITE AND VINYL RAILINGS

Manufacturers of composite decking products are increasingly offering matching railing components. Solid composites can be found in standard railing sizes and can be cut and installed much like wood. Some extruded tubular products allow you to snake wiring runs through the railing to supply lights.

PVC railing systems are also available from a number of manufacturers. The glossy, smooth surface is not likely to be mistaken for wood, but with the growing popularity of vinyl siding and composite decking, a PVC railing can look right at home on many decks. A PVC railing is bought and assembled as a system; you can find components sized to match conventional railings, such as 4 × 4 posts, 2 × 2 balusters, and more. Similar systems are available in formulations other than PVC, including urethane foam, fiberglass, and other plastics.

Deck railings do not have to obstruct the view. Above, large glass panels fill the straight sections of a railing, while below, thick metal cables provide reasonably unobtrusive protection.

OTHER RAILING MATERIALS

If you want to maximize the view from your deck, it is hard to beat clear acrylic or tempered glass panels like those shown here. Some manufacturers offer a post-and-railing system that can accommodate clear panels, matching balusters, or a combination of both. Stainless-steel cable is also great for viewing the scenery, although some building codes prohibit the use of such horizontal railing systems.

preparing posts

Railing posts are usually made from 4 × 4s, although you can use 6 × 6s if you prefer a heftier appearance. Decorative milled posts are available (left), but you can also install regular posts and cut your own decorative pattern, or add a separate cap or finial (above).

Space the posts no more than 6 feet apart; a 4- or 5-foot spacing will create an even stronger railing. While operating within these guidelines, make an effort to keep the posts equally spaced along each side.

Posts should be bolted, not nailed, to the deck. To create a trimmer profile, railing posts are often notched to fit over the decking and joist. This practice does weaken the post connection, however, and is prohibited by some building codes. If you like the notched approach but are restricted by code, you may be able to notch $1\frac{1}{2}$ inches off 6 × 6 posts, but check with your building inspector before doing so.

Plan to keep a 2-inch gap between the house and the end post, which will make it easier to paint or replace the siding at a later date.

POST ATTACHMENT OPTIONS

Railing posts need to be attached to the rim joist and the end joists, and the method varies slightly for the two types of joists. Blocking is often necessary at post locations to strengthen the structure; use joist stock for the blocking. Plan to use two $\frac{1}{2}$-inch carriage bolts to attach each post unless your code says otherwise. Note that if access to the bottom of the deck will be difficult, you should plan to add the blocking before installing the decking.

Solid posts can be attached most easily to the outside of the joists. This approach allows you to finish the decking before having to worry about posts. But many people do not like the appearance of bulky posts hanging off the sides of their deck. With a little more planning, you can install solid posts inside the joists. You will need to do so before installing all of the decking (and you may want to do it before installing any of the decking). Notched posts are usually attached to the outside of the joist, with the $1\frac{1}{2}$-inch notch resting against the side of the joist and on top of the decking.

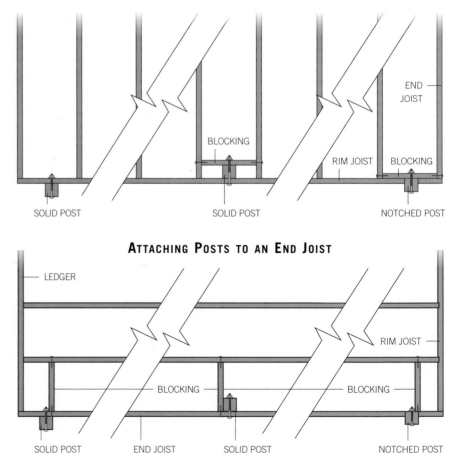

ATTACHING POSTS TO A RIM JOIST

BLOCKING
END JOIST
RIM JOIST
BLOCKING
SOLID POST
SOLID POST
NOTCHED POST

ATTACHING POSTS TO AN END JOIST

LEDGER
RIM JOIST
BLOCKING
BLOCKING
SOLID POST
END JOIST
SOLID POST
NOTCHED POST

NOTCHING POSTS

Properly planned and built, notched posts can produce a strong and attractive railing. The notch permits the post to be moved in closer to the deck by having the unnotched portion rest on top of the decking above the joist. Begin by cutting all posts to length, then follow the steps below for each one.

1 Lay Out the Post

From the bottom of each railing post, measure up the joist depth plus the decking thickness, subtract $\frac{1}{2}$ inch, and make a mark across the post.

2 Cut the Post

Set your circular saw to cut exactly $1\frac{1}{2}$ inches deep. Make a series of closely spaced cuts between the line marked in Step 1 and the post bottom. You can also make these cuts on a table saw or radial arm saw.

3 Clean Out the Notch

With a hammer, knock out the pieces of cut wood. Use a chisel to clean out the notch. Work carefully to create a notch that is squarely cut and the same depth throughout; avoid gouging out too much with the chisel.

4 Cut the Bevel

The exposed bottom edge of the post will look better if it is beveled. You can make this cut with a circular saw, with the blade tilted to make a 45-degree cut, but it will be easier to make a clean, accurate cut on a power miter saw.

installing posts and rails

The strength of the railing is determined first and foremost by the connection of the post to the deck frame. If the posts are plumb and evenly spaced, installing the rails and balusters will also proceed much more smoothly. For most railing styles, it is best to attach all the posts before assembling the rest of the railing.

ATTACHING POSTS

The procedures for attaching posts are similar regardless of whether they are notched or solid, or going on the inside or outside of the joists. Be sure to add any needed blocking, as shown in the illustrations on page 156.

If the posts are going on the inside, however, you can skip the first step at right. Cut and support decking to fit around the posts as shown on page 137.

1 Cut the Decking

If your decking overhangs the edge, you need to cut a notch so that the post can rest against the joist. For 4 × 4 posts, cut the notch about 3¾ inches wide, leaving a ⅛-inch gap between the decking on both sides. A jigsaw is the best tool for this job.

2 Set the Post in Place

If you are using notched posts, set the post in place with the top of the notched portion resting on the decking. With solid posts, you will have better luck having a helper hold the post in place. Use a level to ensure that the post is plumb. Drill pilot holes for each bolt, using a bit the same size or just slightly larger than the bolt diameter. To minimize the chances of splitting, do not locate the top bolt directly over the bottom one; instead, set each off-center just a bit, as shown.

3 Secure the Post

Slide the carriage bolts through the pilot holes. Next, reach beneath the deck and behind the joist to place washers on the bolts, then tighten the nuts on the bolts using a socket wrench or an adjustable wrench.

TURNING CORNERS WITH A RAILING

Handling railings at the corners of a deck takes some advance planning. Although it requires extra posts, a double post design is generally the easiest to install, especially when using continuous rails installed "on edge," with the wide side vertical. If you prefer the look of a single post at the corner, it is best to install all railing posts inside the joists, with rails set "on flat," as shown.

ADDING RAILS

The easiest way to install rails is to attach them on edge to the inside faces of the posts. Unless your deck is particularly long, you can probably accomplish this with a single board for each rail. A top rail and bottom rail are sufficient, but you may prefer to add a cap rail, which provides a flat surface along the top of the railing.

Somewhat more involved are rails installed on flat between the posts. Rails can be toenailed to the posts or attached with metal brackets designed for the job. This technique allows you to create decorative post tops and attach milled balusters between the rails, but keep in mind that the flat rails are not nearly as secure (when stepped on, for example) as rails set on edge. Although it requires a bit of work, you can create a stronger connection by placing the rails in dadoes cut into the posts, as shown at right. Alternatively,

you can install rails on flat, with a flat cap rail.

When rails are to be installed on flat, it is usually best to build entire rail sections, as described on page 162, and then attach the sections to the posts.

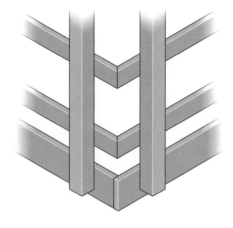

DOUBLE CORNER POSTS WITH RAILS ON EDGE

SINGLE CORNER POST WITH RAILS ON FLAT

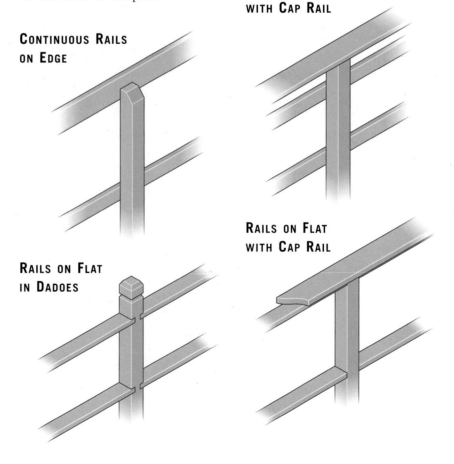

CONTINUOUS RAILS ON EDGE

RAILS ON FLAT IN DADOES

CONTINUOUS RAILS ON EDGE WITH CAP RAIL

RAILS ON FLAT WITH CAP RAIL

installing balusters

MILLED
BALUSTERS

Balusters are commonly made with 2 × 2 lumber and installed vertically. You can buy precut 2 × 2s or milled balusters in lengths that will fit standard railings. If you want to save a few dollars, you can cut your own balusters from long 2 × 2s. If you have access to a table saw, you can also rip balusters from straight 2 × 4s or 2 × 6s. Another good choice for wood balusters is 1 × 4s or 1 × 6s. If you want to maximize privacy, use wide boards and space them closely together.

If you cut your own balusters, make sure they are all the identical length. The most efficient way to do this is to use a power miter saw and construct a simple stop block, as shown in the photograph on page 71.

Balusters attached to the sides of rails look much nicer (and shed water better) if the ends are beveled. Keep the size and angle of the bevels consistent from baluster to baluster. If post bottoms will be visible on the deck, try to match the proportion of the bevels on the posts with those on the balusters, as shown below.

Above: When using a power miter saw to cut balusters, first cut them to length. Then move the blade for a 45-degree cut and adjust the stop block so that you can make consistent beveled cuts on each one. *Left:* If both post and baluster ends are exposed on your deck, cut the bevels at the same angle and keep the bevels comparable in proportion.

Building codes usually allow a maximum gap of 4 inches between balusters. Chances are good, however, that using that 4-inch gap will not result in evenly spaced balusters. For consistent spacing, do the following math. Add the width of one baluster ($1\frac{1}{2}$ inches for a 2 × 2) to the maximum allowed spacing (typically, 4 inches). Divide this total ($5\frac{1}{2}$ inches, in most cases) into the measured distance between two posts ($68\frac{1}{2}$ inches in the example). Finally, round up the result (12.45) to the next highest whole number (here, 13) to find the number of balusters you will need between the posts.

Now that you have the number of balusters, you can figure the spacing. Multiply the number of balusters (13) by the width of one ($13 \times 1\frac{1}{2}$ inches = $19\frac{1}{2}$ inches). Subtract that number from the distance

Calculate the Spacing

between the posts ($68\frac{1}{2} - 19\frac{1}{2} = 49$) and divide the result by the total number of spaces, which is always one more than the number of balusters (thus, $49 \div 14 = 3\frac{1}{2}$ inches). The result is the ideal spacing between balusters. Make a spacer as close to that figure as you can (if necessary, convert the number to its fractional equivalent). Double-check your math by making sure your result is less than the maximum baluster spacing allowed by code.

If the distance between posts varies by a small amount, you should not have to calculate different spacings for the balusters. People are not likely to notice small differences in the spaces between balusters. But you must keep all the gaps between balusters, or balusters and posts, at or below the maximum allowed by your code.

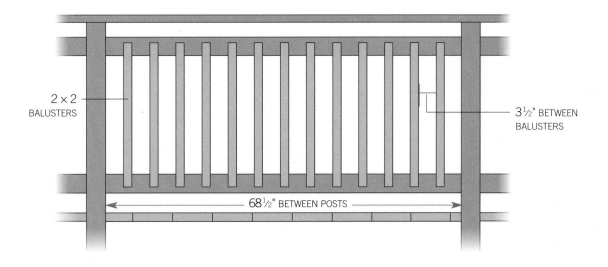

2 × 2 BALUSTERS

$3\frac{1}{2}$" BETWEEN BALUSTERS

$68\frac{1}{2}$" BETWEEN POSTS

ATTACHING THE BALUSTERS

Attaching balusters will proceed much more quickly if you make a spacer. Rip a piece of plywood or 1 × 4 or 1 × 6 lumber to match the desired space between rails. Make the spacer long enough to span from the top to the bottom rail. Press the baluster against the spacer and the neighboring baluster or post as you drive the fasteners.

Begin the installation by grasping a baluster and the spacer in one hand. Hold the spacer tight against the post while driving two screws or nails into each end of the baluster. Move the spacer to the other side of the baluster, pick up another baluster, and repeat the process.

assembling your railing a section at a time

For strong, easy-to-assemble railings, it is hard to beat the system outlined on pages 156–161: install posts, add rails on edge, and finish with balusters. In some areas, building codes insist on this technique. If your code is less strict, and your taste differs, you may prefer the look of a railing with balusters installed between flat rails. This type of railing takes more time to build, and it works best when the posts are perfectly plumb and evenly spaced. These railings are best assembled in full sections, which then are attached as units between posts.

To strengthen the assembly, plan to set the rails into $\frac{1}{2}$-inch-deep dadoes cut into the posts. The rails, therefore, should be cut 1 inch longer than the space between the posts. The dadoes are easiest to cut with a router or table saw before the posts are installed.

Balusters should be cut to identical lengths. To keep them from spinning in place, cut a $\frac{1}{2}$-inch-deep channel along the underside of the top rail just wide enough for the balusters to fit.

When all of the parts have been cut, assemble a railing section on the deck. Position the balusters with a spacer, as described on page 161. Drill a pilot hole at each baluster location, then attach the baluster with 3-inch deck screws driven through the top and bottom rails into the center of the baluster.

Once the balusters have been attached to the rails, lift the section into place, sliding the rail ends into the post dadoes. Fasten with 3-inch deck screws driven at an angle through each rail into the post.

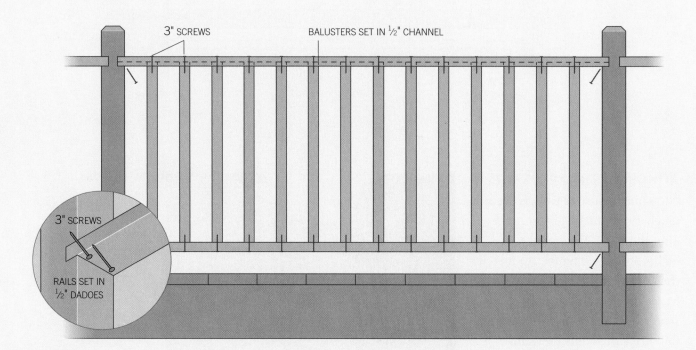

3" SCREWS   BALUSTERS SET IN $\frac{1}{2}$" CHANNEL

3" SCREWS

RAILS SET IN $\frac{1}{2}$" DADOES

INSTALLING METAL BALUSTERS

Metal balusters offer a distinctive look for your deck, and they are not difficult to install. Large home centers, suppliers of stair parts, and online vendors are good places to shop for a suitable product. Powder-coated metal tubing can be found in several colors. A ¾-inch outside diameter is best. Some manufacturers offer matching post caps and decorative centerpieces to dress up the railing. Type K or L copper tubing is another option; use ⅝-inch nominal tubing, which has a ¾-inch outside diameter.

A railing made with metal balusters is easiest to build in sections, as described on page 162, although it can also be built in place on the deck. The main difference is that the rails are installed on edge, so that no dadoes are needed in the posts. Begin by cutting the top and bottom rails to fit between the posts, then clamp them together on edge.

1 Prepare the Holes
Calculate the baluster spacing as explained on page 161. Instead of making a spacer, however, mark an on-center layout for the balusters on the two rails. To drill straight holes to a consistent ¾-inch depth, use a drill guide, as shown, or a drill press. Use a ¾-inch Forstner bit.

2 Assemble the Railing
Unclamp the two rails, clean the chips out of the holes, and put a small amount of silicone caulk into each hole. Insert the balusters tightly into one rail, then fit the other rail over the baluster ends. With one rail clamped in place, use a hammer and a piece of wood to tap the other rail to ensure that all balusters are fully seated in their holes.

3 Attach the Railing Section
Lift the railing section into place. Fasten the rails to the posts with small angle brackets on the rail bottoms and screws or nails driven at an angle through the rail tops into the posts. If you like, install a 2 × 6 cap rail on flat.

installing the stair railing

A railing will make climbing and descending any stairway easier and safer. Even if your local code is lax on the issue, consider adding a railing to at least one side of the stairs leading to your deck. (See page 140 for information on typical code requirements for stair railings.) Stair railings should resemble the deck railing as much as possible, with matching baluster and rail shapes and spacing. The primary difference is that stair railings require a handrail that can be grasped (see the sidebar on page 165). Stairs that are built alongside the house look fine with a single railing, but stairs in any other location are likely to look odd unless both sides have a railing.

PLAN THE POSTS

Stairs should be designed to be evenly spaced between two posts supporting the deck railing. With careful planning, you can use the deck posts as top posts on your stairs. With some railing designs or stair locations, however, it is preferable, or even necessary, to use separate posts for the deck and stair railings. Stair railing posts should be bolted to the stringers in the same manner as posts for the deck railing. Where notched posts are permitted, you can notch stair railing posts to match the posts on the deck railing, but the notch will have to be cut at an angle. Use posts a little longer than you need, then measure and cut them to length after they are installed.

DECK AND STAIR RAILINGS WITH SHARED POST

DECK AND STAIR RAILINGS WITH SEPARATE POSTS

INSTALL THE RAILS AND BALUSTERS

Lay a 2 × 4 across the tread nosings, as shown, and clamp it temporarily to the top post. Determine the height of the top rail (typically between 34 and 38 inches, although building codes often allow a range of 30 to 38 inches). Measure straight up from the bottom of the 2 × 4 on the bottom and top posts, as shown, and mark the distance on the outside edge of each post.

Depending on your railing style, use the marks to determine where to cut the posts or where to align the upper edge of the top rail. With most stairs, the bottom rail can be installed about 1 inch above the line established by the bottom of the 2 × 4 in the illustration and still be acceptable by code. Cut the rails to length and fasten them to the posts. Balusters can then be cut and installed as they were on the deck railing.

If you plan to install a cap rail flat across the tops of the posts, you will need to cut a corresponding angle on the posts to match the top rail. Fasten the cap rail to the stair railing posts in the same way as the cap rail is fastened on the deck railing.

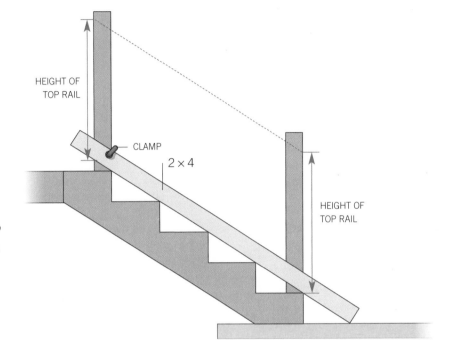

HEIGHT OF TOP RAIL

CLAMP

2 × 4

HEIGHT OF TOP RAIL

Something to Hold On To

The handrail is the critical component of a stair railing. Building codes often require that the handrail be "graspable," by which they mean that a person could grip it securely enough to keep from falling.

Hand sizes differ, of course, so it is best to use a handrail that is small enough to be grasped comfortably by as many people as possible. While codes may allow a handrail to be larger, the most sensible width (or diameter) is 1½ to 2 inches.

Few people could grasp a flat 2 × 6, but most people could benefit from the same 2 × 6 on edge. Even better are handrails that allow the fingers to curl around the bottom. This can be accomplished by ripping a board to a 2-inch width or less, then fastening it to the top of a 2× rail, as shown.

Another good choice is to use a standard round handrail, attached to posts with metal brackets. This approach allows you to build the stair railing to look exactly like the deck railing (with, for example, a 2 × 6 cap rail), and then attach the handrail, somewhat inconspicuously, to the top rail or the posts.

If the stairs to your deck are adjacent to the side of the house and the deck is low enough that it does not require a full railing, you can still make the few steps up and down easier to maneuver by attaching a handrail with brackets to the house itself. Just be sure that fasteners for the bracket are driven into the house framing or foundation.

HANDRAIL OPTIONS

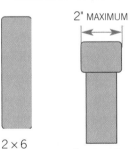

2" MAXIMUM

2 × 6

2 × 4 OR 2 × 6

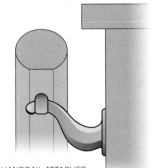

HANDRAIL ATTACHED TO POST OR TOP RAIL

installing the cap rail

With most railing designs, the final step is to attach the cap rail. Since it is so visible, try to use reasonably straight and clean boards for the cap. And since hands and bodies will likely be touching and leaning against it, make a special effort to smooth the edges to avoid cuts or snags; this is especially important on the stair railing.

ON FLAT A cap rail set on flat provides a smooth, consistent surface along the perimeter of the deck and hides the tops of the posts. Whenever possible, try to hide the fasteners by driving them through the bottom. (This will be most successful if you use screws and pre-drill holes for them; nails may push the joints apart.) Just be careful that the tips do not poke through the top surface.

When flat cap rails meet at a corner, join them with miter cuts, which neatly hide the end grain. If you need to join pieces of cap rail on a long run, use a scarf joint and be sure to locate it over a post.

ON EDGE Cap rails set on edge should be attached with fasteners driven through the cap and into the posts. Set the top of the cap at least an inch above the top of the post, and make sure that it is installed level around the deck.

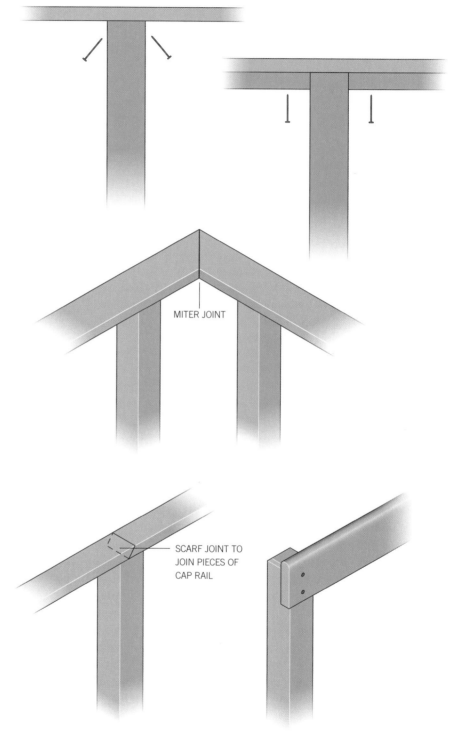

MITER JOINT

SCARF JOINT TO JOIN PIECES OF CAP RAIL

upgrades and options

AS WITH CARS AND WARDROBES, sometimes what separates the merely okay from the exceptional is the choice of accessories. While no deck really requires these additions, most decks will look better and provide more comfort if they include one or more of the projects described in this chapter. ■ Most enhancements to a deck are best thought of as built in rather than added on. With careful forethought and planning, you can tie your seating or an overhead into the deck's frame, which is the best way to ensure a solid connection. If you want to add some low-voltage lighting to a deck built low to the ground, you will find it easier to snake cables through the framing before you install the decking. Other options require still more pre-planning. If you have seen too many rectangular decks for your taste, you should consider the suggestions and instructions for building a curved deck on pages 180–184.

adding benches

Every deck needs some seating. Many people are content to buy standard patio furniture, which can be moved on, off, and around the deck at will. Others prefer the more rustic look of Adirondack chairs with matching tables, or picnic tables, which can be bought or built on site. If the latter option intrigues you, you might want to take a look at some books on constructing out-door furniture, including Sunset's *Building Garden and Patio Furniture*.

Still another popular choice is a hand-built bench, often made to match the decking. A couple of relatively simple bench projects are shown here. The built-in bench shown in two forms at right requires some work before the decking is installed, while the portable bench on the facing page can be put together any time.

A BUILT-IN BENCH

This simple but attractive bench is solidly supported by four 2×8 legs that are bolted to the joist framing. The basic design can be adapted for benches that run either perpendicular or parallel to the joists, as shown. The illustrations show a comfortable seating length of 5 feet, but the version built to run across the joists can be lengthened with additional supports spaced no more than 4 feet apart. Lengthening is not a good idea for the variation at bottom, however, since all of its weight rests on a single joist.

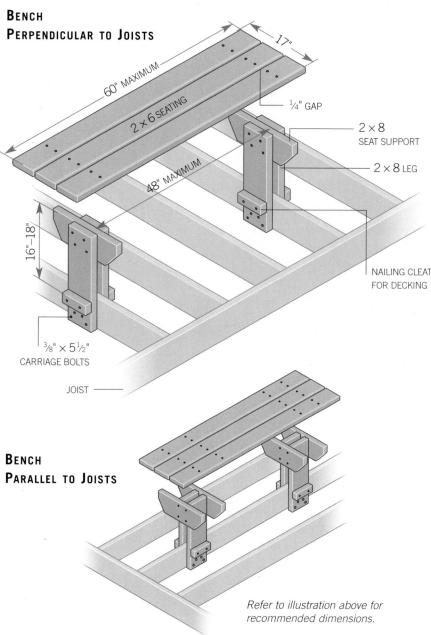

BENCH PERPENDICULAR TO JOISTS

17"

60" MAXIMUM

2 × 6 SEATING

¼" GAP

2 × 8 SEAT SUPPORT

2 × 8 LEG

48" MAXIMUM

16"–18"

NAILING CLEAT FOR DECKING

⅜" × 5½" CARRIAGE BOLTS

JOIST

BENCH PARALLEL TO JOISTS

Refer to illustration above for recommended dimensions.

Built-in perimeter benches can offer abundant seating on a deck. The matching tables on the deck above almost guarantee that the deck will be used regularly for eating meals and playing games.

A PORTABLE BENCH

This bench design is great for seating both on and off the deck. The 4 × 4 posts provide ample support. Build the leg and seat assemblies separately, then attach the two. You may want to build several portable benches for your deck, in varying lengths up to 4 feet.

PORTABLE BENCH

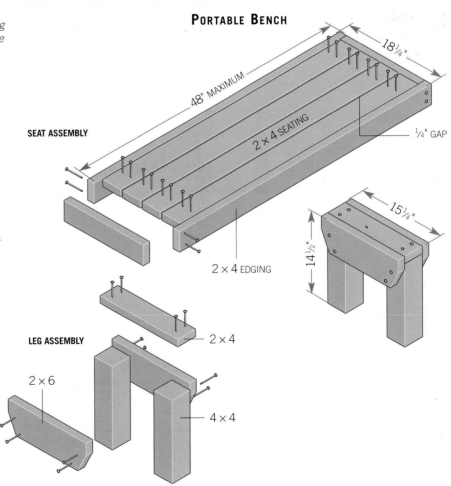

SEAT ASSEMBLY

18¼"

48" MAXIMUM

2 × 4 SEATING

¼" GAP

2 × 4 EDGING

15¼"

14½"

2 × 4

LEG ASSEMBLY

2 × 6

4 × 4

building overheads

An overhead structure can dramatically alter the character of a deck. It can provide some shade and protection from rain, which means that the deck can be used more often and more comfortably. But of equal importance is the fact that an overhead, no matter how modest, creates a more intimate sense of space, much like the canopy of a tree. More elaborate designs can become major visual statements of their own, making a deck seem much more than a simple flat surface.

Although there is almost no limit to the possible variations on an overhead design, the two illustrations at right present the basic issues you should consider right away. For most people, the key decision is to determine how much cover they want over their deck. The top design only hints at cover. It sets the space beneath it apart from the rest of the deck and adds a bit of visual interest, but it has virtually no effect on views or the elements. The specific design shown is composed entirely of 4 × 4s, but you can experiment with different sizes of lumber.

You can get more coverage by reducing the spacing between components and by adding additional layers. The overhead at lower right is an example of a particularly popular three-layer style, with each layer composed of differently sized and spaced members (beam, rafters, and slats).

The second big decision you need to make is how the structure will be supported. A freestanding overhead can be located anywhere on the deck. But overheads are more often placed over the transition from the deck to the house, an arrangement that allows one end to be supported by a ledger, just like the deck itself.

BEAM

RAFTER

POST

SLAT

POST

BEAM

LEDGER

RAFTER

FRAMING AN OVERHEAD

Deck overheads are sometimes built entirely above the deck surface, with the posts set in post bases attached to the decking and with bracing that ties the upper parts together. This approach works best when one side of the overhead is attached to a ledger on the house. Brace the frame as shown on page 106. For an overhead with a double 2 × 8 beam, it will be easier to use 4 × 4 braces as shown at top. For a more finished look, cover the metal post bases with wood trim, as shown at right.

Bolting the posts to the deck joists produces a stronger structure and may be required by your building code. It usually demands very little additional work and often eliminates the need for bracing at the top of the posts. If the decking has already been installed, remove a few boards to install the posts. Bolt and brace the posts to the joists as shown below. See page 156 for more information on attaching posts.

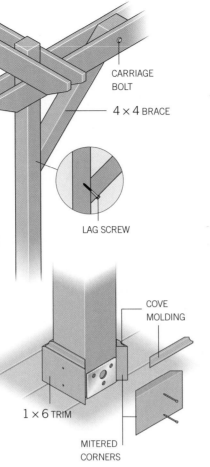

CARRIAGE BOLT

4 × 4 BRACE

LAG SCREW

COVE MOLDING

1 × 6 TRIM

MITERED CORNERS

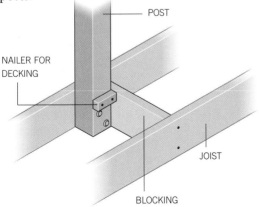

POST

NAILER FOR DECKING

JOIST

BLOCKING

Deck overheads can range from substantial and functional to minimal and even whimsical. The hefty example at top adds shade and enclosure, while the lighter one below defines the spa area of an otherwise wide-open deck.

PLANNING FOR SHADE

One way to increase the amount of shade from your overhead is to add more boards and space them closer together. Another method is to use angled louvers, which achieve the same effect with less expense and weight.

The more you tilt the boards, the fewer of them you will need. As a general rule, orienting louvers east to west and slanted away from the sun will block midday sun while admitting morning and afternoon sun. Running them north to south will admit either morning or afternoon sun, depending on the louvers' slant.

LESS CAN BE MORE

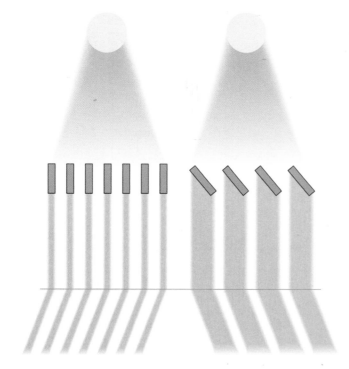

LESS SHADE FROM MORE BOARDS   FEWER BOARDS BUT MORE SHADE

Let the Snow Fall Through

If you live in snow country, plan your overhead so that it does not allow snow to pile up. Snow, accumulating through the winter on a flat surface, can develop into a heavy and dangerous addition to your deck. You can prevent this from occurring by keeping the boards on your overhead spaced at least 3 inches apart. Another approach is to use some form of removable panels (such as lattice), which can be fastened to the rafters during the summer and removed in winter.

DRESSING UP THE POSTS

The long posts supporting an overhead can be made to look less plain and leggy quite easily. Adding trim and molding at the bottom (see page 171) and at the top is one approach.

On relatively open overheads, you can run the post tops a foot or two above the rafters and decorate them with bevels and grooves, as shown in the illustration. You might want to mimic the style of your deck's railing posts.

Another idea is to train vines to grow up the posts. Twining vines are a good choice as they will spiral around the posts as they grow upward. You can choose between deciduous and evergreen vines, and vines that stay green or bear colorful fruits and flowers. If you cover the top of the overhead with closely spaced slats or lattice panels, you can also have the vines grow over the top. Do some research on the ultimate size and weight of a vine before you put it to work on your deck.

DRESSING UP THE RAFTERS

Overhanging rafter and beam ends are highly visible features of a deck overhead, so one simple way to give the structure its own look is to cut the ends in a decorative pattern. Some popular examples are shown here, but you can easily come up with your own. Once you settle on a pattern, make a plywood template to trace the pattern onto the boards before cutting them.

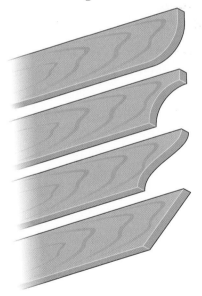

What better way to enhance the garden-like atmosphere of this deck than by running vines up the posts and along the simple overhead.

around for custom-made lattice that is strong enough to function as a railing. You can also make your own lattice by ripping 1× boards into strips of about 2 inches each, then fastening them together in a grid. Another option is to use narrower strips of standard lattice installed above a regular railing.

Lattice panels can be installed between 4 × 4 posts and 2 × 4 rails. Space these components carefully so that you can fit a 4 × 6 panel between them vertically. Set the lattice between 1-inch-square wood stops (or similarly sized pieces of molding), as shown in the illustration.

building a privacy fence

If you do not like the prospect of seeing and being seen by neighbors and passersby while enjoying your new deck, a privacy fence may be just what you need. A fence can also block an unpleasant view or annoying breezes.

A privacy fence is really just a modified section of the deck's railing, and as such it may be governed by the local code requirements for railings. Usually you can achieve the results you are after by adding the fence to one side of the deck, or even just one section of a side.

Additional privacy can be gained by building your railing a bit higher and by spacing balusters very close together. If you want the fence to be a foot or more

higher than the regular railing, it makes sense to design it separately. The fence should be attached to posts that are bolted securely to the deck's frame or otherwise anchored to the ground.

INSTALLING LATTICE PANELS

Lattice offers an easy way to screen a section of your deck. Standard lattice panels are not especially strong, however, so do not substitute the lattice for a required, secure railing. Instead, use it on low decks that would not otherwise need a railing, or shop

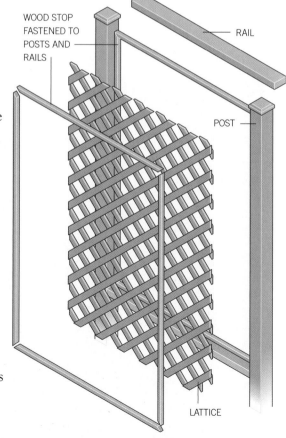

WOOD STOP FASTENED TO POSTS AND RAILS

RAIL

POST

LATTICE

BUILDING A HIGH RAILING

To support a high railing that doubles as a privacy fence, you may want to install a line of posts set on concrete piers along one side of your deck. With the solid connection to the earth and to the deck framing that this provides, you can create a sizable wall of privacy. You can create a higher version of the design used on the rest of the railing or, as shown in the illustration, give the privacy fence a look of its own. Here, wide and narrow boards alternate, but with a uniform and minimal gap between them. The design can be strengthened for use on a deck requiring a railing by adding one or more middle rails.

Unsightly views or a desire for less exposure to public view can be addressed by adding a privacy fence to a deck. Solid walls (opposite) or high, filled-in railing sections offer the most privacy, while more open styles like this one provide a less obstructive barrier.

installing skirting

Visually speaking, perhaps the weakest link on a deck is the space between the bottom of the deck and the ground. If this view of the deck frame is not to your liking, it is easy to cover it up with skirting. The area can also be put it to work as storage.

SKIRTING MATERIALS Lattice, the most popular material for deck skirting, is inexpensive and easy to install. Lattice can usually be attached to the posts beneath the deck. You can also attach 2 × 4 rails between the posts, inset just enough to allow the lattice to rest flush with the post faces. Fasten the lattice to the rails.

If space permits, you can build larger, removable lattice panels that permit the underside of the deck to be used for storage of outdoor items such as grills and lawn or deck furniture. Attach the lattice to a 1 × 4 frame to give it strength, then use hook-and-eye connectors or other hardware to attach the panels to a suitable frame under the deck.

A common alternative to lattice is wood siding or other solid boards. For any wood skirting that will touch the earth, make sure to use treated wood or wood rated for ground contact and apply water-repellent finish annually.

Top: *Lattice panels can be attached to the deck posts or a sturdy frame beneath the deck to hide the deck's framing while allowing for plenty of ventilation.*
Bottom: *On some decks, a more solid type of skirting looks best. Wood siding, perhaps chosen to match the siding on the house, is one easy option.*

FRAMES TO SUPPORT SKIRTING One very sturdy way to attach skirting is to build a modest 2 × 4 frame that can be attached to the deck joists. The top frame here works well for fairly narrow strips of lattice, while the bottom frame is ideal for skirting made of wood siding or boards.

FOR LATTICE

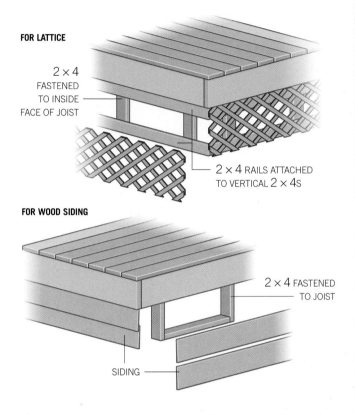

2 × 4 FASTENED TO INSIDE FACE OF JOIST

2 × 4 RAILS ATTACHED TO VERTICAL 2 × 4S

FOR WOOD SIDING

2 × 4 FASTENED TO JOIST

SIDING

The space beneath most decks eventually winds up being used to store at least a few outdoor items. If you would rather plan for a less haphazard result, secure the space with solid walls, a door that can be locked, and a dry floor of concrete or gravel.

Add a Planter

Planters are popular accessories for decks. They can be used on the deck to line the perimeter—a particularly attractive option on low decks without railings—or set on the ground around the deck as skirting to conceal the deck's underside. Often you will have enough leftover pieces of decking to make at least a few small planters. The illustration below shows a basic construction technique that can be adapted to planters of almost any size you like. This planter is designed to hold potted plants. If you would like to be able to add potting soil directly into the planter, line the sides and bottom with plastic sheeting or roofing felt, and poke some drainage holes through the bottom of the lining.

Always provide air space between planters and decking by setting the planters on ½-inch-high decay-resistant spacers; if possible, avoid placing planters over the deck's supporting members, since ongoing drainage could lead to structural rot. Spacers are also a good way to avoid ground contact for planters used as skirting.

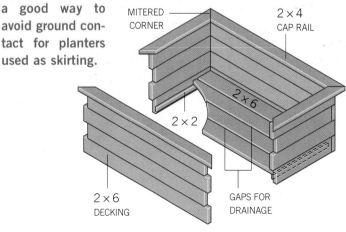

MITERED CORNER

2 × 4 CAP RAIL

2 × 6

2 × 2

2 × 6 DECKING

GAPS FOR DRAINAGE

lighting the deck

Well-planned lighting can make your deck safer and much more inviting after the sun sets. For occasional illumination, a camping lantern might suffice. But most people will want a more permanent source of light, and if your deck includes stairs, you may be required to supply it.

Since decks sit alongside the house, it is usually an easy task to install one or more outdoor fixtures that are tied into the normal household wiring. For versatility combined with safety, low cost, and easy installation, however, it is hard to beat low-voltage lighting.

LOW-VOLTAGE LIGHTING

A low-voltage system uses a transformer to reduce household current to 12 volts. You can buy low-voltage kits, or assemble your own system out of individual components. Just install the transformer, plug it into a GFCI receptacle, then connect the cable to the fixtures. Although each fixture can provide only a modest amount of illumination, a series of fixtures can add just the amount of light you need. And since the voltage passing through the cable is so low, you do not have to worry about curious children or pets suffering harmful shocks.

The transformer can be located inside the house (in the basement, for example), but most often it is placed outside, as shown here. Attach it to an inconspicuous part of the house or, if you can get under the deck, place it on a joist beneath the deck (top photo, right). The cable can be snaked through holes drilled in the framing and channels routed in posts or rails. Railing systems made from extruded composite materials provide ideal runways for cable, as do railings made with tubing.

Low-voltage fixtures can be attached in a number of ways to many locations. Among other things, they can be secured to stakes

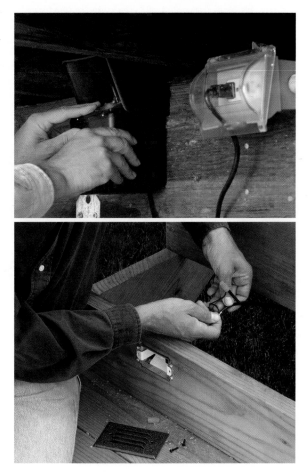

stuck in the ground around the deck, mounted to railing posts, or recessed into stair risers or stringers. Products from different manufacturers vary somewhat, so be sure to buy components that are compatible with your transformer and cable and to follow all instructions.

Top left: *A low-voltage transformer must be installed next to a GFCI outlet. If necessary, first install a GFCI receptacle in an electrical box rated for exterior use and for a permanent plug-in connection.*
Left: *Low-voltage cable can be snaked through holes drilled in the deck's framing. Here a recessed light is being installed in a stair riser.*

building a curved deck

If your idea of outdoor relaxation favors gentle bends over 90-degree corners, a curved deck could be ideal. A deck-in-the-round is certain to stand out, and, while building one does require a bigger commitment, it might be an easier project than you imagine.

Designing a foundation for a curved deck is relatively straight-forward. The rules for sizing and spacing footings, piers, and posts are the same as for a rectangular deck. Curved decks can also be framed and covered with decking without much fuss. But if the deck needs a railing, the workload can increase substantially. Before committing yourself to a curved deck with a railing, take a look at the information on page 184, and make sure you have a thoroughly designed railing in mind before you begin the construction.

FRAMING A ROUNDED CORNER

If you want to round only one or two corners on an otherwise rectangular deck, the framing is the same as for a simple mitered corner (see page 116). Just cantilever the joists well beyond a standard beam, then cut the joists at an angle, as shown in the illustration, and add an angled rim joist. Install the decking as you would for the corner of a rectangular deck, not worrying about the curve. Then mark the curve on the decking, as shown below, and cut with a jigsaw.

A corner curve such as this one requires minimal framing adjustments. To mark the cut line for the curve, drive a nail temporarily into the decking at a point equidistant from both sides, then tie a string to the nail. Tie the other end of the string around a pencil. With the string taut, mark the decking as shown.

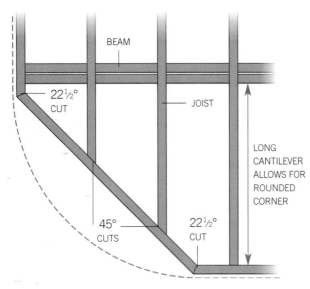

FRAMING ADJUSTMENTS FOR BIGGER CURVES

For bigger curves at the corners, or in order to round an entire side of the deck, you cannot support the deck with one or two long straight beams. This is the biggest framing difference from a rectangular deck. Because the joists must cantilever over the main beam by different amounts, you need to plan for additional beams to keep the joists from exceeding the allowable overhang distance. The angle of each added beam should approximate the outline of the curved deck, but the curve itself comes from the joists and decking.

In planning the deck, you can adjust the size of the arc by playing with different beam alignments and different joist overhang lengths. The illustration at lower left demonstrates what a big impact the addition of even one short beam can make in the overall curve of the deck. Just be sure that all the beam and joist spans, as well as the joist overhangs, do not exceed code limitations.

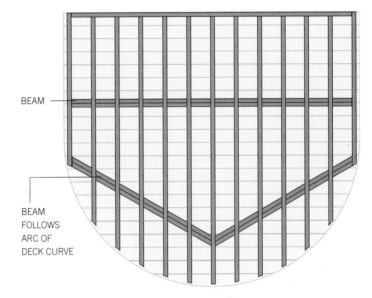

BEAM

BEAM FOLLOWS ARC OF DECK CURVE

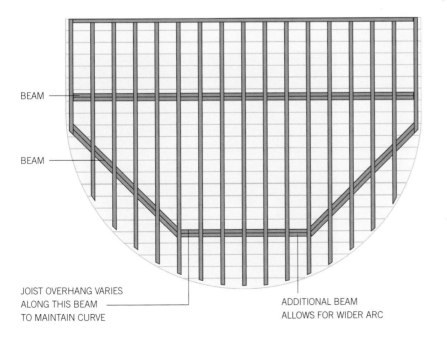

BEAM

BEAM

JOIST OVERHANG VARIES ALONG THIS BEAM TO MAINTAIN CURVE

ADDITIONAL BEAM ALLOWS FOR WIDER ARC

LAYING OUT A CURVE

The string and pencil method for marking a curve (see page 181) works well enough for small curves on the deck surface. To lay out a larger curve on joists, however, you may have better luck with one of the two methods shown here. Begin by installing joists with a large overhang, then mark and cut the joists before installing decking.

Determine the size and degree of radius you want and locate the center point. Place a temporary brace across the two nearest joists. Make a trammel (essentially a large compass) with a long 1 × 4. Drive a nail through one end of the trammel at the center point and place a pencil through a drilled hole at the other end. Mark the curve on the joists by pivoting the trammel.

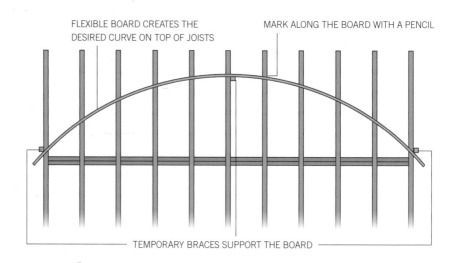

FLEXIBLE BOARD CREATES THE DESIRED CURVE ON TOP OF JOISTS

MARK ALONG THE BOARD WITH A PENCIL

TEMPORARY BRACES SUPPORT THE BOARD

For less circular curves, use a long piece of flexible material, such as paneling or thin wood siding. Bend the strip across the tops of the joists, adjusting the position and arc until you find a curve you like. Attach the ends and middle of the strip to temporary braces attached vertically to the joists, and mark the cut line on the joists by tracing alongside the strip.

CUTTING THE JOISTS

With a combination square, extend the cut line marks down both sides of each joist. Set your circular saw for the angle of the cut, then cut the joist as shown. Note that each joist will probably have to be cut at a different angle, requiring you to readjust the saw for each one. Some cuts may need to be at an angle that exceeds the range of your circular saw, in which case you should use a reciprocating saw.

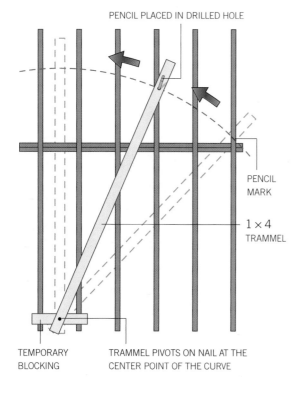

PENCIL PLACED IN DRILLED HOLE

PENCIL MARK

1 × 4 TRAMMEL

TEMPORARY BLOCKING

TRAMMEL PIVOTS ON NAIL AT THE CENTER POINT OF THE CURVE

With the saw adjusted for the necessary angle, cut the joists. If necessary, clamp a straightedge to the joist to guide the saw.

ADDING THE BLOCKING

Blocking between the joists will keep them from flexing as you bend the skirting around the ends. It also provides a solid nailing surface for the skirting and supports railing posts. If you do not plan to install a railing, you may be able to avoid adding the blocking, but you will need to take extra care in fastening the fascia directly to the joist ends.

INSTALLING THE FASCIA

You can make a curving fascia from several materials, and you should try to match the other materials on your deck as closely as possible. Thin strips of attractive, exterior-grade plywood (¼- or ⅜-inch-thick) can be bent into place easily. If you have access to a band saw, you can saw solid boards into thinner pieces for use in covering the joist ends. Be sure to apply finish to the plywood on the back, edges, and front before installing.

A standard 2× rim joist can be turned into a bendable fascia by cutting a series of 1⅜-inch-deep kerfs, spaced 1 inch apart, across the back side of the board. Soak the board for a couple of hours to make it easier to bend.

Perhaps the easiest approach is to use composite fascia boards. Many manufacturers of composite decking now offer matching 10- or 12-inch-wide boards that are ½ inch thick or even less, making them extremely easy to bend.

Blocking ends need to be cut at angles for a good fit between joists. On one side, drive nails through the joist and into the blocking. On the other side, nail through the outside face of the blocking into the joist.

Thin pieces of wood or composite fascia board are easy to install on a curved deck. Try to find fascia material that matches the decking or visible framing lumber.

ADDING THE DECKING

Decking can be installed largely as described in Chapter Six. The major difference here is that you should lay the decking in place around the curve without fastening it. Make sure the boards are spaced properly, then trace along the fascia on the underside of the decking to mark the outline of the curve. Turn the decking over, cut the curves, then turn it over again and install it.

MARK AND CUT THE CURVE ON THE DECKING BEFORE FASTENING TO JOISTS

DECKING OVERHANGS DECK FRAME

BUILDING A CURVED RAILING

If it is high enough, a curved deck needs a curved railing. Posts for the railing can be installed as described on pages 156–159. Because of the extra pressure that bent rails can exert on the posts, however, it is best to space them on 4-foot centers, or even less for a tight radius. For maximum strength, plan to use unnotched posts secured to the joists with blocking on all sides. Once the posts are installed, you can put in the decking (see page 183).

The easiest way to install rails is to use thin wood or composite boards, attached to the insides of the posts. Alternatively, several layers of ¼-inch-thick wood can be glued together to form a strong, bendable rail. For best results, clamp the rail to the post temporarily before fastening with screws. If your code allows, you could use a series of horizontal rails to complete the railing. To minimize the potentially dangerous ladder effect this creates, however, install regular balusters to the outside faces of the rails.

If you choose to install a flat cap rail, cut segments of 2× lumber at angles that roughly correspond to the curve of the deck. First glue the segments together, then mark the curves and cut them with a jigsaw. Attach the cap rail to a double top rail, as shown.

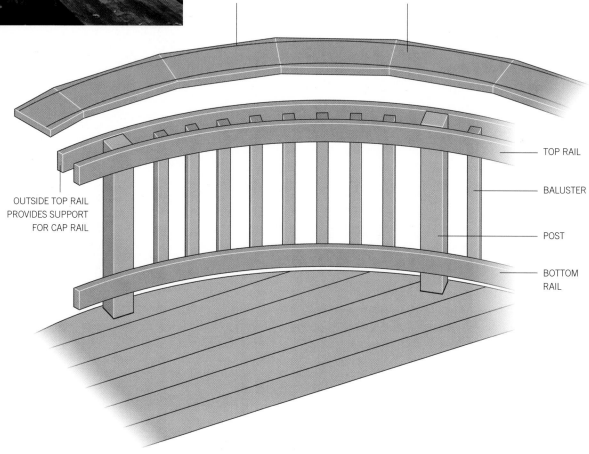

RAIL MARKED FOR DESIRED CURVE

CAP RAIL SEGMENTS MITERED AND GLUED TOGETHER

TOP RAIL

BALUSTER

POST

BOTTOM RAIL

OUTSIDE TOP RAIL PROVIDES SUPPORT FOR CAP RAIL

finish, maintenance, and repair

WHILE SOME OF THE ADS FOR NEWER COMPOSITE DECK MATERIALS may make you think otherwise, the maintenance-free deck has yet to materialize. Composites can eliminate the task of applying new finish to the decking, but the wood frame of your deck still needs to be tended to on a regular basis. And all-wood decks still require regular cleaning and refinishing every year or two. ■ This chapter offers advice on which finishes work best and how they should be applied. You will also find practical advice on how to inspect a deck so that you can identify and fix minor problems before they become major ones. Finally, if you have inherited an old deck that has deteriorated beyond the point of salvation, you will find advice on how to remove it before building a replacement.

choosing a finish

Wood decks need a finish to protect them from sun, rain, mildew, and insect damage. The shelves at your local home improvement or hardware store are probably filled with various products suitable for deck finishing. Some are much more durable and effective than others. Fortunately, determining which finish is best for your deck is not particularly difficult.

Broadly speaking, there are two categories of wood finishes. Penetrating finishes provide protection by soaking through the surface of the wood, while film-forming finishes create a protective coating on the wood's surface.

PENETRATING FINISHES

Most products sold as deck finishes do not form a film on the wood, which means the deck can breathe and the surface of the wood can show through. Wood preservatives, water repellents, and pigmented deck stains are the major types of penetrating finishes.

Clear penetrating finishes are very popular. They are widely available and affordable, and many people appreciate the ability of such finishes to retain the natural color of the decking. But clear finishes are also the least durable and need to be reapplied every year. Clear finishes containing a mildewcide and ultraviolet

(UV) stabilizers provide added protection.

Semi-transparent stains provide a degree of protection against sun damage that clear finishes, even those containing UV stabilizers, cannot match. Consequently, you can expect these coatings to last two to three years between applications. A wide range of colors is available.

Don't Wait on the Finish

Do-it-yourselfers and building professionals alike can often be heard offering the advice to let a deck weather in the sun awhile before applying the first coat of finish. For most decking, it is bad advice. The most important coat of finish your deck will ever receive is the first one, and you want to get it on as quickly as possible, which means as soon as the wood is dry to the touch. Pressure-treated wood may need to dry for a week or two, and untreated wood can often be finished right away. Test the wood for dryness by sprinkling it with some water. If the water soaks in quickly, the wood is ready to be finished.

If you use lumber with a factory-applied water repellent, however, you may need to wait two or three months before applying a semi-transparent stain to it. Check with the dealer to obtain specific recommendations.

PRESSURE-TREATED PINE

Finishes vary in appearance depending on the type of wood to which they are applied. On these two boards, clear, redwood, and gray stains produce very different results.

REDWOOD

FILM-FORMING FINISHES

Paint and solid-color stain are finishes that seal wood with a protective film on the surface. They are used successfully to protect wood siding and trim on houses, but they should be approached with some caution for use on a deck. Because they do not allow the wood to breathe, the surface is prone to cracking and peeling, and foot traffic can turn a painted deck surface into an eyesore in very little time.

If you want to apply paint or solid-color stain to your deck, restrict it to the most visible parts, such as posts, rails, and balusters. Even there, be sure to coat the wood with a paintable water-repellent preservative first.

The beauty of a painted deck can begin to fade almost as soon as the deck is put into service. Without frequent refinishing, the wood may begin deteriorating much sooner than it should.

TEST THE FINISH

If you are using a stain on your deck, be aware that the same stain can look very different when applied to different types of wood, and it is hard to gauge the final color by looking at the color strips at the store. For an accurate test, apply some stain to a scrap piece of the same wood you used on the deck.

Adding Color to a Deck

Deck design has traditionally leaned toward the rustic look, with natural-wood tones dominating the color palette. But there is really no reason why your deck should follow suit. As composite decking products begin to alter our image of what a deck is "supposed" to look like, many people are taking the change a step further by using increasingly vibrant colors on their decks. Bright, cheerful exterior stains suitable for use on decks are available at home centers, paint stores, and through online sources. These stains may be most effective if used in moderation, such as on some balusters or other railing components. Test the stains on a sample of the wood you are using on your deck before making any final decisions.

applying the finish

Once you have selected the right finish for your deck, applying it is a matter of getting the right tools, waiting for the right weather, and allowing yourself the time to do it correctly.

CHOOSING AN APPLICATOR

Deck finish can be applied quickly with a roller or a pump sprayer. You can usually buy pump sprayers at paint stores and home improvement centers. Brushing is more effective, however, since the finish is more likely to be worked into the wood. You will need a brush to apply finish to railings and other smaller sections of the deck. For best long-term results, use a brush to apply at least the first coat of finish to your new deck.

For a nice combination of speed and thoroughness, have a partner use a roller or sprayer to apply the finish while you work it into the wood with a brush. If you are brushing on an oil-based stain, use a natural-bristle brush for best results. For water-borne finishes, synthetic-bristle brushes work best.

While composite decking does not require a finish, it can usually take a stain if you wish to apply one (see page 133).

Finishing Below?

Obviously, you will want to apply the finish to all visible parts of the deck. What do-it-yourselfers often overlook, however, is that the underside of the deck can also benefit from a coating of finish. Sun and foot traffic do not often affect the joists, ledger, beams, and posts, but moisture, temperature variations, and insects can. So if it is at all possible—especially on a new deck—apply finish to all the wood surfaces that can be reached on a deck. A pump sprayer can be particularly useful for reaching remote sections of the deck's underside.

GETTING STARTED

The ideal weather for applying deck finish is slightly overcast, with no rain in the immediate forecast. Most finishes should not be applied when the temperature is below 50 or above 90 degrees. Follow the steps below to apply a fairly thin layer of finish. Let it dry, then add a second coat. Take care to work the finish into exposed end grain and into any joints where water could be trapped.

1 Sand the Wood

New lumber tends to have a slight glaze on the surface from the milling process. The wood will better absorb finish if you lightly sand the surface before applying the first coat. A pole sander, with 120-grit sandpaper, allows you to sand while standing up. Alternatively, use an orbital sander.

2 Clean the Wood

Sweep the deck thoroughly with a broom. Use a shop vacuum or a putty knife to clean out sawdust and other debris between boards.

3 Add the Finish

Wear eye protection when using a sprayer or when applying finish to overhead surfaces. If you are using a stain, try to minimize lap marks, which occur when you brush new finish over previously applied finish that has begun to dry. Instead, apply the stain along the full length of a couple of boards at a time. Never let the stain puddle on the surface.

cleaning and refinishing

Left alone, a wood deck will turn driftwood-gray in color as it weathers. This natural process can begin within days after the wood has been exposed to the sun. While many people prefer the weathered look to the appearance of freshly sawn lumber, it is better for the long-term survival of the deck if the wood is regularly cleaned and refinished as shown here. You can always simulate the weathered look without compromising that protection by using a gray-tinted semi-transparent stain.

STRIPPING A DECK If the old finish on your deck has worn out inconsistently, with stain or sealer visible in some areas but scraped away in others, you will have better success with a deck cleaner if you first use a deck stripper. Used as directed on the container, a stripper will remove the old finish entirely, allowing the deck cleaner to do a more thorough job. And if you just do not like the color of the old finish, a deck stripper is also the best way to get rid of it.

Paint can be removed from a deck easily with a water-neutralized paint stripper. Brush the stripper onto the deck, let it sit awhile, then rinse the deck with a power washer or the spray nozzle on a garden hose. Scrapers and sandpaper can remove paint from parts of the deck where it remains.

1 Clean Out the Recesses
Use a putty knife or small screwdriver to remove debris that has accumulated on joists between deck boards and other nooks and crannies on the deck. Although this may seem like a relatively minor step, it is actually vital. These spots are prime candidates for rot to set in.

2 Apply Deck Cleaner
Specially formulated deck cleaners effectively cut through dirt and kill mold and mildew. Some cleaners should be diluted with water, others are applied full strength. Wait for a cool, overcast day (cleaners tend to evaporate too quickly under dry, sunny conditions) and apply the deck cleaner with a pump sprayer.

3 Scrub the Deck

Let the cleaner sit on the deck for about 15 minutes, then scrub it thoroughly with a stiff-bristled brush. Use a large brush for the deck surface and a smaller one for the railing and stairs. Brush the wood in the direction of the grain.

4 Rinse the Deck

A pressure washer is ideal for rinsing the deck, but only if you know how to use it without damaging the wood; consult the directions carefully. A spray nozzle on a garden hose is a perfectly suitable, and less risky, alternative. Be sure to rinse all of the cleaner from the deck.

5 Apply New Finish

Let the deck dry for a day or two (but not much longer). Apply the finish as described on pages 188–189. If you use a roller for the deck surface, you should plan to use a brush to work the finish between the boards and on other parts of the deck.

inspecting and repairing a deck

Even the best-built decks require periodic maintenance. Wood shrinks and expands, making once-tight joints separate. Fasteners lose their grip and may start rusting. Rot can develop in out-of-sight parts of the deck. While you cannot stop the aging process, you can slow it down by performing a thorough inspection at least once a year.

Top: *All nuts, bolts, screws, and nails on a deck will need to be tightened from time to time. If the fastener no longer seems to be holding tight, check for rot in the wood.* **Bottom:** *Check for rot in wood by probing questionable spots with a pocket knife or other sharp object. Soft, spongy areas should be repaired or replaced right away; otherwise, the rot will continue to spread.*

INSPECTION CHECKLIST

Use this checklist to assess the most important and trouble-prone parts of the deck. If your answers suggest a problem, consult the following pages for repair methods; for damaged or missing railing parts, install replacements as shown on pages 156–161. For significant foundation problems or other major structural concerns, consult a professional.

DECKING
- ✓ Have the fastener heads worked their way above the deck surface?
- ✓ Is the wood free of rot and splitting?
- ✓ Have the ends of deck boards begun warping?
- ✓ Is the wood decking free of splinters and excessive cupping?

JOISTS
- ✓ Is the wood free of rot and splitting, especially at the ends and where the joists contact the beams and decking?
- ✓ Are the joist hanger connections and fasteners tight and secure?
- ✓ Is the rim joist tight against the joist ends?

POSTS
- ✓ Are the posts free of rot and splitting, especially at the ends?
- ✓ Are the fasteners tight and secure?
- ✓ Do the posts appear to be plumb?

STAIRS
- ✓ Do the stairs meet current code?
- ✓ Have mold and mildew made the treads slippery?
- ✓ Is the wood free of rot and splitting, especially the stringers?
- ✓ Are the treads fastened securely to the stringers?

RAILINGS
- ✓ Does the railing wobble when you lean against it?
- ✓ Does it meet current code?
- ✓ Are the posts securely bolted to the deck frame?
- ✓ Is the wood free of rot and splitting?
- ✓ Are the rail and baluster connections tight and solid?

LEDGER AND BEAM
- ✓ Is the ledger free of rot and splitting?
- ✓ Are the bolts connecting the ledger to the house tight and secure?
- ✓ Is there any sign that the ledger has separated from the house?
- ✓ Is the flashing solid, with its edges sealed?
- ✓ Is the beam sagging, cracked, or rotted?

FOUNDATION
- ✓ Are the concrete piers free of major cracks or deterioration?
- ✓ Is there any sign that footings and piers have sunk or shifted (for example, has the deck developed a slope)?

REPAIRING DECK BOARDS

When deck boards splinter, you can smooth them with a small sander or some sandpaper. Cups and small warped areas can often be eliminated with a plane or sander. When the board is severely warped, rotted, or split, however, it should be replaced.

Far-sighted deck builders prepare for this eventuality by keeping some extra decking material on hand, even leaving a few boards to weather in an inconspicuous location outdoors so that they will look right at home when added to the deck. If you have not made this kind of preparation, however, do not worry. Just be sure to use the same type of decking and finish as you originally installed, and the new board or boards will eventually weather to match the rest of the deck.

Begin by removing all nails or screws holding the board in place. You may need a cat's paw to grasp nail heads and to pry the decking away from the joists. Fasten a new board in place with deck screws, then trim it to length.

If you find that nails keep pulling away from the decking, replace them with deck screws. If you are unable to pull the nails out with a cat's paw or hammer claws, use a nail punch to drive them farther into the joist.

Let the replacement decking board overhang the side of the deck while it is being attached. Then you can accurately cut it to length.

REPAIRING JOISTS

If you detect rot on a joist early enough, the repair is easy to make. Remove the rotted material with a hammer and chisel, then coat the newly exposed wood with a water-repellent preservative. Cut a "sister" joist to the same length as the damaged joist, using the same size lumber. Slide the sister joist into place against the old joist and attach with 10d nails every 2 feet. Attach the decking to the sister joist. If the underside of the deck is inaccessible, you will need to remove deck boards to attach the sister joist.

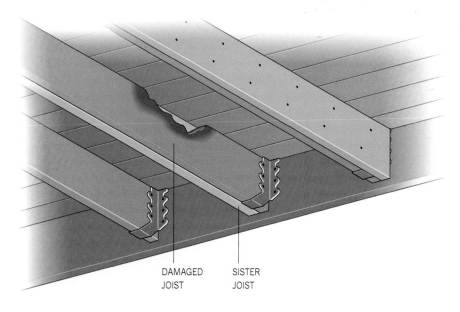

DAMAGED JOIST   SISTER JOIST

REPLACING POSTS

Replace a failing deck post as soon as you can. Begin by jacking up the beam. On a low deck, use a hydraulic bottle jack and concrete block along with pieces of wood, as shown at near right. For a higher deck, use a telescoping jack. Apply just enough pressure to lift the beam very slightly off the post. Remove the post and install a new post base. Cut the new post to length and set it in place, with a new post cap on top. When it is plumb, lower the beam so that it is resting on the post, but keep the jack in place for the moment. Attach the post to the beam, then remove the jack.

For an old post that was buried in concrete, dig out as much of the buried wood as possible, fill up the cavity with fresh concrete, and add a new anchor bolt and a new post base. Then attach the new post to the post base.

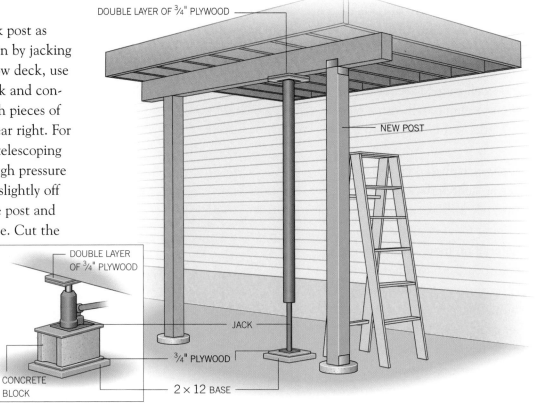

REPLACING STAIR TREADS

Damaged stair treads should also be replaced as soon as they are discovered. Pry loose a nailed-in tread or back the screws out of a screwed-in tread. With the tread removed, take this opportunity to check the condition of the stringers. Cut a replacement tread to length, using the same material as the old tread, and attach it to the stringer.

Attach a replacement tread with screws driven into the stringers. If the stringers are too rotted to hold a screw, they should be replaced.

REPLACING A BEAM

Beams can crack or rot, which requires that they be replaced. If you inherited an old deck with a sagging beam, it is possible that the beam was undersized when the deck was built, in which case it also should be replaced.

Replacing a beam is not particularly difficult if you work carefully and give the job your full attention. First build a temporary replacement beam by nailing together three 2 × 8s that are at least as long as the old beam. It is also smart to have the new beam ready to install before you start removing the old one (see pages 102–105 for a full discussion of beams).

Set the temporary beam on top of jacks (see page 194) close to the old beam, but leave enough room to work. Use at least as many jacks as there are posts supporting the old beam. Raise the jacks just enough to release the pressure of the old beam on the posts. Remove fasteners and hardware securing the beam to the posts and joists, then remove the beam. Cut the beam into smaller sections beforehand, if that makes the removal easier.

Set the new beam and new post caps in place. Make sure the beam spans the full width of the deck and all posts are plumb. Fasten the beam to the joists and the posts. Then remove the temporary beam and the jacks.

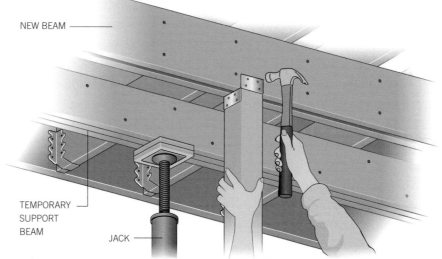

NEW BEAM

TEMPORARY SUPPORT BEAM

JACK

REVIVING A DECK

Years of neglect resulted in this deck becoming an eyesore and even a potentially dangerous place to be (left). The homeowner was able to bring the same deck back to life by replacing the 1 × 4 fir decking with new pressure-treated ⁵⁄₄ × 6 boards, adding a sturdy new railing, and lining the perimeter with functional benches and attractive planters. The revitalized deck was stained after this photograph was taken.

removing an old deck

Often the first step in building a new deck is to dismantle an old deck. Some major deck problems can be fixed without taking such a drastic measure: decking can be replaced, railings and stairs can be rebuilt, joists and posts can be repaired, beams can be replaced, and wood can be revitalized. But if the frame and foundation are failing or inadequate (see page 45), or if the overall design does not meet your needs, removal of the deck is the only option.

The quickest way to tear apart a deck is to cut it into pieces. If you try to remove fasteners one at a time, the job will take much longer. The most important tools for the job are a reciprocating saw with a demolition blade, a circular saw, a large pry bar, and a sledge-hammer. Be sure to wear long sleeves, gloves, a dust mask, ear protection, and eye protection to cope with flying dust and debris.

Have a local garbage disposal service place a dumpster as close to the deck as possible. Cut up the deck into pieces that you can throw into the dumpster. If the deck contains pressure-treated lumber, be sure to mention that fact to the disposal service.

In general, you should remove the deck in the reverse order in which it was built. Concrete footings may serve for a new deck, or may simply be left in place unused; removing them is usually very costly in time or money.

The following sequence will work for most decks:

- Cut off power to any electrical fixtures on the deck, disconnect the wiring, and remove the fixtures. Also remove any plumbing.
- Remove overheads, benches, planters, or other features that were added to the original deck.
- Cut the railings into removable sections.
- Snap chalk lines on the decking to identify joist locations, then cut through the decking on each side of the joists.
- Cut and remove the joists, one at a time.
- Remove treads and risers from stairs, and cut stringers loose from the deck.
- Cut up the beam and then the posts.
- Remove fasteners holding the ledger to the house and carefully pull or pry it off.
- Remove old flashing.

This old deck has seen better days. Since there is such a great view, however, the decision to rebuild the deck is easy to make.

deck plans

THE REAL-LIFE DECK DESIGNS IN this chapter can simplify planning for your own deck and help you to produce a more beautiful and effective result. In addition to the plans, you will find photographs of the finished projects and lists of the materials used to build them. ■ Differences in styles, foundations, materials, and details reflect the designers' preferences and local conditions. You will probably need to make adjustments to suit your own situation. Some basic approaches to adapting the plans are described on pages 198–199, and each project also includes notes on particular variations. ■ Whether or not one of the plans suits your needs, you can also look through the projects to find ideas for the aspects of any deck. Take a look at building details such as unusual railings, stairs, or other features.

adapting custom plans

Chances are that none of the plans in this book will fit your needs exactly. You will probably have to adjust the deck size to fit your site, and adapt the layout to such specific house details as the location and height of doors. Often, you may need to change aspects of the foundation to adapt to the terrain. You may also want to adjust aspects of the deck's style or specific details. Even if you wish to use a plan "as is," your local building code and local conditions may require some changes.

To get started, think about your new deck from the top down. Draw exactly what you want the decking to look like, and then make any needed changes to the existing plan: first to the framing, then to the foundation. Check pages 60–63 for lumber and fastener choices.

Practical considerations, such as lumber availability, may also dictate changes. If you want to use a different decking material than the one specified, you may find that structural changes are necessary. This is especially true for composite decking, which often requires tighter joist spacing, but even switching from one species of wood to another can have a ripple effect on the joists, beams, posts, and foundation.

READING THE PLANS

The plans provided in this book include plan views, elevations (including elevation sections), and detail drawings (see pages 56–57). Three-dimensional renderings offer additional information for some details. Where appropriate, the drawings are linked together with a reference symbol, as shown below.

CHECKING LOCAL CODES

In most areas, you will need a building permit to begin construction on almost any deck (see pages 52–53). Share the plans for your deck with your local building department and find out the requirements for a permit, including any needed inspections. Each of the deck plans that follow was approved by a building department in the jurisdiction where the deck was built, but the plans may require modification in your area.

PLAN VIEW

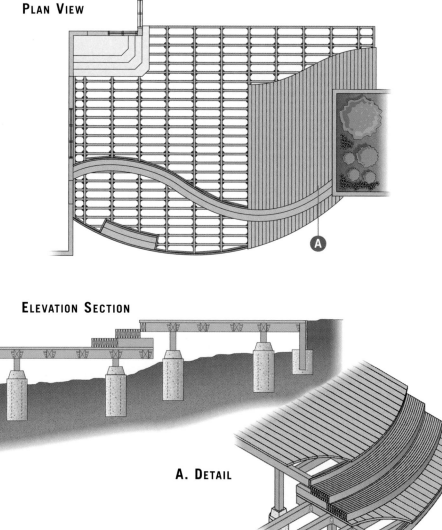

ELEVATION SECTION

A. DETAIL

MAKING CHANGES

Some of the most common optional plan adaptations are described below. You will need to make any such adjustments to your plans before they are approved by your local building department.

RAISING OR LOWERING Increasing the height of the deck surface will likely mean more than just using taller posts. If a deck is 30 or more inches above the ground, codes often require railings for safety, and railings are common even at slightly lower heights. If you go above 36 inches, you will probably need to cross-brace the perimeter posts.

If you lower a deck, it is a good idea to leave at least 6 inches between the ground and wood members, even if you are using pressure-treated lumber. This clearance is only mandatory for untreated wood, however. Treated lumber or rot-resistant species such as redwood or cedar heartwood are sometimes used closer to the ground for appearance.

ENLARGING, REDUCING, OR RESHAPING Enlarging a deck is often easy. You can add posts, piers, and footings and increase the length (and sometimes the size) of the ledgers, beams, and joists. Always check span and spacing tables for the type of lumber involved to be sure you are working within allowable limits, and remember that larger decks may require bigger joists, beams, posts, and foundations.

Reducing the size of a deck may only involve shortening structural members, and in some cases using smaller lumber. You may also be able to eliminate some posts, piers, and footings.

Changing the shape of a deck can be more complicated, although in the case of a rectan-gular design you will simply follow the rules for enlarging and reducing. In some cases, you can look at the plans as modules to be adapted to the shape you want. Connect modules by extending ledgers alongside end joists and by doubling joists so that they become beams, as shown below.

ATTACHING OR DETACHING Most attached decks can be made freestanding, and most freestanding decks can be attached to a house. Detach a deck from a house by replacing the ledger with a beam of the same length, supported by posts; for additional modifications that may be required, see page 79. To attach a freestanding deck design, you can usually replace a beam with a ledger of suitable size. Make sure to anchor the ledger securely to the house framing, as described on pages 80–84.

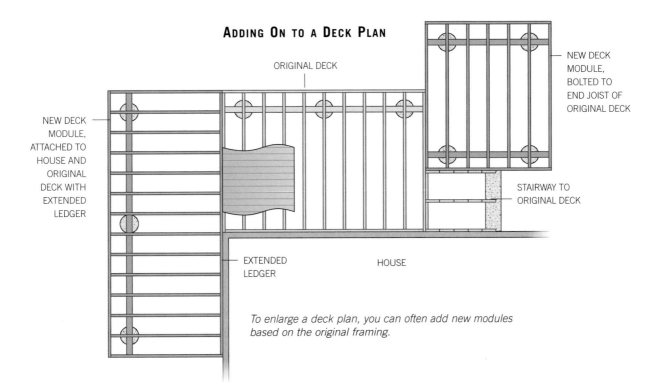

ADDING ON TO A DECK PLAN

ORIGINAL DECK

NEW DECK MODULE, BOLTED TO END JOIST OF ORIGINAL DECK

NEW DECK MODULE, ATTACHED TO HOUSE AND ORIGINAL DECK WITH EXTENDED LEDGER

STAIRWAY TO ORIGINAL DECK

EXTENDED LEDGER

HOUSE

To enlarge a deck plan, you can often add new modules based on the original framing.

poolside paving deck

This handsome, irregular, and extremely simple deck hides a worn pool coping from view and provides a welcome spot for sunning and relaxing. On the pool side, the heavy 3 × 6 deck boards are cut to a smooth contour. On the garden side, they are cut at random lengths. A simple support system of concrete piers and beams makes the deck quick and easy to build. There are no posts or joists. Gravel and stones over landscape fabric keep weeds at bay.

TO ADAPT THIS PLAN

This deck is adaptability itself, almost as much a wood paving system as a deck plan. It is at home in any garden, with or without a pool. Add piers to extend the structure in any direction.

MATERIALS LIST

Designed for pressure-treated lumber (beams), Construction Heart redwood (decking), and galvanized hardware.

LUMBER	
Beams	4 × 6
Decking	3 × 6
MASONRY	
Concrete	Piers
Stone/gravel	Mulch under and around deck
HARDWARE	
Nails	As appropriate for connectors
Connectors	Saddle brackets
Other	Hidden metal-bracket fasteners

BUILDING NOTES

Because there are no posts, you must keep the tops of the piers level with each other to ensure that the beams will be level as well. You can make up for minor discrepancies with pressure-treated shims, but taking special care with the foundation will be time well spent.

DESIGNER
Ransohoff, Blanchfield, Jones, Landscape Architects

Plan View—Decking

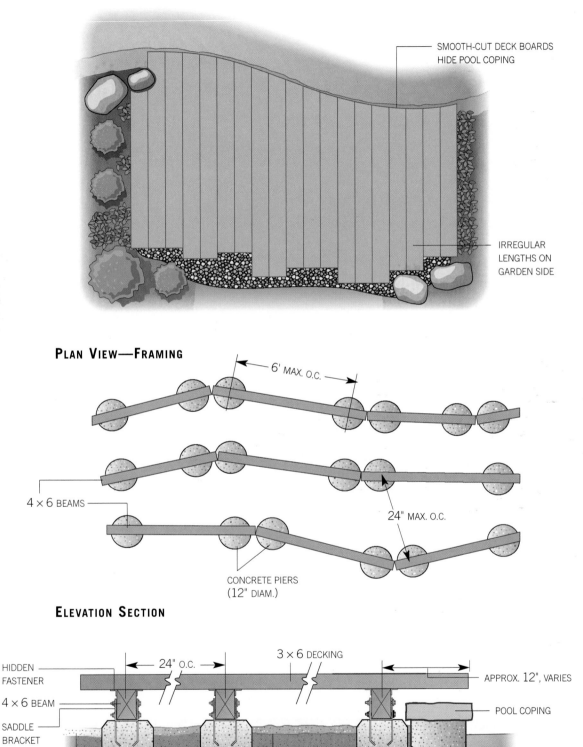

SMOOTH-CUT DECK BOARDS
HIDE POOL COPING

IRREGULAR
LENGTHS ON
GARDEN SIDE

Plan View—Framing

6' MAX. O.C.

4 × 6 BEAMS

24" MAX. O.C.

CONCRETE PIERS
(12" DIAM.)

Elevation Section

HIDDEN
FASTENER

24" O.C.

3 × 6 DECKING

APPROX. 12", VARIES

4 × 6 BEAM

POOL COPING

SADDLE
BRACKET

STONE OR
GRAVEL

CONCRETE PIER (12" DEEP)

LANDSCAPE FABRIC

simple deck with modern materials

This deck is as basic as it can be, but it is solid, functional, and family friendly. Attached to the master bedroom, the deck has high railings and gates to keep children and pets safe. For low maintenance, a solid composite was used for the decking, fascia, balusters, rails, treads, and risers, and even as a matching "skin," or cladding, over the wood gate frames.

TO ADAPT THIS PLAN

The deck can be built low to the ground or, with cross-braced posts, can be made higher. Stairs can be left off or attached at any point on the perimeter. The gates probably will not be needed if children and pets are not a concern.

BUILDING NOTES

The framing and foundation in this deck are textbook simple and should pass code in most areas. As with any deck-building project, however, be sure the location, size, and spacing of your foundation, posts, beams, and joists are appropriate to the materials you use and meet local code.

DESIGNER
Tibor Ambrus

MATERIALS LIST

Designed for pressure-treated lumber (structural supports), Construction Heart redwood (railing posts, gate frames), solid composite (decking, railings, gate cladding, and other visible members), and galvanized hardware.

LUMBER	
Posts	4 × 6
Beams	4 × 6
Joists and ledgers	2 × 6
Fascia and borders	2 × 2, 2 × 6
Decking	2 × 6
Stairs	2 × 12 stringers; 2 × 6 treads
Railings	4 × 4 posts; 2 × 4 rails; 2 × 2 balusters; 2 × 6 cap rails
Gates	2 × 4 frames; 2 × 2 balusters, nailers, and braces; composite cladding
MASONRY	
Concrete	Piers, footings
HARDWARE	
Nails	16d (framing); as appropriate for connectors
Bolts and screws	2½" stainless-steel screws (decking); ½" lag screws (ledger)
Connectors	Post connectors; joist hangers
Other	Gate hardware

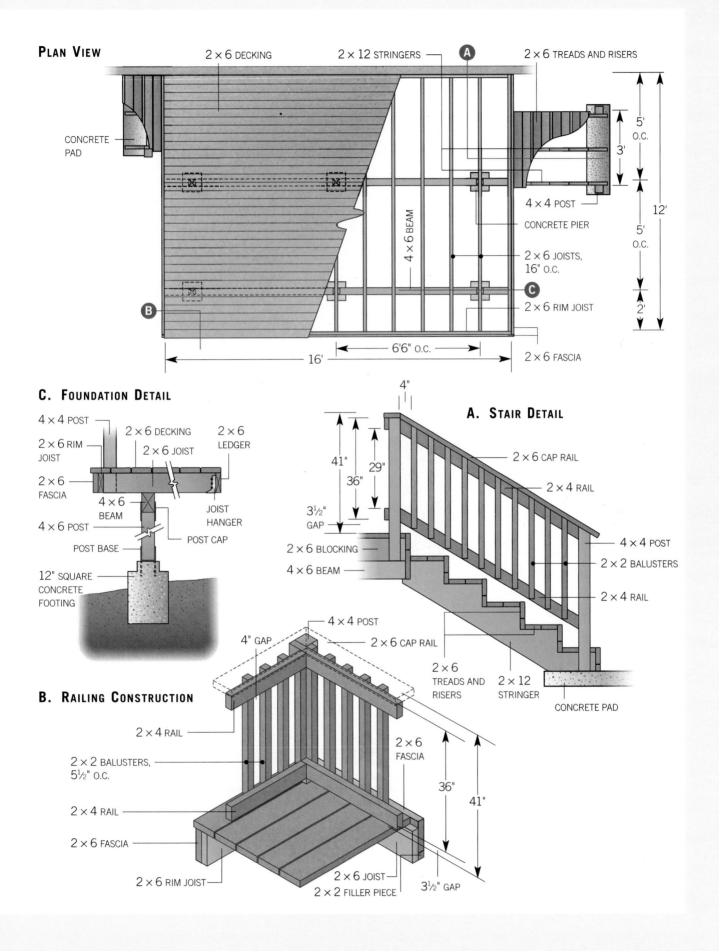

PLAN VIEW

2 × 6 DECKING
2 × 12 STRINGERS
Ⓐ
2 × 6 TREADS AND RISERS

CONCRETE PAD

4 × 6 BEAM

4 × 4 POST
CONCRETE PIER

2 × 6 JOISTS, 16" O.C.

Ⓒ

Ⓑ

2 × 6 RIM JOIST

2 × 6 FASCIA

5' O.C.
3'
12'
5' O.C.
2'

6'6" O.C.
16'

C. FOUNDATION DETAIL

4 × 4 POST
2 × 6 DECKING
2 × 6 LEDGER
2 × 6 RIM JOIST
2 × 6 JOIST
2 × 6 FASCIA
4 × 6 BEAM
JOIST HANGER
4 × 6 POST
POST CAP
POST BASE
12" SQUARE CONCRETE FOOTING

A. STAIR DETAIL

4"
41"
29"
36"
3½" GAP
2 × 6 BLOCKING
4 × 6 BEAM
2 × 6 CAP RAIL
2 × 4 RAIL
4 × 4 POST
2 × 2 BALUSTERS
2 × 4 RAIL
2 × 6 TREADS AND RISERS
2 × 12 STRINGER
CONCRETE PAD

B. RAILING CONSTRUCTION

4 × 4 POST
2 × 6 CAP RAIL
4" GAP
2 × 4 RAIL
2 × 2 BALUSTERS, 5½" O.C.
2 × 4 RAIL
2 × 6 FASCIA
2 × 6 RIM JOIST
2 × 6 JOIST
2 × 2 FILLER PIECE
2 × 6 FASCIA
36"
41"
3½" GAP

transitional deck

This partly sheltered deck serves as an indoor-outdoor space connecting a family room with a patio. Classically simple, it is a great transitional element for nearly any style of house.

TO ADAPT THIS PLAN

You can wrap this deck plan around almost any house on fairly flat ground. The key lies in establishing the shape of the deck. As shown here, wide places invite socializing, while traffic areas are narrower. If the floors in your home are higher than in this design, you can set the beams on posts with appropriate piers and footings, and then add steps as needed. For a higher deck, check whether a railing may be necessary. This plan includes a perimeter foundation to support the beams, an arrangement that provides maximum support and ease in leveling the structure, but you could use individual piers and footings instead.

BUILDING NOTES

Where a perimeter trim board runs perpendicular to the rest of the decking, an extra joist must be provided beneath the joint, as shown.

DESIGNER
Todd Fry, ASLA

MATERIALS LIST

Designed for pressure-treated lumber (structural members), Clear Heart redwood (decking and other visible members), and galvanized hardware.

LUMBER	
Beams	4 × 6
Joists and ledgers	2 × 6
Decking	2 × 6, with 2 × 8 trim boards
Steps	2 × 12 treads; 2 × 6 risers; 1 × 4 and 1 × 6 fascias
MASONRY	
Concrete	Perimeter foundation
HARDWARE	
Nails	16d (framing), 10d finish (blind-nailed decking); as appropriate for connectors
Connectors	Joist hangers
Other	#4 rebar

PLAN VIEW

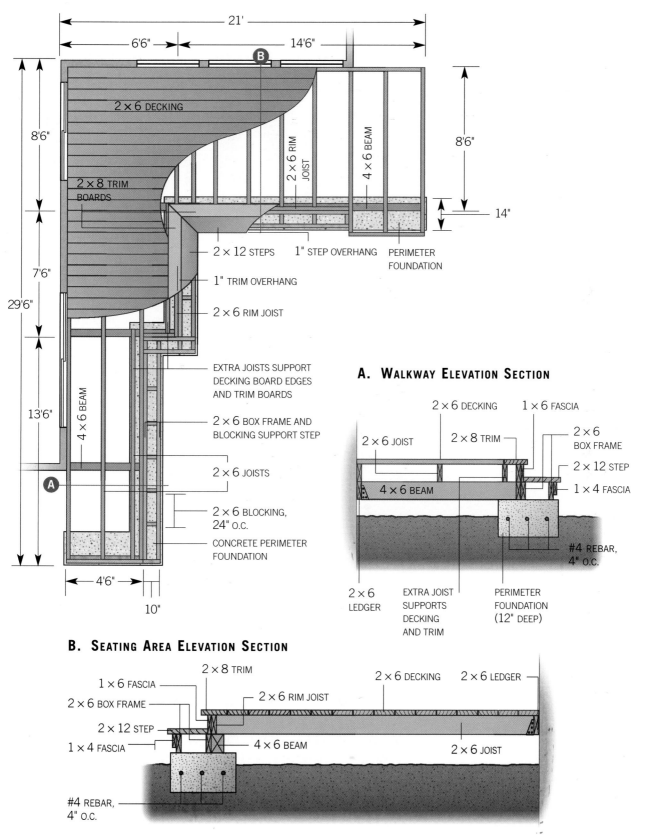

21'

6'6"   14'6"

2 × 6 DECKING

8'6"

2 × 8 TRIM BOARDS

7'6"

29'6"

13'6"

4 × 6 BEAM

4'6"

10"

2 × 6 RIM JOIST

4 × 6 BEAM

8'6"

14"

2 × 12 STEPS

1" STEP OVERHANG

PERIMETER FOUNDATION

1" TRIM OVERHANG

2 × 6 RIM JOIST

EXTRA JOISTS SUPPORT DECKING BOARD EDGES AND TRIM BOARDS

2 × 6 BOX FRAME AND BLOCKING SUPPORT STEP

2 × 6 JOISTS

2 × 6 BLOCKING, 24" O.C.

CONCRETE PERIMETER FOUNDATION

A. WALKWAY ELEVATION SECTION

2 × 6 DECKING   1 × 6 FASCIA

2 × 6 JOIST   2 × 8 TRIM

2 × 6 BOX FRAME

2 × 12 STEP

4 × 6 BEAM

1 × 4 FASCIA

#4 REBAR, 4" O.C.

2 × 6 LEDGER

EXTRA JOIST SUPPORTS DECKING AND TRIM

PERIMETER FOUNDATION (12" DEEP)

B. SEATING AREA ELEVATION SECTION

2 × 8 TRIM

1 × 6 FASCIA

2 × 6 BOX FRAME

2 × 6 RIM JOIST

2 × 6 DECKING   2 × 6 LEDGER

2 × 12 STEP

1 × 4 FASCIA

4 × 6 BEAM

2 × 6 JOIST

#4 REBAR, 4" O.C.

garden deck

TO ADAPT THIS PLAN

Since the lot for this deck is level, the foundation and framing are relatively simple. The design could be adapted to more challenging terrain, however, by adjusting the height of the posts. The design wraps around a bay window, which requires a separate ledger for each angle. It could just as easily be attached to a straight wall with a single ledger. If you increase the deck's height at any point, be sure to check your local code, as railings may become necessary. The long cantilever of the angled edge may not meet code in all areas.

BUILDING NOTES

The piers and footings in this plan are designed for a region where frost is rare and earthquakes are not a concern. Be sure to check with your building department to confirm that the piers and footings are sufficiently deep and robust for your area. The joist spacings, set at 18 inches on the deck and 24 inches on the bridge, are designed for 2 × 3 cedar decking. If you are using another type of wood, or composite material, you may need to adjust these spacings.

DESIGNER
Scott Lankford, Lankford Associates Landscape Architects

This crisp, low-lying platform seems to float out from the house and over the garden. Built-in benches outline the deck and serve much the same function as railings, which are not required at this low height. Beneath them, light fixtures provide subtle illumination. On one side, the deck steps down to a low bridge over a small pool. On the other, it connects to a patio.

PLAN VIEW—DECKING

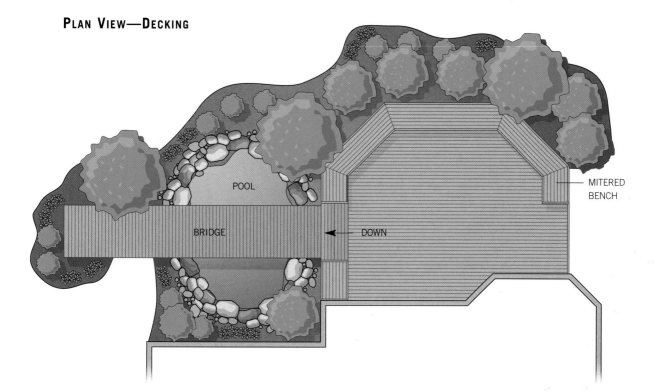

MATERIALS LIST

Designed for pressure-treated lumber (structural members), tight-knot surfaced cedar (decking), clear cedar (fascia and other visible members), and galvanized hardware.

LUMBER	
Beams	4 × 8
Joists and ledgers	2 × 8
Decking and bench seating	2 × 3
Bench supports	4 × 12
Fascia	1 × 6, 2 × 4, 2 × 8
MASONRY	
Concrete	Piers, footings
HARDWARE	
Nails	16d (framing); 10d galvanized finish (decking and fascia); as appropriate for connectors
Bolts and screws	½" bolts (framing)
Connectors	Beam-to-footing connectors; joist hangers; post connectors
Other	#5 rebar
OTHER	
Surface-mount low-voltage lights (under bench)	

PLAN VIEW—FRAMING

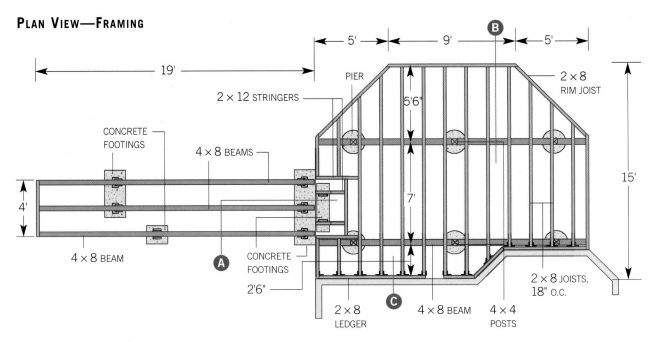

19'

5' — 9' — **B** — 5'

2 × 12 STRINGERS

PIER

5'6"

2 × 8 RIM JOIST

CONCRETE FOOTINGS

4 × 8 BEAMS

15'

4'

7'

4 × 8 BEAM

A

CONCRETE FOOTINGS

2'6"

C

2 × 8 LEDGER

4 × 8 BEAM

4 × 4 POSTS

2 × 8 JOISTS, 18" O.C.

BRIDGE ELEVATION SECTION

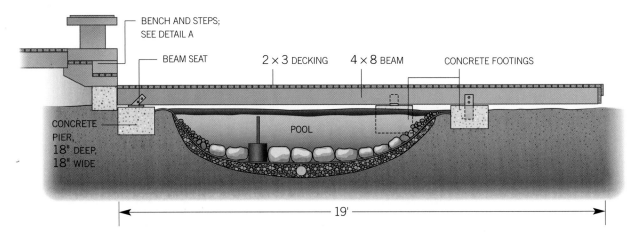

BENCH AND STEPS; SEE DETAIL A

BEAM SEAT

2 × 3 DECKING

4 × 8 BEAM

CONCRETE FOOTINGS

CONCRETE PIER, 18" DEEP, 18" WIDE

POOL

19'

A. BENCH AND STEPS DETAIL

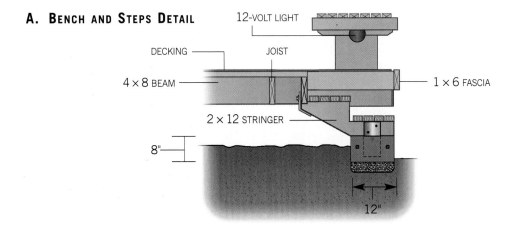

12-VOLT LIGHT

DECKING

JOIST

4 × 8 BEAM

1 × 6 FASCIA

2 × 12 STRINGER

8"

12"

PLAN VIEW—BENCH FRAMING

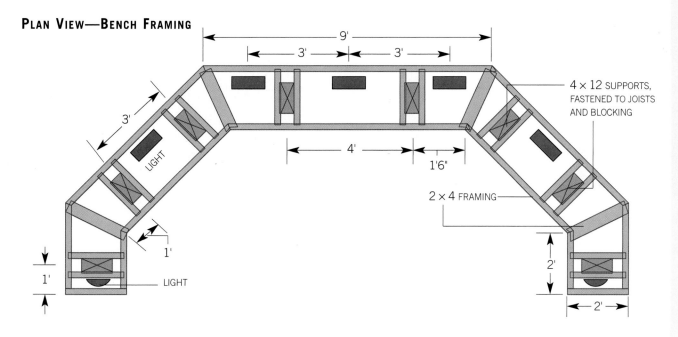

9'

3'   3'

3'

LIGHT

4'   1'6"

4 × 12 SUPPORTS, FASTENED TO JOISTS AND BLOCKING

2 × 4 FRAMING

1'

1'   LIGHT

2'

2'

C. LEDGER AND BEAM DETAIL

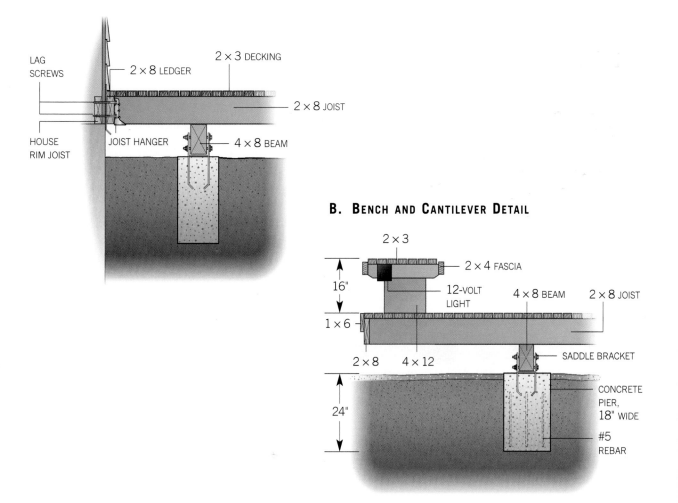

LAG SCREWS

2 × 8 LEDGER

2 × 3 DECKING

2 × 8 JOIST

HOUSE RIM JOIST

JOIST HANGER   4 × 8 BEAM

B. BENCH AND CANTILEVER DETAIL

2 × 3

2 × 4 FASCIA

16"

12-VOLT LIGHT

4 × 8 BEAM   2 × 8 JOIST

1 × 6

2 × 8   4 × 12

SADDLE BRACKET

24"

CONCRETE PIER, 18" WIDE

#5 REBAR

seating deck

Set above a large deck on an angled platform, this handsome seating unit is in effect a mini-deck itself. The design provides front-row seats for eight or more with cantilevered benches that are easy to sweep under. The sturdy overhead can support heavy, mature foliage for shade in summer.

TO ADAPT THIS PLAN

This versatile design could be adapted in several ways. It was originally built as a platform on top of a large deck, but you can adapt it to stand alone by setting the joists on beams supported by posts, piers, and footings, with a stair added if necessary. You can also extend the deck, benches, and overhead in either direction; be sure to stick to the same spacing. The unit need not be angled and could instead be built straight. Finally, the bench and overhead alone could make a handsome addition to a new or an existing deck. Be sure to provide a strong connection between the overhead posts and the framing underneath them. In this deck, the posts are attached to plates atop a perimeter foundation that supports the main deck below.

BUILDING NOTES

Be sure to buy good-quality, straight-grain seasoned lumber for this project. Since the assembly is exposed to view, any warping or other defects will show clearly. Accurate cutting and assembly are important, too. A power miter saw set up as shown on page 71 is ideal for reproducing the many identical parts required in this design.

DESIGNER
Ward-Young Architecture & Planning

MATERIALS LIST

Designed for pressure-treated lumber (structural members), Construction Heart redwood (overhead, benches, and other visible members), composite decking, treads and risers, and galvanized hardware.

LUMBER	
Joists	2 × 10
Fascia	2 × 12
Decking	2 × 6
Stairs	2 × 6 treads and risers
Overhead	4 × 6 (posts, beams), 4 × 4 (braces, rafters)
Bench	4 × 4 (supports); 2 × 4 with ¼" spacers (seating); 2 × 6 (trim)
HARDWARE	
Nails	16d (framing), 10d (fascia and risers); as appropriate for connectors
Bolts and screws	2½" stainless-steel screws (decking); ½" bolts (framing)
Connectors	Joist hangers; post caps; angle clips
OTHER	
Recessed, low-voltage stair lights	

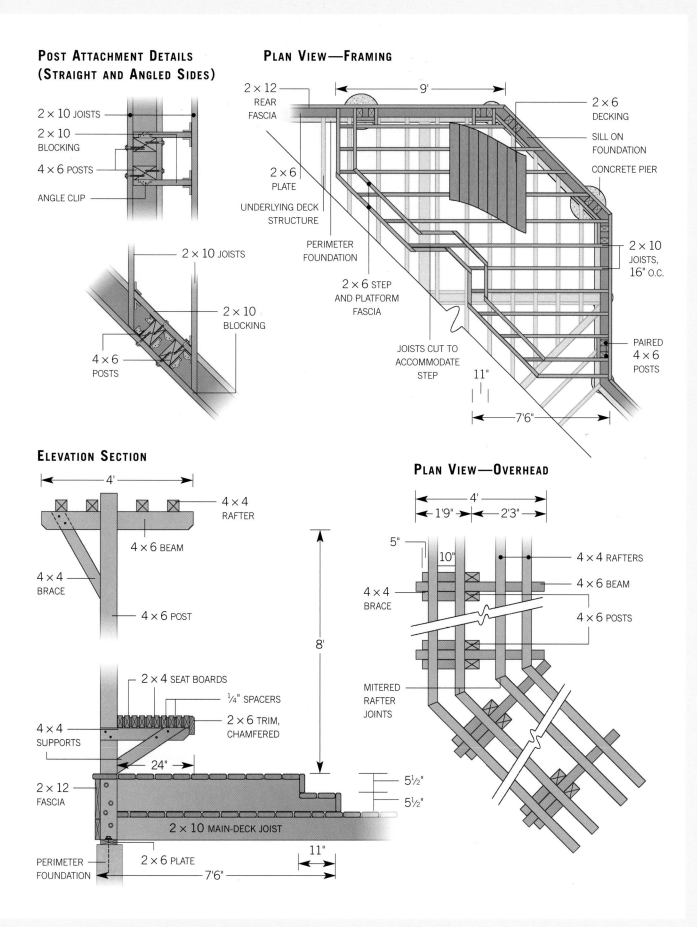

Post Attachment Details (Straight and Angled Sides)

2 × 10 JOISTS

2 × 10 BLOCKING

4 × 6 POSTS

ANGLE CLIP

2 × 10 JOISTS

2 × 10 BLOCKING

4 × 6 POSTS

Plan View—Framing

2 × 12 REAR FASCIA

2 × 6 PLATE

UNDERLYING DECK STRUCTURE

PERIMETER FOUNDATION

2 × 6 STEP AND PLATFORM FASCIA

JOISTS CUT TO ACCOMMODATE STEP

9'

2 × 6 DECKING

SILL ON FOUNDATION

CONCRETE PIER

2 × 10 JOISTS, 16" O.C.

PAIRED 4 × 6 POSTS

11"

7'6"

Elevation Section

4'

4 × 4 RAFTER

4 × 6 BEAM

4 × 4 BRACE

4 × 6 POST

8'

2 × 4 SEAT BOARDS

¼" SPACERS

2 × 6 TRIM, CHAMFERED

4 × 4 SUPPORTS

24"

2 × 12 FASCIA

2 × 10 MAIN-DECK JOIST

5½"

5½"

PERIMETER FOUNDATION

2 × 6 PLATE

11"

7'6"

Plan View—Overhead

4'

1'9"

2'3"

5"

10"

4 × 4 RAFTERS

4 × 6 BEAM

4 × 4 BRACE

4 × 6 POSTS

MITERED RAFTER JOINTS

hardwood entry deck

This elegant entry deck along the front of a suburban home was built to replace a small concrete porch, which was left in place underneath the deck. The tropical hardwood surface of pau lope is practical, beautiful, and enduring. Crisply painted white railings add a tailored look appropriate for the public side of the house.

TO ADAPT THIS PLAN

The deck is designed to fit a particular house front, and the outer edge is angled to provide useful space, create visual interest, and distinguish between areas. The shape of your house face is undoubtedly different, so you will need to adjust the deck plan accordingly.

BUILDING NOTES

Since the concrete porch was not removed, the system shown in the plans was used to cover it up. If you are building from scratch (or tearing out a porch), you will need to fill in that area with framing and foundations. The hardwood decking permits 24-inch joist spacing. Different decking materials may require a different joist spacing.

DESIGNER
Peter Koenig Designs, with Bryan Gordon, B. Gordon Builders

MATERIALS LIST

Designed for pressure-treated lumber (structural members), hardwood decking and fascia, Clear redwood (railings and other visible members), and galvanized hardware.

LUMBER	
Posts	4 × 4
Beams	4 × 6
Joists and ledgers	2 × 6
Decking and fascia	5/4 × 6
Stairs	2 × 12 stringers; 5/4 × 6 treads and risers
Railings	6 × 6 posts, with caps; 2 × 2 balusters; 2 × 4 rails; 2 × 6 cap rails
Other	Lattice skirting; 2 × 4 nailers
MASONRY	
Concrete	Piers
HARDWARE	
Nails	16d (framing); as appropriate for connectors
Bolts and screws	Metal-bracket screws (decking); 1/2" bolts and lag screws (framing/ledgers)
Connectors	Metal-bracket fasteners (decking); post connectors; joist hangers; seismic ties
Other	#4 rebar; #3 hoops

PLAN VIEW

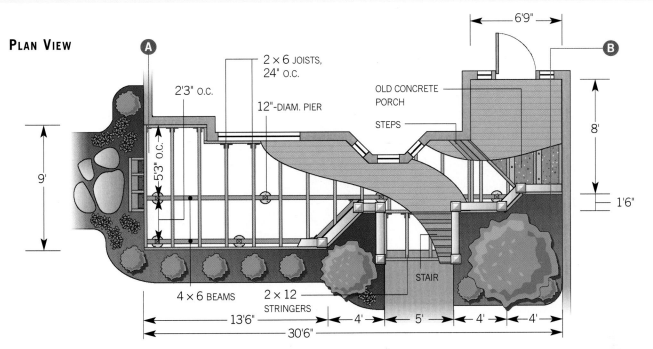

- 2'3" O.C.
- 2 × 6 JOISTS, 24" O.C.
- 12"-DIAM. PIER
- 5'3" O.C.
- 6'9"
- 8'
- 1'6"
- OLD CONCRETE PORCH
- STEPS
- 4 × 6 BEAMS
- 2 × 12 STRINGERS
- STAIR
- 9'
- 13'6"
- 4'
- 5'
- 4'
- 4'
- 30'6"

B. BUILT-OVER PORCH DETAIL

- 2 × 6 CAP RAIL
- DECORATIVE CAP
- 2 × 4 RAIL
- 2 × 2 BALUSTER
- 6 × 6 POST
- 2 × 4 RAIL
- ⁵⁄₄ × 6 DECKING USED AS FASCIA
- BRICK VENEER
- OLD CONCRETE PORCH
- 2 × 4 NAILER SCREWED TO CONCRETE
- HOUSE
- 2 × 6 JOIST, SHAPED TO FOLLOW SLOPE OF PORCH
- LAG SCREW

The new deck covers an old concrete porch, now hidden beneath the stairs and platform at rear. Besides being useful, the extra length of the deck gives the house a much more graceful presence from the street.

A. FRAME AND RAILING CONSTRUCTION

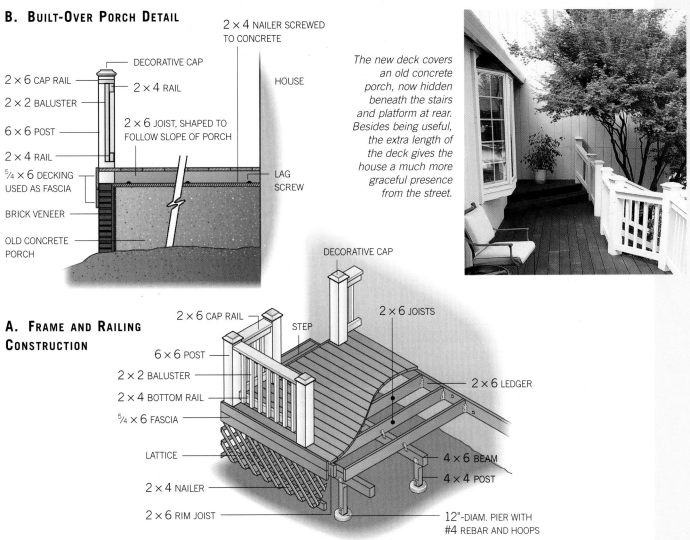

- 2 × 6 CAP RAIL
- STEP
- DECORATIVE CAP
- 2 × 6 JOISTS
- 6 × 6 POST
- 2 × 2 BALUSTER
- 2 × 4 BOTTOM RAIL
- ⁵⁄₄ × 6 FASCIA
- 2 × 6 LEDGER
- LATTICE
- 2 × 4 NAILER
- 2 × 6 RIM JOIST
- 4 × 6 BEAM
- 4 × 4 POST
- 12"-DIAM. PIER WITH #4 REBAR AND HOOPS

curving composite deck

Filling in a backyard niche, this curving deck uses solid composite decking in an unusual way. Two broad, curving steps made of edge-up composite boards divide the deck surface into two levels. Another stair made the same way is notched into the deck's edge, giving access to the yard. Both stairs rely on the flexibility of the composite material.

TO ADAPT THIS PLAN

This deck can take on nearly any size and shape by adapting its framing of beams, posts, piers, and footings. Bear in mind, however, that if you raise either level past 30 inches, most local codes will require railings. You may also want to incorporate railings for a deck at a somewhat lower height.

BUILDING NOTES

Many short joist lengths were used in this deck so that the joists and beams could be on the same level, keeping the deck low. In a higher version of the deck, you could run longer joists over the beams, saving considerable time and labor.

DESIGNER
Bruce Jett Associates,
Landscape Architects

MATERIALS LIST

Designed for pressure-treated lumber (structural members), solid composite (decking and edging), and galvanized hardware.

LUMBER	
Posts	4 × 6
Beams	4 × 6
Joists and ledgers	4 × 6
Decking and fascia	2 × 6
MASONRY	
Concrete	Footings, pre-cast piers
HARDWARE	
Nails	16d (framing); as appropriate for connectors
Bolts and screws	2½" stainless-steel screws (decking); ½" galvanized screws (step fastening)
Connectors	Post connectors; joist hangers
Other	#4 rebar

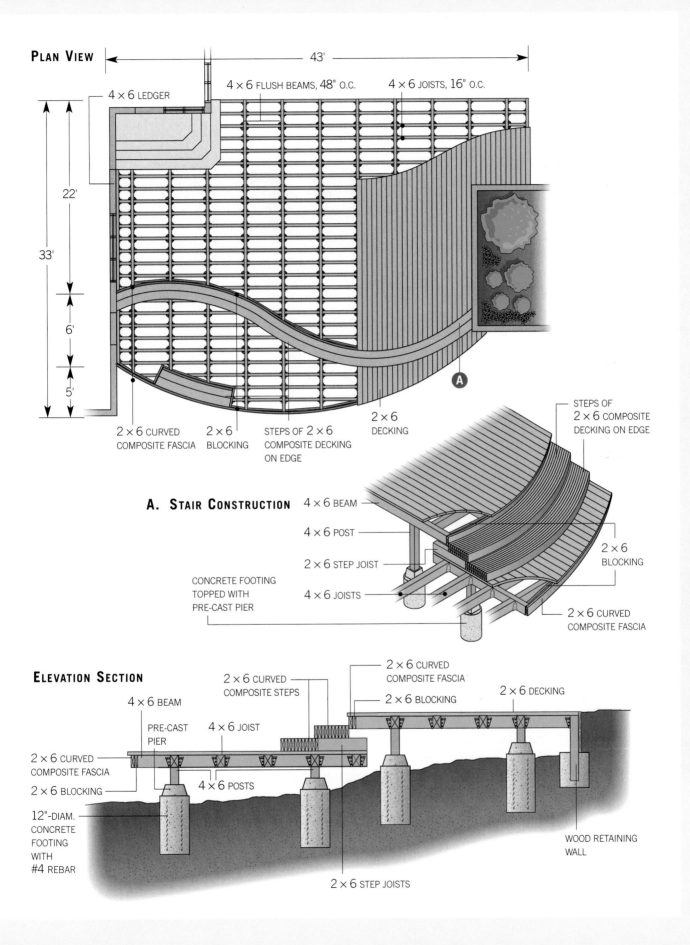

PLAN VIEW

43'

4 × 6 LEDGER

4 × 6 FLUSH BEAMS, 48" O.C.

4 × 6 JOISTS, 16" O.C.

33'

22'

6'

5'

2 × 6 CURVED
COMPOSITE FASCIA

2 × 6 BLOCKING

STEPS OF 2 × 6
COMPOSITE DECKING
ON EDGE

2 × 6 DECKING

STEPS OF
2 × 6 COMPOSITE
DECKING ON EDGE

A

A. STAIR CONSTRUCTION

4 × 6 BEAM

4 × 6 POST

2 × 6 STEP JOIST

CONCRETE FOOTING
TOPPED WITH
PRE-CAST PIER

4 × 6 JOISTS

2 × 6 BLOCKING

2 × 6 CURVED
COMPOSITE FASCIA

ELEVATION SECTION

2 × 6 CURVED
COMPOSITE STEPS

2 × 6 CURVED
COMPOSITE FASCIA

2 × 6 BLOCKING

2 × 6 DECKING

4 × 6 BEAM

PRE-CAST
PIER

4 × 6 JOIST

2 × 6 CURVED
COMPOSITE FASCIA

2 × 6 BLOCKING

4 × 6 POSTS

12"-DIAM.
CONCRETE
FOOTING
WITH
#4 REBAR

WOOD RETAINING
WALL

2 × 6 STEP JOISTS

deck for a sloping site

Built at the edge of a hill, this deck serves as an outdoor room that carries the home's floor level outward to light, fresh air, and a fine view. A balcony supported by angled "kicker" posts punctuates the far side of the deck. A pathway deck leads around the house on one side, while a simple step gives access to the backyard on the other side. A "saddlebag" storage unit on that same side supports a built-in

barbecue. Simple details—such as the water-shedding bevels on the top rails and post tops—distinguish the design and add to its character.

TO ADAPT THIS PLAN

A single, floating platform like this is adaptable to houses of nearly any size and shape. Reduced in size, it could become as simple as the deck on pages 202–203. Enlarging it is a matter of extending the framing and foundations. The barbecue unit and pathway deck are optional and can be replaced with sections of railing.

BUILDING NOTES

This deck was built on a hillside in a zone where earthquakes may occur, so it required a substantial pier-and-tie-beam foundation that might be excessive in your location. (A tie beam is a reinforced concrete beam that ties together individual piers or footings so as to distribute forces among them.) Your local building department can advise you on the most suitable approach for your situation. You will need a table saw to create the beveled rails.

DESIGNER
Bill Remick, Remick Associates
Architects/Builders

MATERIALS LIST

Designed for pressure-treated hem-fir (structural members), Construction Heart redwood (decking, railings, and other visible members), and galvanized hardware.

LUMBER	
Posts	6 × 6
Beams	6 × 8
Joists	2 × 8
Ledgers	3 × 8
Braces	2 × 6
Decking	2 × 6
Railings	6 × 6 posts; 4 × 4 top rails; 3 × 4 bottom rails; 2 × 2 balusters; $\frac{5}{8}$" × $\frac{5}{8}$" stops; 1" × 1$\frac{1}{2}$" spacers
Other	Clapboard siding
MASONRY	
Concrete	Tie beams, piers
HARDWARE	
Nails	16d (framing), 10d (decking); as appropriate for connectors
Bolts	$\frac{1}{2}$" bolts (framing)
Connectors	Post connectors; joist hangers
Other	#3, #4, #5 rebar
OTHER	
Built-in barbecue unit; gas lines	

PLAN VIEW—DECKING

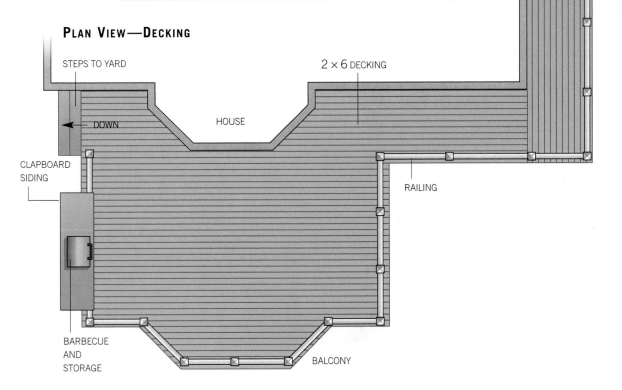

STEPS TO YARD

2 × 6 DECKING

DOWN

HOUSE

CLAPBOARD SIDING

RAILING

BARBECUE AND STORAGE

BALCONY

DOWN

PATHWAY DECK

PLAN VIEW—FRAMING

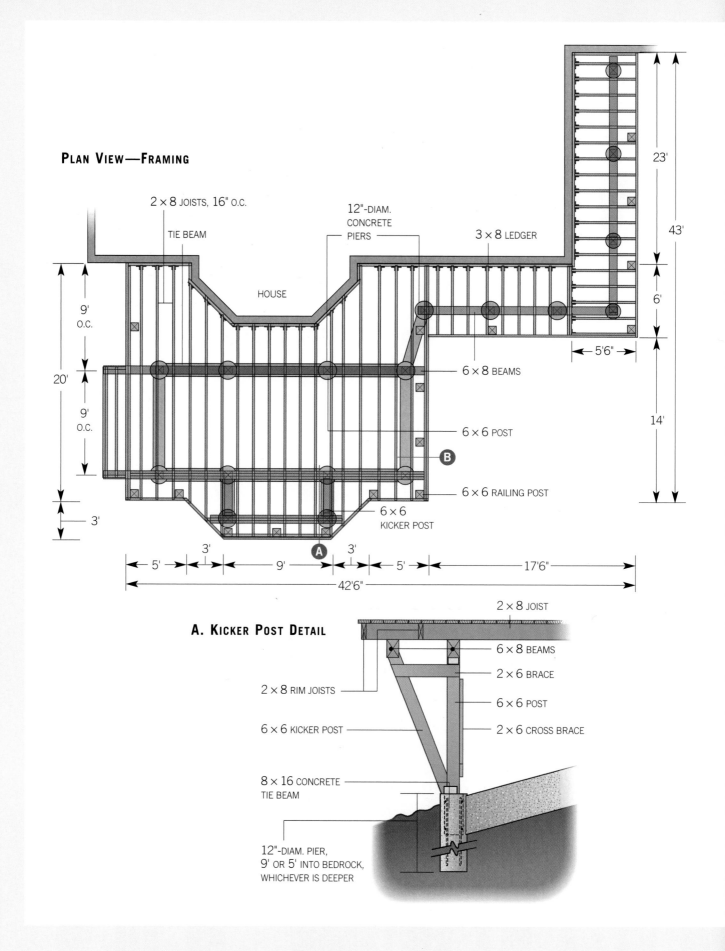

2 × 8 JOISTS, 16" O.C.

TIE BEAM

12"-DIAM.
CONCRETE
PIERS

3 × 8 LEDGER

HOUSE

23'

43'

6'

5'6"

9'
O.C.

6 × 8 BEAMS

20'

9'
O.C.

14'

6 × 6 POST

B

6 × 6 RAILING POST

6 × 6
KICKER POST

3'

3'   3'

5'   9'   5'   17'6"

A

42'6"

A. KICKER POST DETAIL

2 × 8 JOIST

6 × 8 BEAMS

2 × 6 BRACE

2 × 8 RIM JOISTS

6 × 6 POST

6 × 6 KICKER POST

2 × 6 CROSS BRACE

8 × 16 CONCRETE
TIE BEAM

12"-DIAM. PIER,
9' OR 5' INTO BEDROCK,
WHICHEVER IS DEEPER

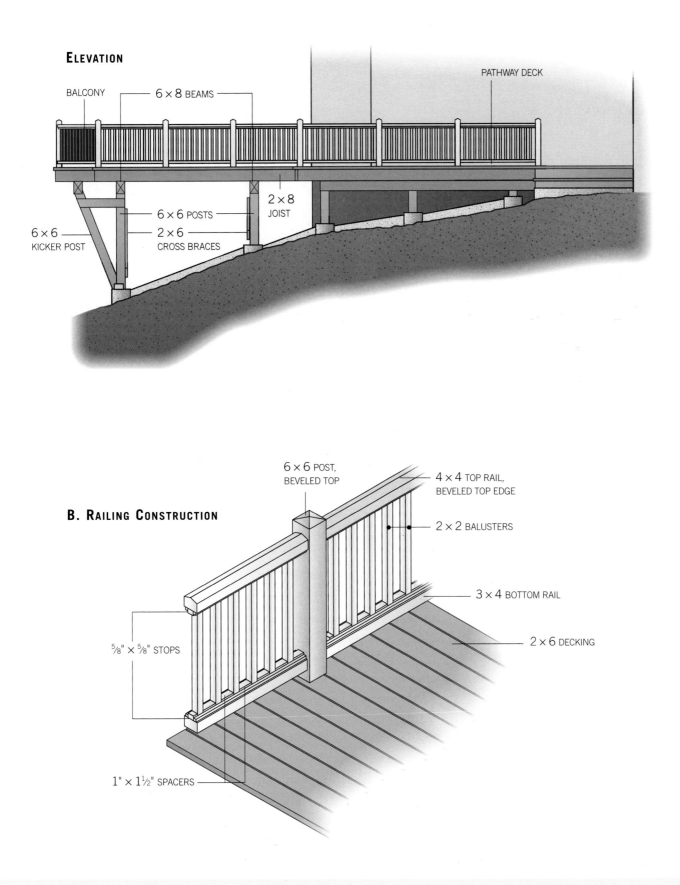

ELEVATION

BALCONY

6 × 8 BEAMS

PATHWAY DECK

2 × 8 JOIST

6 × 6 POSTS

6 × 6 KICKER POST

2 × 6 CROSS BRACES

B. RAILING CONSTRUCTION

6 × 6 POST, BEVELED TOP

4 × 4 TOP RAIL, BEVELED TOP EDGE

2 × 2 BALUSTERS

3 × 4 BOTTOM RAIL

2 × 6 DECKING

$\frac{5}{8}$" × $\frac{5}{8}$" STOPS

1" × 1$\frac{1}{2}$" SPACERS

octagonal decks for a hill

TO ADAPT THIS PLAN

The larger of the two decks is 16 feet across; the smaller deck is 10 feet across. You can also adapt the structure to other sizes. If you are enlarging it, however, check the appropriate span tables. You may need deeper joists or an inner ring of posts, piers, and footings to handle the longer spans. You could also adapt this structure to a hexagonal plan, reducing framing costs and building time, but bear in mind that a hexagon incorporates much less space than an octagon of the same width.

BUILDING NOTES

As built, the pressure-treated deck/roof posts run straight from the eaves into the ground. This detail may not comply with code in your area, so be sure to check with your local building department. The joists also attach directly to the posts, rather than to separate beams.

If cedar is not available in your area, redwood or Southern pine should make a good substitute; check the span tables for the type of decking you choose.

DESIGNER
Robert Carlson, Pacific Northwest Construction

Two octagonal decks, one with a gazebo roof, step smartly down a hillside. The simple stick styling gives a nod to the Victorian past without copying its ornate quality. The solid roof provides protection in a mild, rainy climate and is set high enough to admit plenty of welcome sunshine. Built in two sizes from the same basic framing plans, the two decks work as modules that can be changed in size and rearranged.

MATERIALS LIST

Designed for pressure-treated lumber (structural members), #2 hem-fir (rafters and collar ties), clear Western red cedar (decking, roof deck, benches, railings, and other visible members), and galvanized hardware.

LUMBER	
Posts	4 × 4, 6 × 6
Joists and blocking	2 × 6, 2 × 8
Fascia	1 × 8
Decking	2 × 6
Headers	4 × 4
Rafters and collar ties	2 × 6
Roof	1 × 6 tongue-and-groove substrate; $7/16$" oriented-strand board (OSB) underlayment
Stairs	2 × 12 stringers; 2 × 6 treads
Railings	4 × 4 posts; 2 × 4 rails; 1 × 3 nailers; 2 × 2 balusters
Benches	2 × 4 supports; 2 × 6 seats
Other	Roof finial; lattice
MASONRY	
Concrete	Piers
HARDWARE	
Nails	10d finish (decking); 16d (framing); 6d (balusters); as appropriate for connectors
Bolts	½" bolts (framing)
Connectors	Post connectors; joist hangers
OTHER	
Shingles (wood or composite)	

ELEVATION

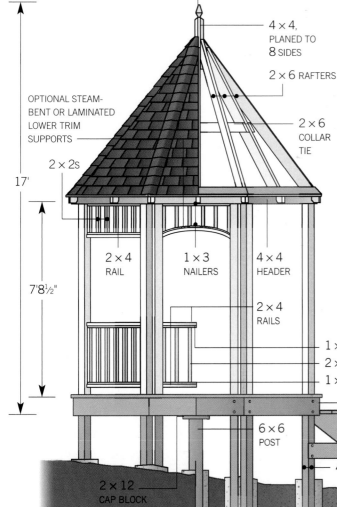

- FINIAL
- 4 × 4, PLANED TO 8 SIDES
- 2 × 6 RAFTERS
- 2 × 6 COLLAR TIE
- OPTIONAL STEAM-BENT OR LAMINATED LOWER TRIM SUPPORTS
- 2 × 2s
- 17'
- 7'8½"
- 2 × 4 RAIL
- 1 × 3 NAILERS
- 4 × 4 HEADER
- 2 × 4 RAILS
- 1 × 3 NAILER
- 2 × 2 BALUSTER
- 1 × 3 NAILER
- 1 × 8 FASCIA
- 2 × 12 STRINGER
- 6 × 6 POST
- 2 × 8 JOIST
- 4 × 4 POSTS SET DIRECTLY IN CONCRETE
- 2 × 12 CAP BLOCK
- 12"-DIAM. PIER (MIN. 30" DEEP)

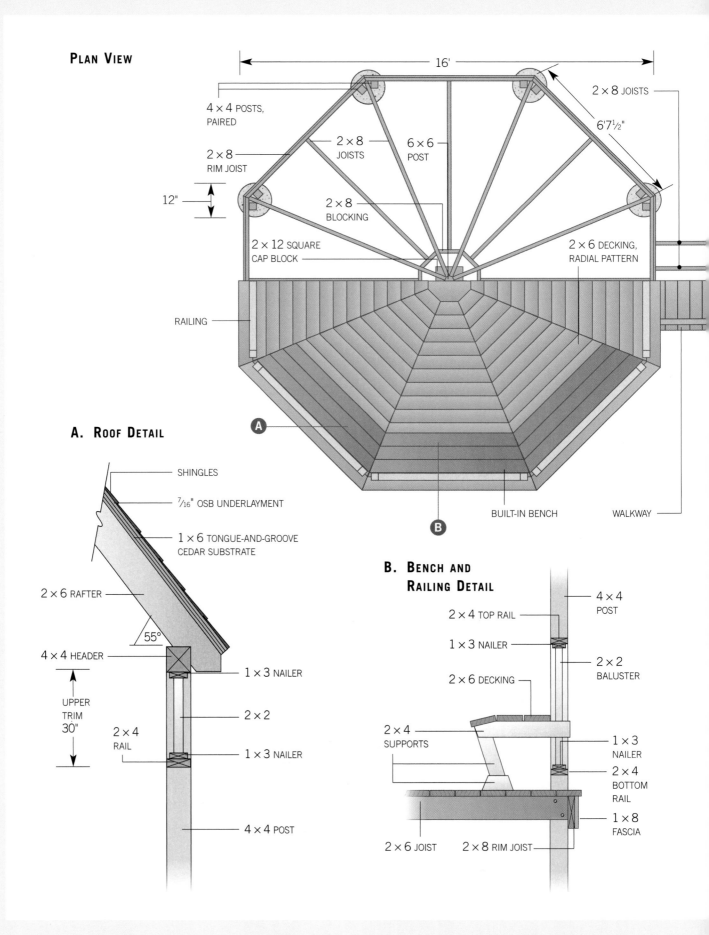

PLAN VIEW

16'

4 × 4 POSTS, PAIRED

2 × 8 JOISTS

2 × 8 RIM JOIST

2 × 8 JOISTS

6 × 6 POST

6'7½"

12"

2 × 8 BLOCKING

2 × 12 SQUARE CAP BLOCK

2 × 6 DECKING, RADIAL PATTERN

RAILING

A

B

BUILT-IN BENCH

WALKWAY

A. ROOF DETAIL

SHINGLES

⁷⁄₁₆" OSB UNDERLAYMENT

1 × 6 TONGUE-AND-GROOVE CEDAR SUBSTRATE

2 × 6 RAFTER

55°

4 × 4 HEADER

1 × 3 NAILER

UPPER TRIM 30"

2 × 4 RAIL

2 × 2

1 × 3 NAILER

4 × 4 POST

B. BENCH AND RAILING DETAIL

2 × 4 TOP RAIL

4 × 4 POST

1 × 3 NAILER

2 × 2 BALUSTER

2 × 6 DECKING

2 × 4 SUPPORTS

1 × 3 NAILER

2 × 4 BOTTOM RAIL

1 × 8 FASCIA

2 × 6 JOIST

2 × 8 RIM JOIST

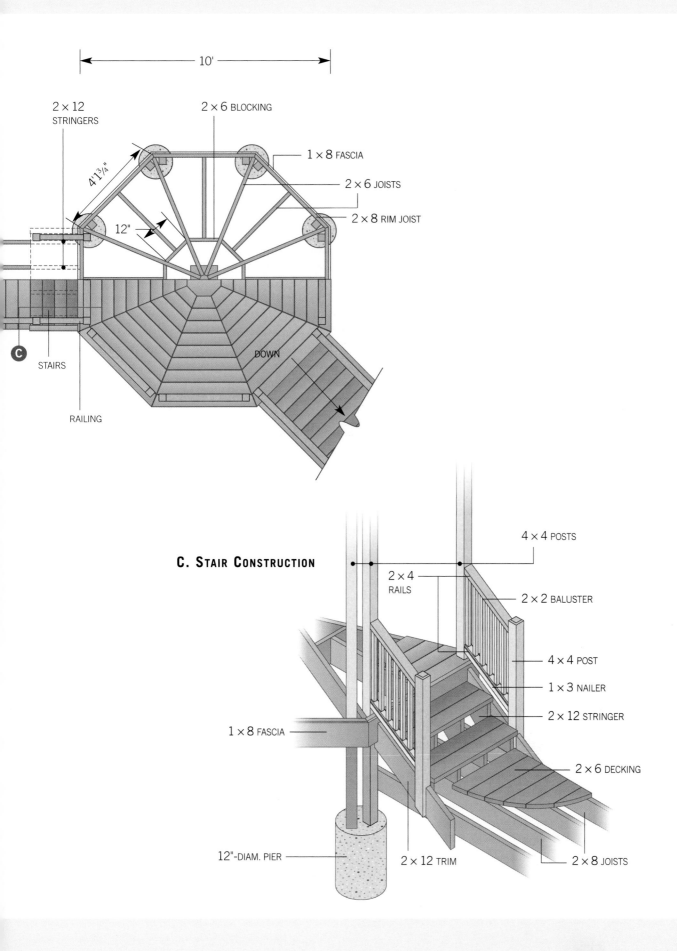

10'

2 × 12 STRINGERS

2 × 6 BLOCKING

1 × 8 FASCIA

2 × 6 JOISTS

2 × 8 RIM JOIST

4'1¾"

12"

C

STAIRS

RAILING

DOWN

C. STAIR CONSTRUCTION

4 × 4 POSTS

2 × 4 RAILS

2 × 2 BALUSTER

4 × 4 POST

1 × 3 NAILER

2 × 12 STRINGER

2 × 6 DECKING

1 × 8 FASCIA

12"-DIAM. PIER

2 × 12 TRIM

2 × 8 JOISTS

split-level spa deck

MATERIALS LIST

Designed for pressure-treated Douglas fir (structural members), composite decking, Clear redwood (wood railing, deck border, and other visible members), and galvanized hardware.

LUMBER	
Posts	4 × 4
Beams	4 × 8, 4 × 10
Joists and ledgers	2 × 8
Decking and fascia	2 × 6, 2 × 8
Stairs	2 × 12 stringers; 2 × 6 treads; 1 × 6 risers
Railings	4 × 4 posts; 1 × 6 boards with 1 × 2 stops; 2 × 6 cap rails
MASONRY	
Concrete	Piers
HARDWARE	
Nails	16d (framing); as appropriate for connectors
Bolts and screws	2½" stainless-steel screws (decking); ½" bolts (framing)
Connectors	Post connectors; joist hangers
Other	#4 rebar; 2" steel pipe (stair handrail)

This deck combines a broad, level expanse that extends over a highly uneven backyard, with an upper level that houses a spa. Composite decking provides a low-maintenance, splinter-free surface that also handles chlorinated splashes from the spa without discoloring, as wood might do.

TO ADAPT THIS PLAN

This deck is tailored to a very particular backyard full of challenging slopes, but you can adapt its outline and bi-level structure to suit any similar situation. You may even turn the deck around to work as a down-slope solution. Adjust deck levels and their relationship to each other by adding or subtracting stairs and changing post heights (as always, these changes will have ripple effects on other parts of the framing). You can also take out the spa and its re-inforced framing. If you do that, you will need to fill in the space where the spa was with the framing found on either side and extend the stairs to full width.

BUILDING NOTES

The 16-inch joist spacing was specified to handle solid composite decking. Wider spacing can suffice for wood.

DESIGNER
Gary Marsh, All Decked Out

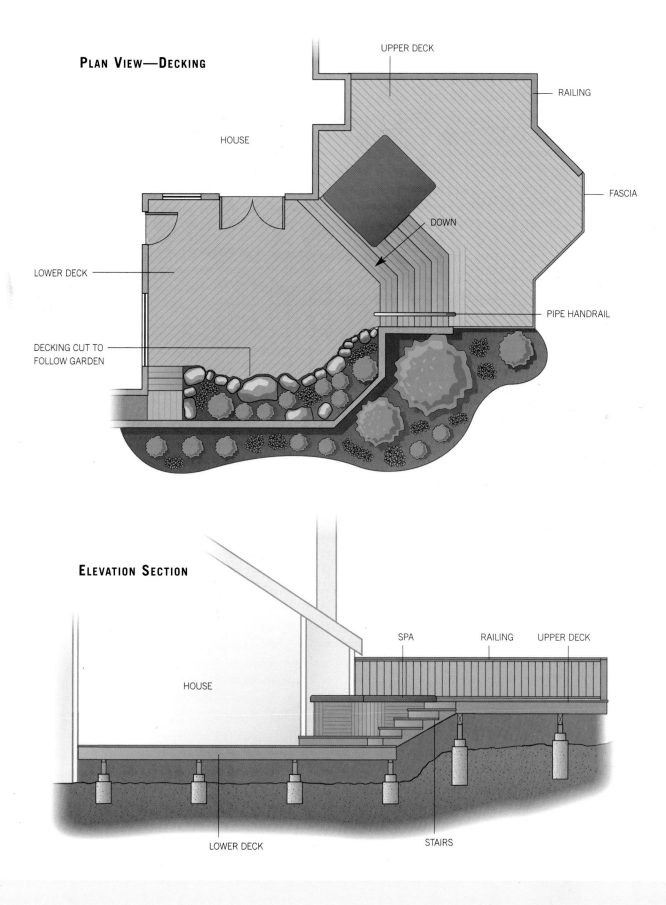

PLAN VIEW—DECKING

UPPER DECK

RAILING

HOUSE

FASCIA

DOWN

LOWER DECK

PIPE HANDRAIL

DECKING CUT TO
FOLLOW GARDEN

ELEVATION SECTION

SPA   RAILING   UPPER DECK

HOUSE

LOWER DECK

STAIRS

PLAN VIEW—FRAMING

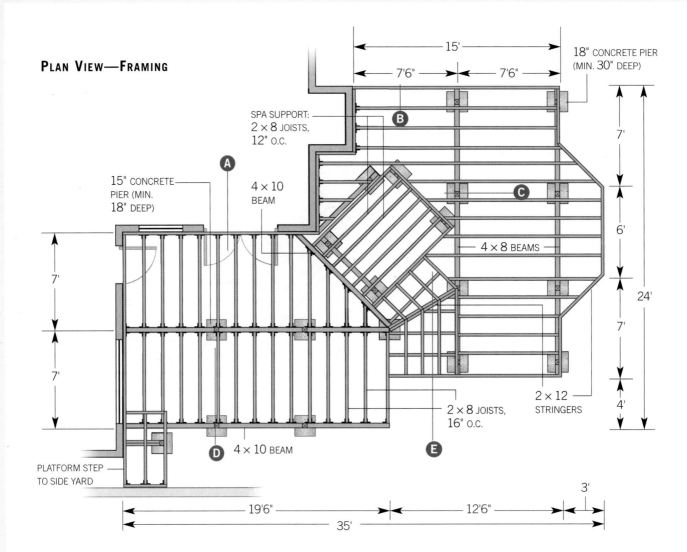

15'

7'6"   7'6"

18" CONCRETE PIER
(MIN. 30" DEEP)

SPA SUPPORT:
2 × 8 JOISTS,
12" O.C.

B

15" CONCRETE
PIER (MIN.
18" DEEP)

A

4 × 10
BEAM

C

7'

4 × 8 BEAMS

6'

24'

2 × 8 JOISTS,
16" O.C.

7'

7'

7'

2 × 12
STRINGERS

4'

D   4 × 10 BEAM

E

PLATFORM STEP
TO SIDE YARD

19'6"   12'6"   3'

35'

A. LEDGER DETAIL

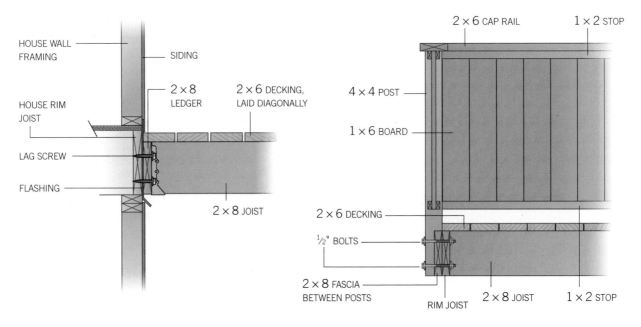

HOUSE WALL
FRAMING

SIDING

2 × 8
LEDGER

2 × 6 DECKING,
LAID DIAGONALLY

HOUSE RIM
JOIST

LAG SCREW

FLASHING

2 × 8 JOIST

B. UPPER DECK, RAILING

2 × 6 CAP RAIL

1 × 2 STOP

4 × 4 POST

1 × 6 BOARD

2 × 6 DECKING

½" BOLTS

2 × 8 FASCIA
BETWEEN POSTS

RIM JOIST

2 × 8 JOIST

1 × 2 STOP

C. UPPER DECK, SUPPORT DETAIL

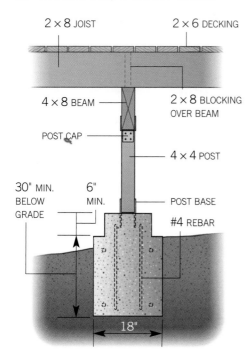

2 × 8 JOIST

2 × 6 DECKING

4 × 8 BEAM

2 × 8 BLOCKING OVER BEAM

POST CAP

4 × 4 POST

30" MIN. BELOW GRADE

6" MIN.

POST BASE

#4 REBAR

18"

D. LOWER DECK, FLUSH BEAM DETAIL

2 × 6 DECKING

JOIST HANGER

POST CAP

2 × 8 JOIST

4 × 10 BEAM

4 × 4 POST

E. STAIR CONSTRUCTION

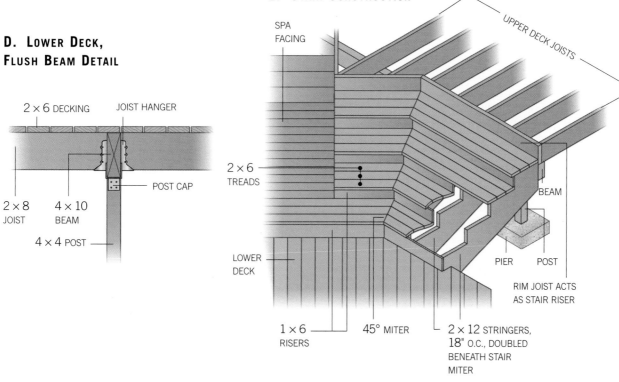

SPA FACING

UPPER DECK JOISTS

2 × 6 TREADS

BEAM

LOWER DECK

PIER

POST

RIM JOIST ACTS AS STAIR RISER

1 × 6 RISERS

45° MITER

2 × 12 STRINGERS, 18" O.C., DOUBLED BENEATH STAIR MITER

two-story deck

This deck provides sunny outdoor living for both floors of the house. Many details contribute to its success. The zigzag perimeter of the lower deck creates natural seating areas with room for plantings, while the upper deck provides some—but not too much—shade for the lower level. Large posts and deep beams under the upper deck are minimally intrusive, and the stair between the two decks is set to one side so as not to steal useful space from the lower deck. What might have been "dead" areas below the upper balcony and stair landing are used for storage and finished with waterproof roofs.

TO ADAPT THIS PLAN

As always, if you substitute another type of decking material, including a different wood species, check to make sure the joist spacing remains appropriate. Modify the size of the deck according to the length of the back of your house and the depth of your lot.

In this design, pressure-treated posts pass directly into the ground, running all the way beneath the frost line. This footing detail may not be appropriate in all areas, so be prepared to modify it if necessary.

MATERIALS LIST

Designed for pressure-treated southern pine (structural members), Construction Heart redwood (decking and other visible members), cedar (storage siding), and galvanized hardware.

LUMBER	
Posts	6 × 6 (upper), 4 × 4 (lower)
Beams	Doubled 2 × 12s (upper), 4 × 6 (lower)
Ledgers	2 × 12 (upper), 2 × 6 (lower)
Joists	2 × 10 (upper), 2 × 6 (lower)
Decking	2 × 6
Fascia	2 × 12
Stairs	2 × 12 stringers; 2 × 6 treads and risers; 4 × 4 posts at landing
Railings	4 × 4 posts; 2 × 4 rails; 2 × 2 balusters; 2 × 6 caps
Benches	4 × 4 legs; 2 × 4 seating and braces; 2 × 6 trim; ³⁄₈" spacers
Storage	1 × 8 siding; 1 × 4 door frame; 2 × 2 sleepers; ½" exterior, pressure-treated plywood; 2 × 4 and 2 × 12 framing; 1 × 8 tongue-and-groove siding
Planters	2 × 6 siding; 2 × 4 caps; 1 × 4 braces
MASONRY	
Concrete	Footings
Gravel	Planter drainage
HARDWARE	
Nails	10d (framing, decking, seating); 8d casing (trim); as appropriate for connectors
Bolts and screws	Expanding anchor bolts (ledgers to masonry); ³⁄₈" lag screws (framing)
Connectors	Post connectors; joist hangers
Other	Hinges and latches for storage areas
OTHER	
Bitumen roofing membrane (storage); waterproof lining (planters)	

BUILDING NOTES

In the lower deck design, the beams run perpendicular to the ledger and the joists are set flush with the beams. These details allow for outward-running deck boards and keep the deck close to the ground.

Be sure to follow the storage-shed roof design; note that the sleepers that carry the decking are only nailed into the 2 × 12 frame, and not through the bitumen roofing membrane (which would cause leaks).

DESIGNER

Milt Charno & Associates

PLAN VIEW (LOWER DECK)—DECKING

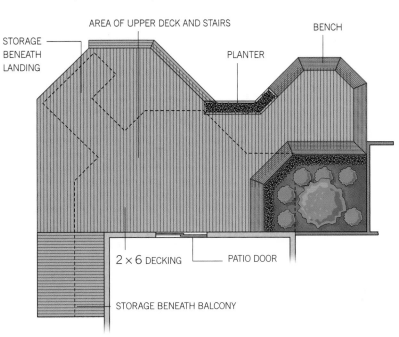

AREA OF UPPER DECK AND STAIRS

STORAGE BENEATH LANDING

BENCH

PLANTER

2 × 6 DECKING

PATIO DOOR

STORAGE BENEATH BALCONY

PLAN VIEW (LOWER DECK)—FRAMING

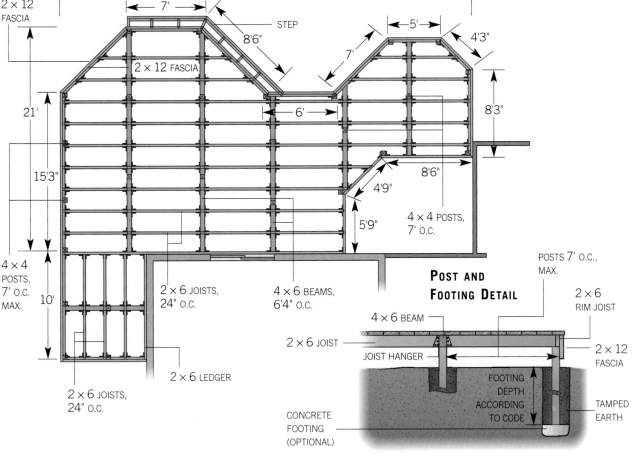

2 × 12 FASCIA

38'

7'

STEP

8'6"

2 × 12 FASCIA

5'

4'3"

7'

21'

6'

8'3"

15'3"

8'6"

4'9"

5'9"

4 × 4 POSTS, 7' O.C.

4 × 4 POSTS, 7' O.C. MAX.

10'

2 × 6 JOISTS, 24" O.C.

4 × 6 BEAMS, 6'4" O.C.

2 × 6 LEDGER

2 × 6 JOISTS, 24" O.C.

POST AND FOOTING DETAIL

POSTS 7' O.C., MAX.

2 × 6 RIM JOIST

4 × 6 BEAM

2 × 6 JOIST

JOIST HANGER

2 × 12 FASCIA

FOOTING DEPTH ACCORDING TO CODE

TAMPED EARTH

CONCRETE FOOTING (OPTIONAL)

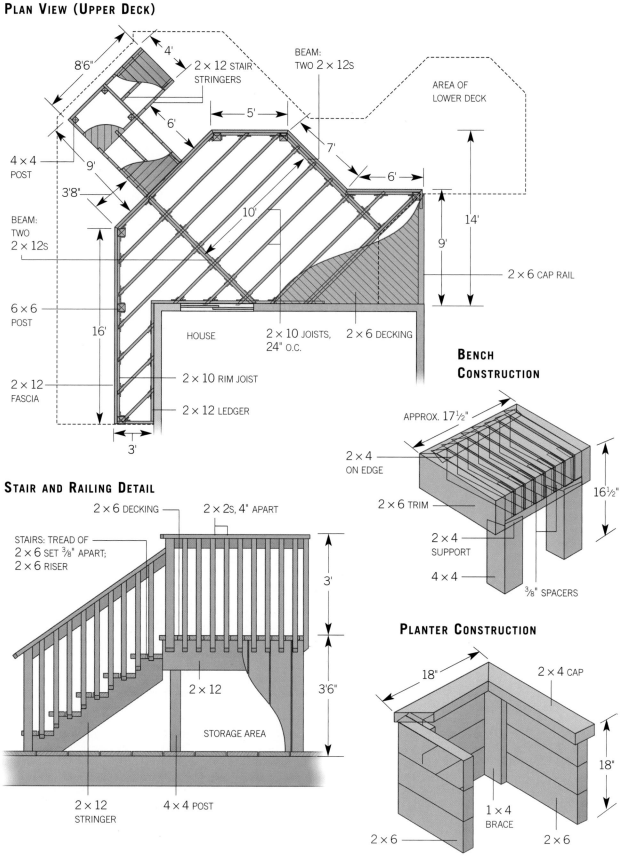

PLAN VIEW (UPPER DECK)

8'6"

4'

2 × 12 STAIR STRINGERS

BEAM: TWO 2 × 12S

AREA OF LOWER DECK

5'

6'

7'

6'

4 × 4 POST

9'

3'8"

10'

14'

9'

2 × 6 CAP RAIL

BEAM: TWO 2 × 12S

6 × 6 POST

16'

HOUSE

2 × 10 JOISTS, 24" O.C.

2 × 6 DECKING

2 × 12 FASCIA

2 × 10 RIM JOIST

2 × 12 LEDGER

3'

STAIR AND RAILING DETAIL

2 × 6 DECKING

2 × 2S, 4" APART

STAIRS: TREAD OF 2 × 6 SET ³⁄₈" APART; 2 × 6 RISER

3'

2 × 12

3'6"

STORAGE AREA

2 × 12 STRINGER

4 × 4 POST

BENCH CONSTRUCTION

APPROX. 17½"

2 × 4 ON EDGE

2 × 6 TRIM

2 × 4 SUPPORT

4 × 4

16½"

³⁄₈" SPACERS

PLANTER CONSTRUCTION

18"

2 × 4 CAP

18"

2 × 6

1 × 4 BRACE

2 × 6

ELEVATION

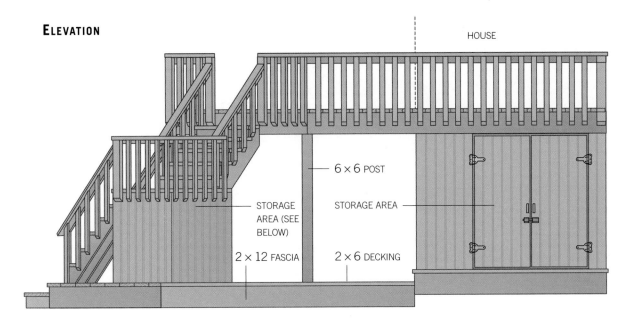

HOUSE

6 × 6 POST

STORAGE AREA (SEE BELOW)

STORAGE AREA

2 × 12 FASCIA

2 × 6 DECKING

UNDER-STAIR STORAGE CONSTRUCTION

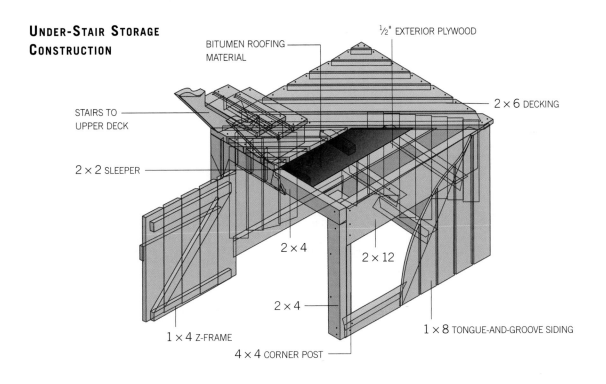

BITUMEN ROOFING MATERIAL

½" EXTERIOR PLYWOOD

STAIRS TO UPPER DECK

2 × 6 DECKING

2 × 2 SLEEPER

2 × 4

2 × 12

2 × 4

1 × 4 Z-FRAME

4 × 4 CORNER POST

1 × 8 TONGUE-AND-GROOVE SIDING

deck with ramps

MATERIALS LIST

Designed for pressure-treated lumber (structural members), Construction Heart redwood (decking, rails, and other visible members), oriented-strand board (fascia, column sheathing), painted pipe (balusters), and galvanized hardware.

LUMBER	
Posts	4 × 4
Beams	2 × 8, 2 × 10
Joists and ledgers	2 × 6 (ramp joists); 2 × 8 (ledger, deck joists)
Decking	2 × 6
Stairs	2 × 12 stringers; 2 × 6 treads
Railings	4 × 4 posts; 2 × 4 rails; 1" pipe balusters; 2 × 6 cap rails
Fascia	Oriented-strand board (OSB)
Columns	OSB (sheathing); 2 × 4 (framing); 2 × 8 (tops)
Other	Lattice skirting
MASONRY	
Concrete	Piers, slabs
Stucco	Columns, fascia
HARDWARE	
Nails	16d (framing); as appropriate for connectors
Bolts and screws	½" bolts (framing); ⅝" lag screws and epoxy anchors (framing-to-masonry)
Connectors	Post connectors; joist hangers
Other	Hidden fasteners (decking); #4 rebar; stucco mesh
OTHER	
Light fixtures and wiring	

Ramps can be a good substitute for stairs on a deck, providing functional access for a wheelchair and a graceful design touch as well. This deck uses three ramps to link separate areas for grilling, dining, and relaxing. The top level, shaded by the home's roof, is close to the kitchen and both indoor and outdoor eating areas. From it, an upper ramp descends to a dining platform with seating for ten. A second ramp then leads to a lower level, which is set low enough to do without railings. A third, shorter ramp connects the deck to the yard.

TO ADAPT THIS PLAN

You can adjust the size, shape, and number of levels of this deck by proper adaptation of the framing—but make sure that any changes you make do not result in steeper ramps than those shown here. Ramps for a commercial establishment would be shallower, and you may choose to reduce the ramp slopes for your deck as well. The stucco-clad pillars are visual elements meant to tie together the look of the deck and the house, and are not needed for structural support; you can keep or omit them as you wish.

BUILDING NOTES

The doubled posts and side-by-side piers and footings serve the same purpose as would larger foundations and single 6 × 6 posts. On this deck a planter functions as a barrier between the top deck and the first ramp; depending on your local codes, you may need to install an additional railing in this area. As built, this deck also includes a tree cutout in the lower deck.

DESIGNER
Russ Sinkola

PLAN VIEW—DECKING

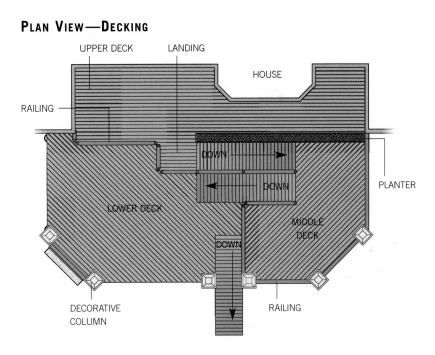

UPPER DECK   LANDING
HOUSE
RAILING
DOWN
DOWN
PLANTER
LOWER DECK
MIDDLE DECK
DOWN
DOWN
DECORATIVE COLUMN
RAILING

PLAN VIEW—FRAMING

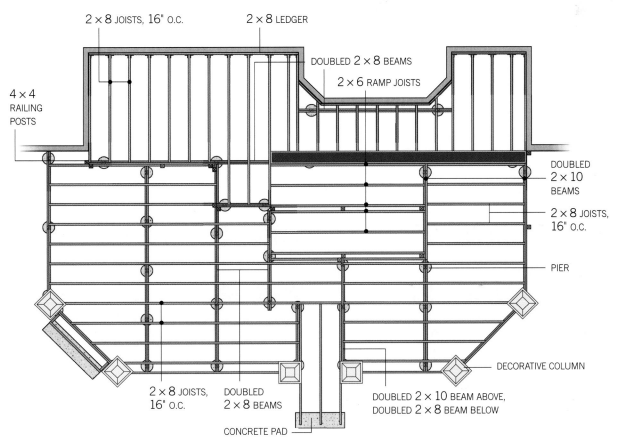

2 × 8 JOISTS, 16" O.C.   2 × 8 LEDGER

DOUBLED 2 × 8 BEAMS

2 × 6 RAMP JOISTS

4 × 4 RAILING POSTS

DOUBLED 2 × 10 BEAMS

2 × 8 JOISTS, 16" O.C.

PIER

DECORATIVE COLUMN

2 × 8 JOISTS, 16" O.C.   DOUBLED 2 × 8 BEAMS

DOUBLED 2 × 10 BEAM ABOVE, DOUBLED 2 × 8 BEAM BELOW

CONCRETE PAD

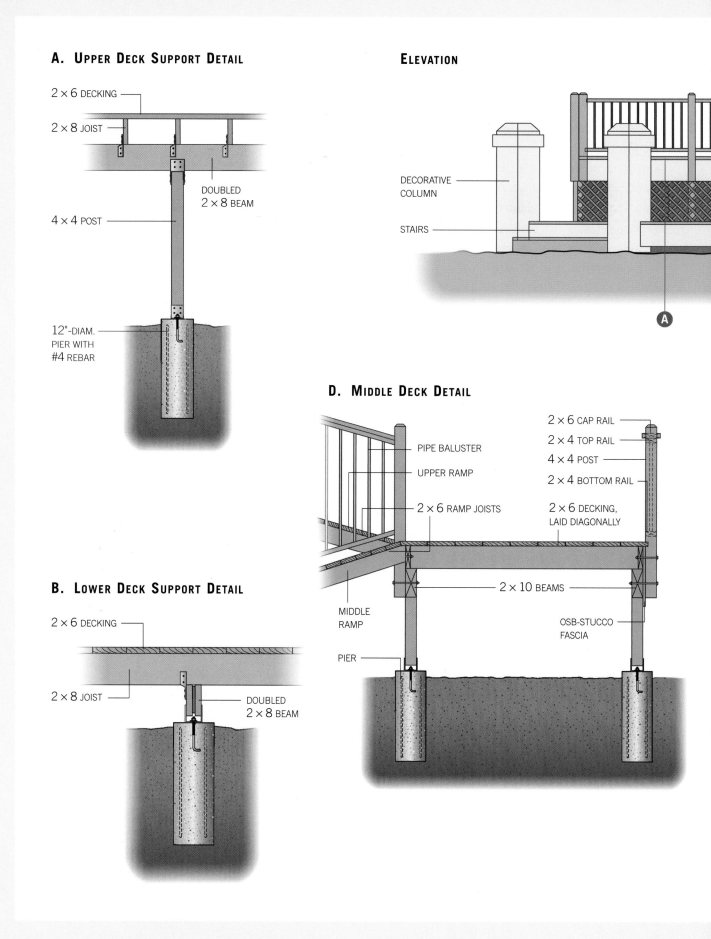

A. UPPER DECK SUPPORT DETAIL

2 × 6 DECKING

2 × 8 JOIST

DOUBLED
2 × 8 BEAM

4 × 4 POST

12"-DIAM.
PIER WITH
#4 REBAR

ELEVATION

DECORATIVE
COLUMN

STAIRS

A

D. MIDDLE DECK DETAIL

2 × 6 CAP RAIL

2 × 4 TOP RAIL

4 × 4 POST

2 × 4 BOTTOM RAIL

2 × 6 DECKING,
LAID DIAGONALLY

PIPE BALUSTER

UPPER RAMP

2 × 6 RAMP JOISTS

2 × 10 BEAMS

MIDDLE
RAMP

OSB-STUCCO
FASCIA

PIER

B. LOWER DECK SUPPORT DETAIL

2 × 6 DECKING

2 × 8 JOIST

DOUBLED
2 × 8 BEAM

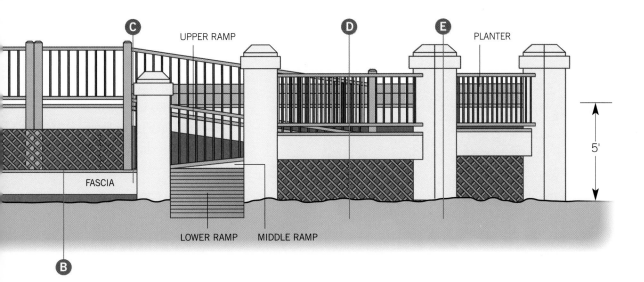

UPPER RAMP

PLANTER

FASCIA

LOWER RAMP

MIDDLE RAMP

5'

C. RAMP FRAMING DETAIL

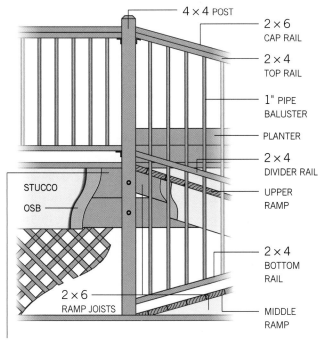

4 × 4 POST

2 × 6 CAP RAIL

2 × 4 TOP RAIL

1" PIPE BALUSTER

PLANTER

2 × 4 DIVIDER RAIL

UPPER RAMP

2 × 4 BOTTOM RAIL

MIDDLE RAMP

STUCCO

OSB

2 × 6 RAMP JOISTS

2 × 8 RIM JOIST ON LANDING

E. DECORATIVE COLUMN DETAIL

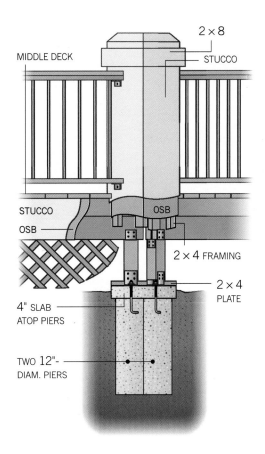

MIDDLE DECK

2 × 8

STUCCO

STUCCO

OSB

OSB

2 × 4 FRAMING

2 × 4 PLATE

4" SLAB ATOP PIERS

TWO 12"- DIAM. PIERS

patio deck for a steep slope

skirtings help create the effect of a very large balcony that looks as if it has always been there. A mature tree grows through the deck, enhancing the effect.

TO ADAPT THIS PLAN

This deck is tailored to its home and site, yet it can be adapted to any home that needs a wraparound deck that turns a corner. You can readily scale it up or down. If you do not need the lattice privacy screen or the bench, you can substitute railing sections.

BUILDING NOTES

The distinctive seat and railings are easy to build, with beveled post and rail tops that are simple but quite distinguished looking. For a less challenging site, you may be able to substitute more typical deck framing and foundations. The underpinnings of this deck, including massive 6 × 12 beams and pier-and-tie-beam foundation (see page 216), are carefully engineered. If you have a similarly difficult site and wish to use or adapt the supporting scheme shown here, consult a structural engineer (see page 55).

DESIGNER
Bill Remick, Remick Associates
Architects/Builders

Mediterranean-style homes often have patios, but, because it was built on a steep slope, the house for which this deck was built had no patio. This ambitious, conservatively engineered deck solved the problem by converting the unusable hillside into a "backyard." From below, the lattice

ELEVATION

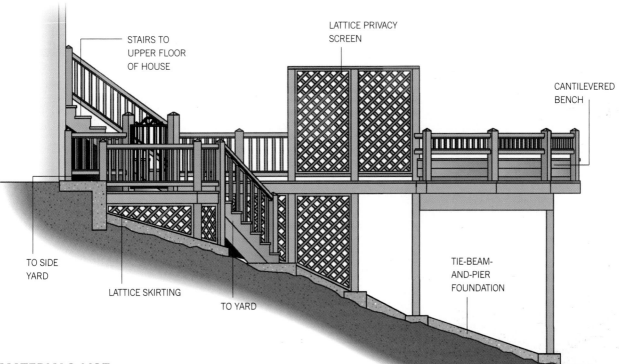

STAIRS TO
UPPER FLOOR
OF HOUSE

LATTICE PRIVACY
SCREEN

CANTILEVERED
BENCH

TO SIDE
YARD

LATTICE SKIRTING

TO YARD

TIE-BEAM-
AND-PIER
FOUNDATION

MATERIALS LIST

Designed for pressure-treated lumber (structural members), Heart B redwood
(decking, bench, fascia, and other visible members), and galvanized hardware.

LUMBER	
Decking	2 × 6
Joists and ledgers	2 × 8
Posts	6 × 6
Beams	4 × 8, 6 × 12
Fascia	1 × 6, 2 × 4, 2 × 8
Bench	2 × 6 seat, ledger, skirting, and fascia; 2 × 4 cripple wall and joists
Stairs	2 × 12 stringers; 2 × 6 treads and risers
Railings	6 × 6 posts; 4 × 4 top rails; 3 × 4 bottom rails; 2 × 2 balusters; ⅝" × ⅝" stops; 1" x 1½" blocking
Other	Redwood lattice; 1 × 2 stops; 2 × 6 lattice frame
MASONRY	
Concrete	Piers, tie beams
HARDWARE	
Nails	16d (framing); as appropriate for connectors
Bolts and screws	½" bolts (framing); 2½" coated screws (decking)
Connectors	Post and beam connectors; joist hangers
Other	#3, #4, #5 rebar

PLAN VIEW—DECKING

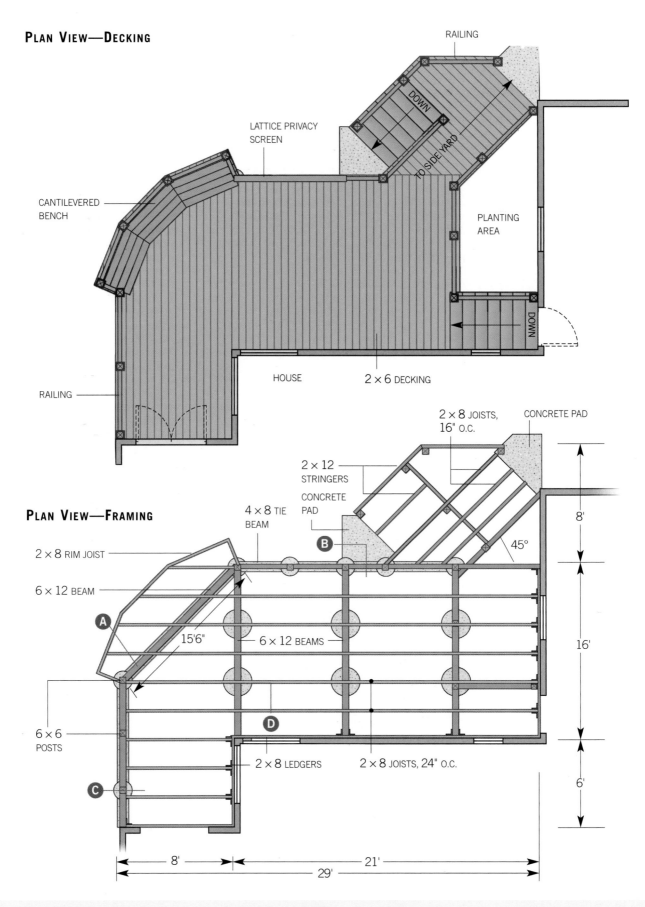

RAILING

LATTICE PRIVACY
SCREEN

TO SIDE YARD

DOWN

PLANTING
AREA

CANTILEVERED
BENCH

DOWN

RAILING

HOUSE

2 × 6 DECKING

PLAN VIEW—FRAMING

2 × 8 JOISTS,
16" O.C.

CONCRETE PAD

2 × 12
STRINGERS

CONCRETE
PAD

4 × 8 TIE
BEAM

2 × 8 RIM JOIST

6 × 12 BEAM

A

B

45°

8'

15'6"

6 × 12 BEAMS

D

16'

6 × 6
POSTS

2 × 8 LEDGERS

2 × 8 JOISTS, 24" O.C.

C

6'

8'

21'

29'

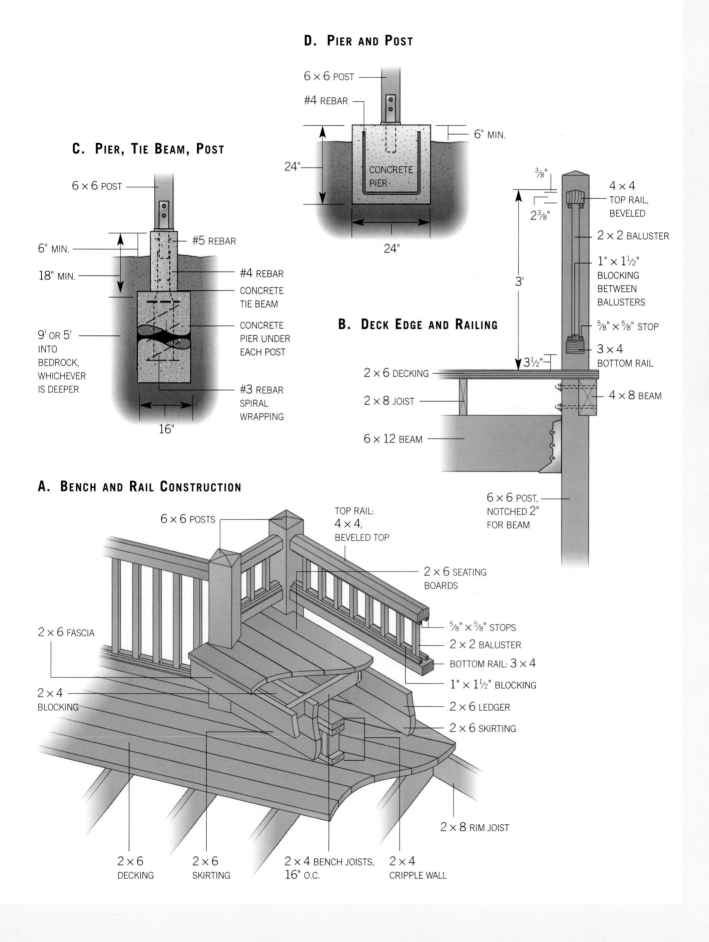

D. PIER AND POST

6 × 6 POST

#4 REBAR

6" MIN.

24"

CONCRETE PIER

24"

C. PIER, TIE BEAM, POST

6 × 6 POST

6" MIN.

18" MIN.

#5 REBAR

#4 REBAR

CONCRETE TIE BEAM

CONCRETE PIER UNDER EACH POST

9' OR 5' INTO BEDROCK, WHICHEVER IS DEEPER

#3 REBAR SPIRAL WRAPPING

16"

B. DECK EDGE AND RAILING

$\frac{3}{8}$"

$2\frac{3}{8}$"

3'

$3\frac{1}{2}$"

4 × 4 TOP RAIL, BEVELED

2 × 2 BALUSTER

1" × 1$\frac{1}{2}$" BLOCKING BETWEEN BALUSTERS

$\frac{5}{8}$" × $\frac{5}{8}$" STOP

3 × 4 BOTTOM RAIL

2 × 6 DECKING

2 × 8 JOIST

6 × 12 BEAM

4 × 8 BEAM

6 × 6 POST, NOTCHED 2" FOR BEAM

A. BENCH AND RAIL CONSTRUCTION

6 × 6 POSTS

TOP RAIL: 4 × 4, BEVELED TOP

2 × 6 SEATING BOARDS

$\frac{5}{8}$" × $\frac{5}{8}$" STOPS

2 × 2 BALUSTER

BOTTOM RAIL: 3 × 4

1" × 1$\frac{1}{2}$" BLOCKING

2 × 6 LEDGER

2 × 6 SKIRTING

2 × 8 RIM JOIST

2 × 6 FASCIA

2 × 4 BLOCKING

2 × 6 DECKING

2 × 6 SKIRTING

2 × 4 BENCH JOISTS, 16" O.C.

2 × 4 CRIPPLE WALL

deck with a view

Designed for large-scale entertaining, this big step-down deck reclaims a largely unusable strip of land next to a house set on a steep hill. The large upper level extends into a built-in sofa bench serving the smaller lower level, which in turn provides a seating area with a canyon view. Built-in planters embrace the sofa and support the seat backs. End tables that also serve as armrests provide convenience. The bi-level plan focuses attention on the view and preserves the outlook from the house.

PLAN VIEW—DECKING

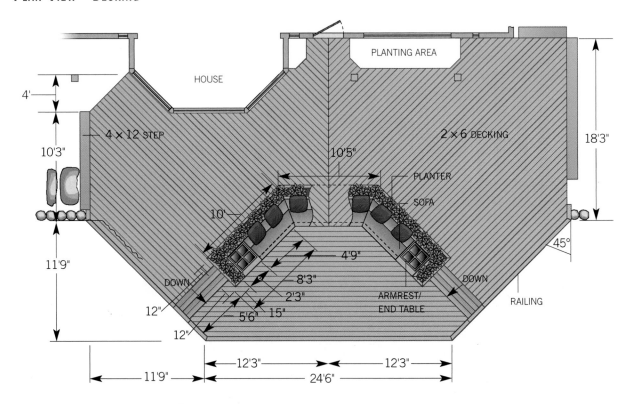

TO ADAPT THIS PLAN

You can straighten out or relocate the ledger breaks and their supports to suit your home, and scale the plan up or down.

BUILDING NOTES

This deck is designed for a problem site in a seismic zone. Built on a steep down-slope and straddling a swale, the deck required reinforced continuous footings throughout. There are no piers. The perimeter footing is faced with stone for appearance and provided with drainage to handle water accumulating in the swale. For maximum stability, a concrete-block wall supports the stone and the perimeter posts. To adapt this elaborate foundation scheme, consult an engineer (see page 55). If your site is less extreme, you may be able to substitute more conventional pier footings throughout. You should also consult an architect or engineer before you make such a change, however, since the foundation is integral to the deck's design.

DESIGNER
Robert Engman, AIA, Architect

MATERIALS LIST

Designed for pressure-treated lumber (structural members), surfaced Western red cedar (decking), Clear Heart redwood (siding), and galvanized hardware.

LUMBER	
Plates	2 × 4
Posts	4 × 4
Beams	4 × 8
Bracing	2 × 6 at stone wall
Joists	2 × 6 (upper deck), 2 × 8 (lower deck)
Ledger	2 × 8
Blocking	2 × 6 atop interior footings
Decking	2 × 6
Interior stairs	2 × 12 stringers; 2 × 6 treads; 2 × 4 risers
Railings	4 × 4 posts; 2 × 3 rails; 2 × 8 caps; 1 × 8 fascia; $\frac{3}{4}$" × $2\frac{1}{4}$" trim
Planter/ bench	2 × 8 armrest/end table frame; 2 × 6 backrest; 2 × 4 frame, caps, armrest trim; 2 × 2 under caps; 1 × 8 siding; 1 × 6 trim; $\frac{3}{4}$" marine plywood planter bottom, armrest top; $\frac{3}{8}$" plywood planter interior sides
Exterior step	4 × 12
MASONRY	
Concrete	Continuous footings
Stone	Wall facing
Gravel	Drain rock at perforated pipe
HARDWARE	
Nails	16d (framing); 10d (decking); as appropriate for connectors
Bolts and screws	$\frac{5}{8}$" bolts at steps; $\frac{1}{2}$" anchor bolts
Connectors	Post connectors; joist hangers
Other	$\frac{1}{2}$" copper pipe balusters; 4" perforated drainpipe at stone wall; $\frac{3}{4}$" drainpipe for planter/sofa; masonry anchors in stone wall; #3 and #4 reinforcing bars; #3 hoops; for sofa/planter: galvanized sheet-metal liner; 12" tiles; bitumen protective coating; all-weather cushions

ELEVATION

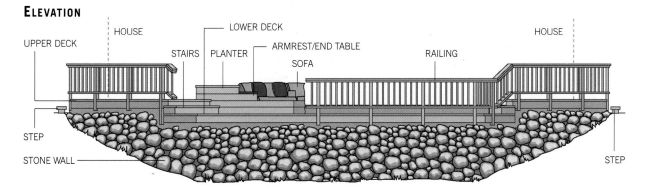

UPPER DECK · HOUSE · LOWER DECK · STAIRS · PLANTER · ARMREST/END TABLE · SOFA · RAILING · HOUSE · STEP · STONE WALL · STEP

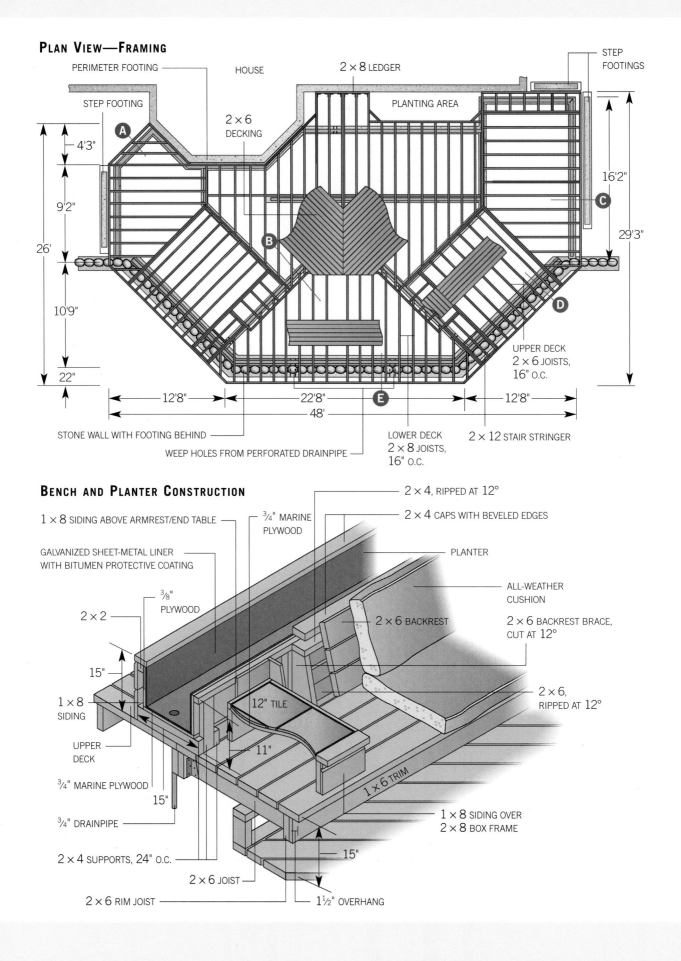

PLAN VIEW—FRAMING

PERIMETER FOOTING

HOUSE

2 × 8 LEDGER

STEP FOOTINGS

STEP FOOTING

PLANTING AREA

A

2 × 6 DECKING

4'3"

9'2"

16'2"

C

26'

B

29'3"

10'9"

D

22"

UPPER DECK
2 × 6 JOISTS,
16" O.C.

12'8"

22'8"

E

12'8"

48'

STONE WALL WITH FOOTING BEHIND

LOWER DECK
2 × 8 JOISTS,
16" O.C.

2 × 12 STAIR STRINGER

WEEP HOLES FROM PERFORATED DRAINPIPE

BENCH AND PLANTER CONSTRUCTION

1 × 8 SIDING ABOVE ARMREST/END TABLE

¾" MARINE PLYWOOD

2 × 4, RIPPED AT 12°

2 × 4 CAPS WITH BEVELED EDGES

GALVANIZED SHEET-METAL LINER
WITH BITUMEN PROTECTIVE COATING

PLANTER

ALL-WEATHER
CUSHION

⅜" PLYWOOD

2 × 2

2 × 6 BACKREST

2 × 6 BACKREST BRACE,
CUT AT 12°

15"

1 × 8 SIDING

12" TILE

2 × 6,
RIPPED AT 12°

UPPER DECK

11"

¾" MARINE PLYWOOD

15"

1 × 6 TRIM

¾" DRAINPIPE

1 × 8 SIDING OVER
2 × 8 BOX FRAME

2 × 4 SUPPORTS, 24" O.C.

15"

2 × 6 JOIST

2 × 6 RIM JOIST

1½" OVERHANG

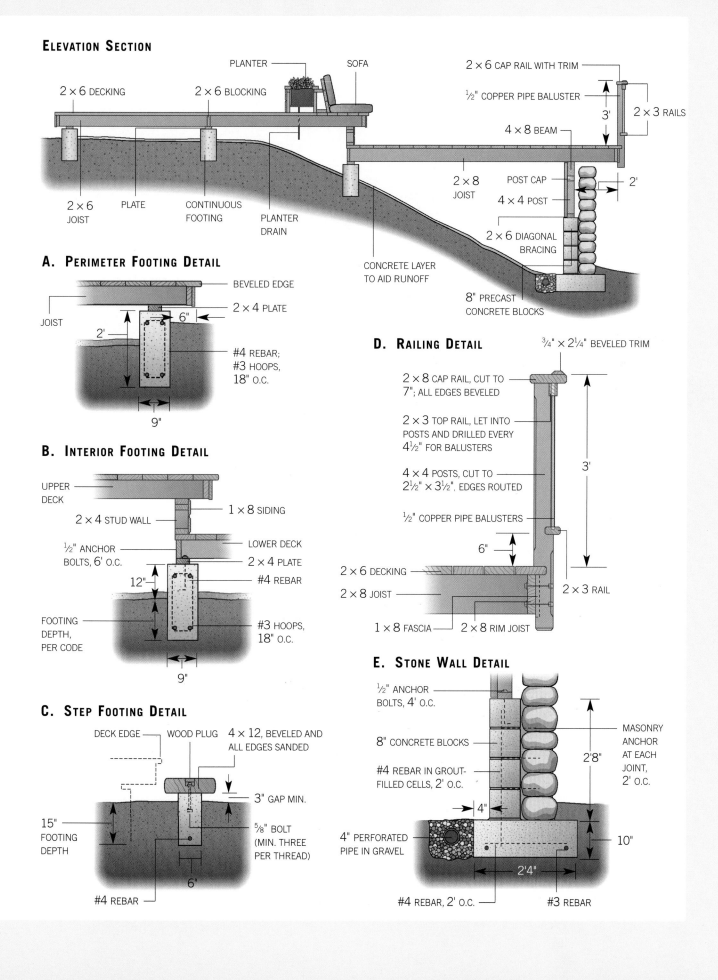

ELEVATION SECTION

PLANTER
SOFA
2 × 6 DECKING
2 × 6 BLOCKING
2 × 6 CAP RAIL WITH TRIM
½" COPPER PIPE BALUSTER
2 × 3 RAILS
3'
4 × 8 BEAM
2 × 6 JOIST
PLATE
CONTINUOUS FOOTING
PLANTER DRAIN
POST CAP
2 × 8 JOIST
4 × 4 POST
2'
CONCRETE LAYER TO AID RUNOFF
2 × 6 DIAGONAL BRACING
8" PRECAST CONCRETE BLOCKS

A. PERIMETER FOOTING DETAIL

BEVELED EDGE
2 × 4 PLATE
6"
JOIST
2'
#4 REBAR; #3 HOOPS, 18" O.C.
9"

B. INTERIOR FOOTING DETAIL

UPPER DECK
2 × 4 STUD WALL
1 × 8 SIDING
½" ANCHOR BOLTS, 6' O.C.
LOWER DECK
2 × 4 PLATE
12"
#4 REBAR
FOOTING DEPTH, PER CODE
#3 HOOPS, 18" O.C.
9"

C. STEP FOOTING DETAIL

DECK EDGE
WOOD PLUG
4 × 12, BEVELED AND ALL EDGES SANDED
3" GAP MIN.
15" FOOTING DEPTH
⅝" BOLT (MIN. THREE PER THREAD)
6"
#4 REBAR

D. RAILING DETAIL

¾" × 2¼" BEVELED TRIM
2 × 8 CAP RAIL, CUT TO 7"; ALL EDGES BEVELED
2 × 3 TOP RAIL, LET INTO POSTS AND DRILLED EVERY 4½" FOR BALUSTERS
4 × 4 POSTS, CUT TO 2½" × 3½", EDGES ROUTED
½" COPPER PIPE BALUSTERS
3'
6"
2 × 6 DECKING
2 × 8 JOIST
2 × 3 RAIL
1 × 8 FASCIA
2 × 8 RIM JOIST

E. STONE WALL DETAIL

½" ANCHOR BOLTS, 4' O.C.
8" CONCRETE BLOCKS
#4 REBAR IN GROUT-FILLED CELLS, 2' O.C.
MASONRY ANCHOR AT EACH JOINT, 2' O.C.
2'8"
4" PERFORATED PIPE IN GRAVEL
4"
10"
2'4"
#4 REBAR, 2' O.C.
#3 REBAR

house-wide deck

This welcoming, asymmetrical design spans the full width of a large house, providing a sunny outdoor space for each room on a south-facing wall. At right, a raised section supplements the master bedroom; the rest of the deck serves the kitchen, family room, and other social spaces. Two stairways flanking a projecting seating area lead to the yard. Stone facings and lattice skirting hide the substructure. A large built-in planter and its contents offer a pleasant counterpoint to the broad expanse of wood.

TO ADAPT THIS PLAN

In dealing with a very wide house, the designer broke up the expanse with angles in the plan view and level changes in the elevation. As a result, the design is in essence a series of interconnected deck modules, and these can be adapted. You could pick and choose among the connected modules, altering their sizes and contours and recomposing the whole to fit your home. The broad left-hand section with stairs would also make a simple, elegant deck of its own. As always for any changes, make sure the framing

and foundations are adjusted to adequately support the changes you have made.

BUILDING NOTES

Built on a level lot in a temperate climate, this deck has a simple, robust frame supported by piers and footings, with block-wall support along the stairs. This foundation scheme

might need to be re-engineered for a more challenging site. The 16-inch joist spacing is conservative and will work for almost all decking materials. For some materials, you could increase the spacing to 24 inches and save on framing material.

DESIGNER
Gary Marsh, All Decked Out

PLAN VIEW—DECKING

FENCE AND SERVICE GATE

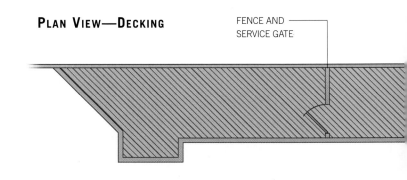

MATERIALS LIST

Designed for pressure-treated lumber (structural members), Heart B redwood (decking, railings, and other visible members), and galvanized hardware.

LUMBER	
Posts	6 × 6
Beams	3 × 8, 6 × 10
Joists and ledgers	2 × 10
Plates	2 × 4, 2 × 6, 2 × 8
Braces	2 × 8
Fascia	1 × 6, 1 × 4, 2 × 4
Decking	2 × 6
Stairs	2 × 4 platform framing; 2 × 12 stringers; 2 × 6 treads; 2 × 6 risers; 2 × 12 fascia
Railings	4 × 4 posts; 2 × 4 rails; 2 × 2 balusters; 2 × 6 cap rails; milled handrails
Other	Redwood lattice cladding; 1 × 2 stops
MASONRY	
Concrete	Footings, filling blocks
Concrete block	8" hollow block (planter walls)
Stone	River rock (block-wall facings)
Gravel	1" (planter drain)
HARDWARE	
Nails	16d (framing); as appropriate for connectors
Bolts and screws	2½" stainless-steel screws (decking); ⅝" bolts (framing); ⅝" lag screws and epoxy anchors (framing-to-masonry)
Connectors	Post connectors; joist hangers; strap ties, beam connectors, beam carriers
Other	#3, #4 rebar; #4 hoops; ⅝" galvanized rod
OTHER	
Recessed low-voltage stair lights	
Soil, charcoal, landscaping fabric, drain, and piping (planter)	

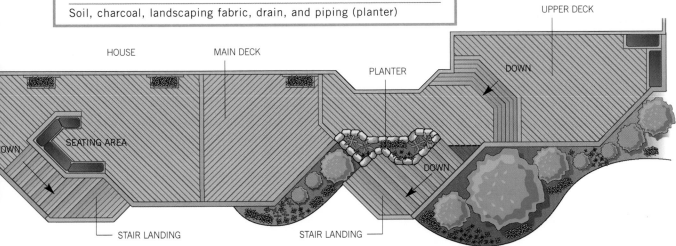

UPPER DECK

HOUSE   MAIN DECK   PLANTER   DOWN

DOWN   SEATING AREA   DOWN

STAIR LANDING   STAIR LANDING

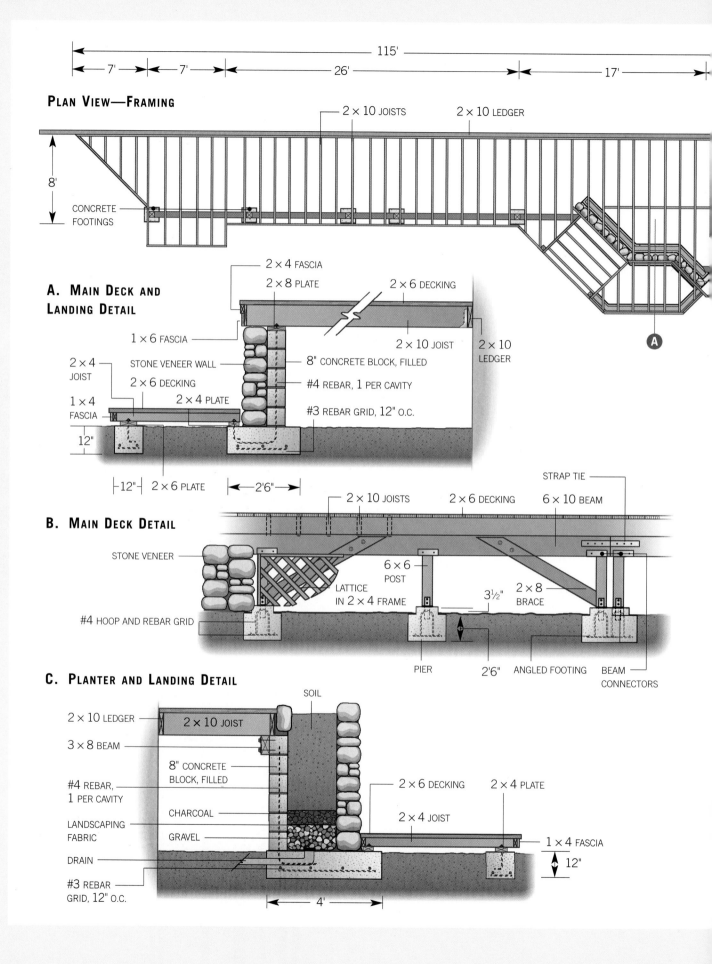

PLAN VIEW—FRAMING

115'

7' · 7' · 26' · 17'

2 × 10 JOISTS
2 × 10 LEDGER

8'

CONCRETE
FOOTINGS

**A. MAIN DECK AND
LANDING DETAIL**

2 × 4 FASCIA
2 × 8 PLATE
2 × 6 DECKING

1 × 6 FASCIA
2 × 10 JOIST
2 × 10 LEDGER

2 × 4 JOIST
STONE VENEER WALL
8" CONCRETE BLOCK, FILLED
2 × 6 DECKING
2 × 4 PLATE
#4 REBAR, 1 PER CAVITY
1 × 4 FASCIA
#3 REBAR GRID, 12" O.C.

12"

12"   2 × 6 PLATE   2'6"

A

B. MAIN DECK DETAIL

STRAP TIE
2 × 10 JOISTS
2 × 6 DECKING
6 × 10 BEAM

STONE VENEER
6 × 6 POST
2 × 8 BRACE
LATTICE IN 2 × 4 FRAME
3½"
#4 HOOP AND REBAR GRID
PIER   2'6"   ANGLED FOOTING   BEAM CONNECTORS

C. PLANTER AND LANDING DETAIL

SOIL
2 × 10 LEDGER
2 × 10 JOIST
3 × 8 BEAM
8" CONCRETE BLOCK, FILLED
#4 REBAR, 1 PER CAVITY
2 × 6 DECKING
2 × 4 PLATE
LANDSCAPING FABRIC
CHARCOAL
2 × 4 JOIST
GRAVEL
1 × 4 FASCIA
DRAIN
12"
#3 REBAR GRID, 12" O.C.
4'

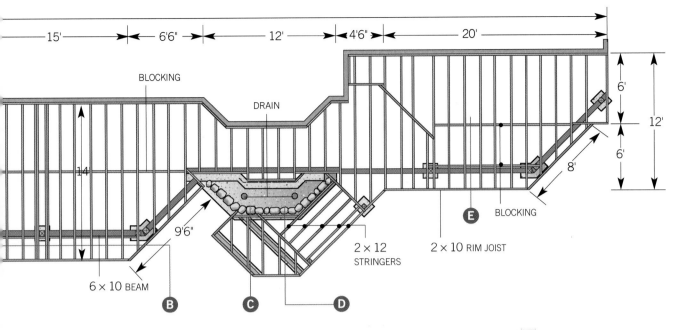

15'   6'6"   12'   4'6"   20'

BLOCKING

DRAIN

6'

12'

6'

14

8'

E

BLOCKING

2 × 10 RIM JOIST

6 × 10 BEAM

9'6"

2 × 12
STRINGERS

B   **C**   **D**

D. RIGHT-SIDE STAIR DETAIL

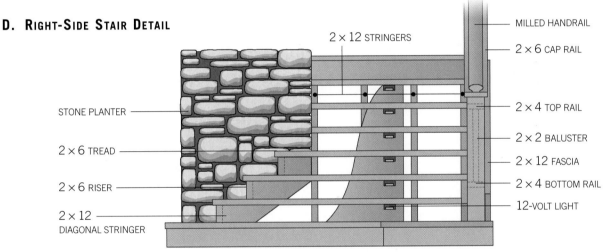

2 × 12 STRINGERS

MILLED HANDRAIL

2 × 6 CAP RAIL

STONE PLANTER

2 × 4 TOP RAIL

2 × 2 BALUSTER

2 × 6 TREAD

2 × 12 FASCIA

2 × 6 RISER

2 × 4 BOTTOM RAIL

12-VOLT LIGHT

2 × 12
DIAGONAL STRINGER

E. UPPER DECK AND STEPS DETAIL

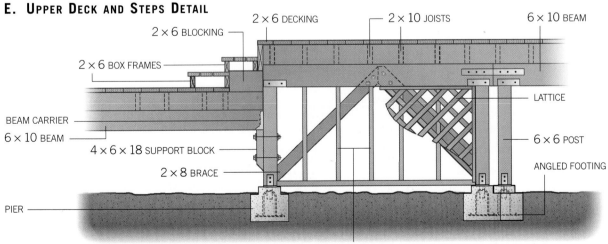

2 × 6 DECKING

2 × 10 JOISTS

6 × 10 BEAM

2 × 6 BLOCKING

2 × 6 BOX FRAMES

LATTICE

BEAM CARRIER

6 × 10 BEAM

4 × 6 × 18 SUPPORT BLOCK

6 × 6 POST

2 × 8 BRACE

ANGLED FOOTING

PIER

2 × 4 SUPPORTS

landscaping deck

Like water itself, this deck seems to flow through its site, tying together a swimming pool, spa, cabana, and patio. Designed in part according to the principles of Chinese feng shui, the deck features an irregular, flowing edge that harmonizes with the Asian-style garden and the watery setting. It runs from grade level near the pool over a ravine at the rear, reclaiming lost space and adding it to the yard.

TO ADAPT THIS PLAN

The ambitious deck scheme bears some similarities to the ultra-simple deck on pages 200–201. Both are based on an adaptable system that is suited to decks of many sizes and shapes. The planting bays and tree cutout show the flexibility of this creative system, which you can adapt to your site in the same way.

BUILDING NOTES

To create the irregular edge for this deck, joist blocking and site-laminated benderboard complete the framing. The deck boards are cut to fit above, their edges routed for a smooth, organic look. This deck is set quite low to the ground where it meets the pool, but at the rear a steep ravine required tall footings set in bedrock. The beams had to parallel the ravine so that the joists could be brought back for a solid connection to the main level. Given less challenging terrain, more conventional framing (like the framing near the pool) could have been used throughout.

In order for the decking to run toward the pool, 2 × 4 stringers, laid flat, were used above the joists so that the deck boards could run parallel to them. You can change the framing to eliminate these non-structural members.

DESIGNER
Bryan Gordon, B. Gordon Builders; Rick Hirsch, architect

MATERIALS LIST

Designed for pressure-treated Douglas fir (structural supports), Heart B redwood (decking and other visible members), and galvanized hardware.

LUMBER	
Posts	4 × 4
Beams	4 × 6, 4 × 12
Joists, blocking, and ledgers	2 × 10; some blocking 2 × 6
Stringers and braces	2 × 4
Fascia	2 × 10 (fascia); ⅜" × 9½" and ⅜" × 5½" benderboard (laminated curved fascia)
Decking	2 × 6
Stairs	2 × 12 stringers; 2 × 6 treads; 2 × 8 risers; 1 × 4 trim
Railings	4 × 4 posts; 2 × 4 rails; 2 × 4 square-welded wire with plastic coating; for curved railing, 2 × 4, 2 × 6, and ⅜" × 3½" or ⅜" × 5½" glued laminated benderboard
MASONRY	
Concrete	Footings
HARDWARE	
Nails	16d (framing); as appropriate for connectors
Bolts and screws	2½" stainless-steel screws (decking); ½" bolts (framing); ½" lag screws (ledger)
Connectors	Post connectors; joist hangers
Other	#3 rebar

PLAN VIEW

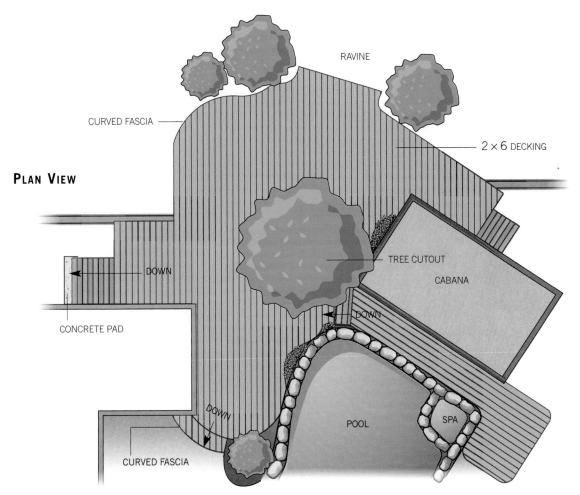

RAVINE

CURVED FASCIA

2 × 6 DECKING

DOWN

TREE CUTOUT

CABANA

CONCRETE PAD

DOWN

DOWN

CURVED FASCIA

POOL

SPA

PLAN VIEW—FRAMING

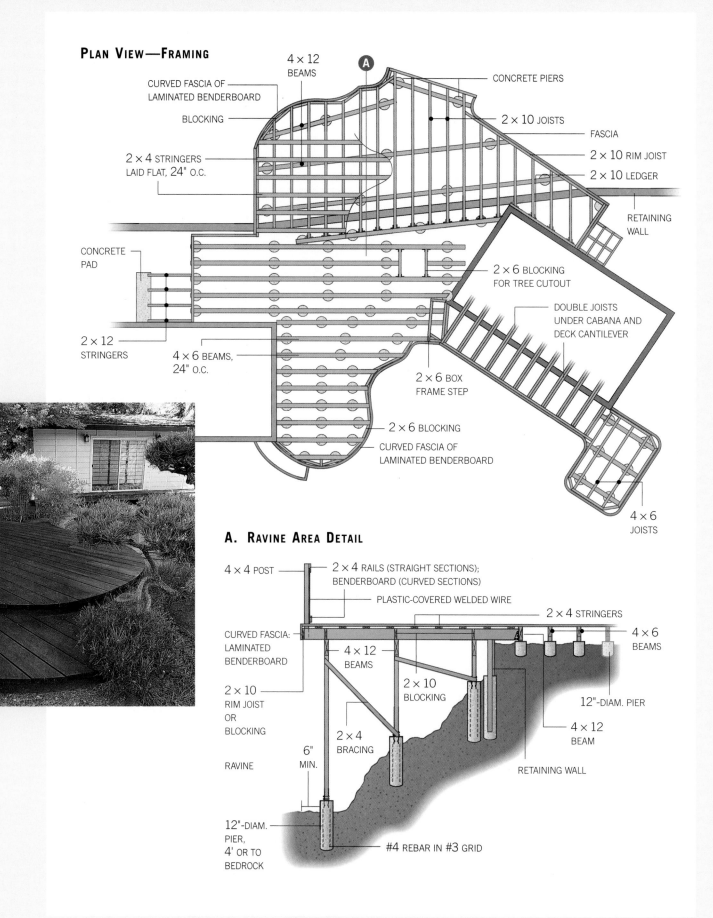

CURVED FASCIA OF
LAMINATED BENDERBOARD

4 × 12
BEAMS

A

CONCRETE PIERS

BLOCKING

2 × 10 JOISTS

FASCIA

2 × 4 STRINGERS
LAID FLAT, 24" O.C.

2 × 10 RIM JOIST

2 × 10 LEDGER

RETAINING
WALL

CONCRETE
PAD

2 × 6 BLOCKING
FOR TREE CUTOUT

DOUBLE JOISTS
UNDER CABANA AND
DECK CANTILEVER

2 × 12
STRINGERS

4 × 6 BEAMS,
24" O.C.

2 × 6 BOX
FRAME STEP

2 × 6 BLOCKING

CURVED FASCIA OF
LAMINATED BENDERBOARD

4 × 6
JOISTS

A. RAVINE AREA DETAIL

4 × 4 POST

2 × 4 RAILS (STRAIGHT SECTIONS);
BENDERBOARD (CURVED SECTIONS)

PLASTIC-COVERED WELDED WIRE

2 × 4 STRINGERS

4 × 6
BEAMS

CURVED FASCIA:
LAMINATED
BENDERBOARD

4 × 12
BEAMS

2 × 10
BLOCKING

2 × 10
RIM JOIST
OR
BLOCKING

12"-DIAM. PIER

4 × 12
BEAM

RAVINE

6"
MIN.

2 × 4
BRACING

RETAINING WALL

12"-DIAM.
PIER,
4' OR TO
BEDROCK

#4 REBAR IN #3 GRID

glossary

Anchor bolt. Used on decks to secure the post base to the concrete foundation.

Baluster. A thin, usually vertical component of a deck railing that is attached to the rails.

Batterboard. A temporary structure of two stakes and a crosspiece that is used to hold strings while a deck is being laid out.

Beam. A large horizontal framing member that usually rests on posts and supports joists.

Blocking. Pieces of framing lumber installed between joists to add rigidity to a deck.

Bracing. Used on some decks to strengthen the connection between posts and beams or joists.

Cantilever. To extend past the edge of a supporting member, such as when joist ends overhang a beam.

Cap rail. A component of some deck railings; the horizontal board laid across the tops of the posts.

Cleat. A small piece of wood used solely to support the end of another piece. Typically used on deck posts to provide a nailing surface for decking.

Composite lumber. Material used for decking and railing components, typically made from a mix of wood products and recycled plastic.

Crown. The high point along the edge of a piece of lumber.

Dead load. The weight of the permanent materials used in constructing a deck.

Decking. The boards used for the top, walking surface of a deck.

Elevation. A drawing of the side view of a structure showing vertical dimensions and relationships.

Fascia. A decorative trim board around the edge of a deck that covers the rim and end joists, and, in some cases, the ends of decking boards.

Flashing. A protective layer of metal or flexible, self-adhering material used at a deck ledger to prevent moisture from getting into the house or its framing.

Footing. The bottom part of a concrete foundation that distributes the weight of the deck to the earth.

Frost line. The maximum depth at which freezing can occur in a particular locale.

Joist. A horizontal framing member that supports the decking.

Joist hanger. A metal connector used to join a joist to a ledger, rim joist, or beam.

Lattice. A gridwork of wood or plastic strips used for skirting, privacy screens, and overheads.

Ledger. A structural member attached to a house or another structure, used to support one end of the joists.

Level. Aligned with the horizon, or perfectly horizontal. Also, a tool used to determine level and plumb (see below).

Live load. The weight of temporary or movable objects on a deck, such as people, furniture, and snow.

Miter joint. A joint formed when two members have been cut at an angle other than 90 degrees, usually at 45 degrees.

On center. A measurement of the spacing between a series of objects as measured from the center of one to the center of the next; usually abbreviated "o.c."

Pier. A vertical, often cylindrical piece of concrete that usually rests on a footing, and that supports a deck post.

Plan view. A view of a structure from above that shows the framing or the decking.

Plumb. Perfectly vertical.

Post. A vertical framing member that supports the beam.

Post base. A metal connector used to join a deck post or beam to a concrete foundation.

Post cap. A metal connector used to join a deck post to a beam.

Rim joist. A joist that is fastened to the ends of the other joists.

Rise. The term for identifying vertical distance in stairs.

Riser. The board attached to the vertical surface of a stair stringer (see below).

Run. The term for identifying horizontal distance in stairs.

Skirting. A screen installed below the deck surface to hide the substructure or to protect items stored beneath the deck.

Span. The distance a member covers from the center of one supporting member to the center of the next.

Square. When one surface is at a perfect 90-degree angle to another. Also, a tool for determining and marking square.

Stringer. A diagonal part of a stairway that supports treads and risers. Also called a "carriage."

Tread. The board or boards attached to the horizontal surface of a stair stringer.

resource guide

Most materials needed to build a deck can be found at local stores. You can locate some more specialized items included in this book through the following sources. The list also includes composite and vinyl decking and railing products, which are still not available in all areas.

FASTENERS AND CONNECTORS

Dec-Klip
BEN Manufacturing
21229 Cypress Way
Lynnwood, WA 98036
425-776-5340
www.premier1.net/~ben69

Deckmaster
P.O. Box 4060
Concord, CA 94524
800-869-1375
www.deckmaster.com

Deck One
1932-B Voorhees Ave.
Redondo Beach, CA 90278-2327
888-335-3217
www.deckone.com

EB-TY
P.O. Box 414
Califon, NJ 07830
888-438-3289
www.ebty.com

McFeely's Square Drive Screws
620 Wythe Rd. / P.O. Box 11169
Lynchburg, VA 24506-1169
800-443-7937
www.mcfeelys.com

Simpson Strong-Tie Connectors
4120 Dublin Blvd., Suite 400
Dublin, CA 94568
800-999-5099
www.strongtie.com

Swan Secure Products Inc.
7525 Perryman Ct.
Baltimore, MD 21226-1752
800-966-2801
www.swansecure.com

USP Lumber Connectors
703 Rogers Dr.
Montgomery, MN 56069
800-328-5934
www.uspconnectors.com

COMPOSITE DECKING AND RAILINGS

Boardwalk
CertainTeed Corp.
750 E. Swedesford Rd. / P.O. Box 860
Valley Forge, PA 19482
800-233-8990
www.certainteed.com

E-Z Deck
Imperial Building Products
2305 8th St.
Nisku, Alberta, Canada T9E 7Z3
800-990-3099
www.ezdeck.com

Fiberon
Fiber Composites LLC
34570 Random Dr.
New London, NC 28127
704-463-7120
www.fibercomposites.com

Nexwood
1327 Clark Blvd.
Brampton, Ontario, Canada L6T 5R5
888-763-9966
www.nexwood.com

SmartDeck Systems
2600 W. Roosevelt Rd.
Chicago, IL 60608
888-733-2546
www.smartdeck.com

TimberTech
894 Prairie Rd.
Wilmington, OH 45177
800-307-7780
www.timbertech.com

Trex Co.
160 Exeter Pl.
Winchester, VA 22603-8605
800-289-8739
www.trex.com

WeatherBest, LP Corp.
805 SW Broadway
Portland, OR 97205
800-521-4316
www.weatherbest.lpcorp.com

Weyerhaeuser ChoiceDek, AERT Inc.
914 N. Jefferson / P.O. Box 1237
Springdale, AR 72764
800-951-5117
www.choicedek.com

VINYL DECKING AND RAILINGS

Brock Deck Systems
Royal Crown Ltd.
P.O. Box 360
Milford, IN 46542-0360
800-365-3625
www.royalcrownltd.com

Color Guard Fence
Poly Vinyl Co.
Drawer 300
Sheboygan Falls, WI 53085
800-832-8914
www.polyvinyl.com

Dream Deck
Thermal Industries Inc.
301 Brushton Ave.
Pittsburgh, PA 15221
800-245-1540
www.thermalindustries.com

Kroy Building Products
P.O. Box 636
York, NE 68467
800-933-5769
www.kroybp.com

Royal Deck
Royal Outdoor Products
100B Royal Group Crescent
Woodbridge, Ontario, Canada L4H 1X9
800-949-7410
www.royaloutdoor.com

Yardcrafters
GSW Thermoplastics Co.
26 Lorena St.
Barrie, Ontario, Canada L4N 4P4
800-662-4479
www.gswthermo.com

SPECIALIZED PRODUCTS

BoWrench
Cepco Tool Co.
P.O. Box 700
Spencer, NY 14883
800-466-9626
www.cepcotool.com

Woodburst Color Co.
1419 20th St. NW, #B
Auburn, WA 48001
253-939-6123
www.woodburst.com

credits

PHOTOGRAPHY

Unless otherwise credited, all photographs are by **Mark Rutherford**.

Courtesy of Arch Wood Company: 30 bottom, 31 bottom, 32 top, 169, 177 top, 178 top; **Mark Bolton/Garden-Image:** 24 top, 173; **Ernest Braun/-California Redwood Association:** 152; **Gay Bumgarner:** 38 top, 38 middle; **Karen Bussolini:** 15 top, 34 bottom; **Karen Bussolini/Positive Images:** 20 top; **Rex Butcher/GardenImage:** 30 left; **Courtesy of California Redwood Association:** 142 bottom; **Milt Charno:** 228; **Glen Cormier:** 42 bottom; **Crandall & Crandall:** 26 bottom, 27 bottom, 33 top, 42 top, 98, 155 bottom, 177 bottom; **Courtesy of Danuser Machine Co.:** 89 bottom; **Ben Davidson:** 202, 210, 212, 213, 214, 216, 224, 227 top, 236, 237, 249, 250; **Janet Davis:** 175; **Catriona Tudor Erler:** 24 bottom, 36 bottom, 49, 117 bottom, 153, 174, 196; **Derek Fell:** 20 middle, 23 bottom, 40, 119 bottom; **Scott Fitzgerrell:** 59, 60, 61, 62 (7), 63 (7), 64, 65, 66 (7), 67, 69 left, 69 middle, 70 bottom, 74, 77, 97, 100 left, 108, 116 center, 121, 126, 127 left, 139, 151, 156, 160 left, 160 middle, 167, 185, 186, 187 bottom, 188, 197; **G.L. French/ H. Armstrong Roberts:** 114 top; **Jay Graham:** 5 middle, 8, 9 top, 10 top, 36 top, 46 top, 120 top, 122, 170, 244, 245; **Courtesy Hadco Lighting:** 178 bottom; **Lynne Harrison:** 22 top; **Phil Harvey:** 2, 13 bottom, 39, 46 bottom, 62 (4), 63 (5), 66 (1), 179 bottom, 200, 240; **Saxon Holt:** 18 left, 19 bottom; **James Frederick Housel:** 155 top, 220; **James Frederick Housel/ California Redwood Association:** 5 top, 6 top; **Jerry Howard/Positive Images:** 187 top, 195 left, 195 right; **judywhite/ GardenPhotos.com:** 34 top; **Philip Wegener Kantor:** 17 bottom; **Dennis Krukowski:** 32 bottom; **David Duncan Livingston:** 6 bottom, 12 top, 27 top; **Craig Lovell/Eagle Visions:** 17 top; **Allan Mandell:** 1, 29 bottom, 34 left, 37 bottom; **Charles Mann:** 5 bottom,

18 right; **Richard Nicol:** 206; **Russell J. Nirella/Thermal Industries, Inc.:** 133 bottom left, 133 bottom right; **Robert Perron:** 10 bottom, 13 top, 37 top, 172, 181 bottom; **D. Petku/ H. Armstrong Roberts:** 176 left; **Norman A. Plate:** 14 bottom, 41, 115 top; **Rich Pomerantz/GardenImage:** 141; **Courtesy of Portland Cement Association:** 91 right; **Courtesy of Punch Software, LLC:** 55 top, 55 bottom; **Jon Reis/PHOTOLINK:** 154, 184; **K. Rice/ H. Armstrong Roberts:** 35 bottom, 171 bottom; **Susan A. Roth:** 14 top, 21 bottom, 29 top, 123; **Marv Sloben:** 16, 20 bottom, 35 top, 128, 129; **Marv Sloben/California Redwood Association:** 9 bottom; **Joe Sohn/Unicorn Photos:** 180 top; **Courtesy of Southern Forest Products Association:** 21 top, 22 bottom; **Graeme Teague:** 23 top; **Tim Street-Porter/Beateworks.com:** 11, 26 top; **Michael S. Thompson:** 7, 28 top; **Courtesy of TREX:** 132; **Courtesy of Trowel Trades Red Lion:** 91 left; **Mark Turner:** 15 bottom, 36 left, 38 bottom, 52, 116 top, 118 top, 171 top; **David Wakely:** 25; **Jessie Walker:** 12 bottom, 168; **Courtesy of Western Wood Products Association:** 142 top; **Peter Whiteley:** 28 bottom, 33 bottom; **David Winger:** 232; **Tom Wyatt:** 204

DESIGNERS

Tibor Ambrus: 202; **The Berger Partnership Landscape Architects:** 46 bottom; **Terry Boyd:** 115; **The Brickman Group:** 40; **Robert Carlson, Pacific Northwest Construction:** 220; **Milt Charno & Associates:** 228; **Churchill & Hambelton:** 2; **Jon Courter/Courter Construction:** 13 bottom; **Davis Construction Services:** 155 top; **Robert Engman, AIA, Architect:** 240; **Steven Erlich:** 26 top; **Todd Fry, ASLA:** 204; **Michael Glassman & Associates, Landscape Architecture:** 28 bottom, 33 bottom; **Ireland-Gannon:** 21 bottom; **Konrad Gauder Garden Design:** 37 bottom; **Bryan Gordon, B. Gordon Builders:** 212, 213, 249, 250; **John Herbst, Jr.:** 26 bottom, 27 bottom, 98; **Rick Hirsch, Architect:** 249, 250; **Bruce Jett Associates, Landscape**

Architects: 214; **Johnsen Design & Planning:** 34 bottom; **Robert Knight, Architect:** 181; **Peter Koenig Designs:** 212, 213; **Garrett Kuhlman:** 14 bottom; **Landgraphics Inc.:** 179 bottom; **Scott Lankford, Lankford Associates Landscape Architects:** 206; **Carl & Tiffany Ledbetter:** 13 bottom; **Mike Lervick & Vicki Mandin:** 6, 155 top; **Tom MacAusland:** 122; **John Montgomery/Garden Architecture:** 179 bottom; **Gary Marsh, All Decked Out:** 8, 9 top, 10 top, 36 top, 46 top, 120 top, 170, 224, 227, 244, 245; **Susan Muszulu:** 15 top; **Scott Padgett Construction:** 9 bottom, 16, 35 top, 42 bottom; **Dr. Robert F. Powers:** 152; **Ransohoff, Blanchfield & Jones Landscape Architects:** 200; **Bill Remick, Remick Associates, Architects/ Builders:** 216, 236, 237; **Russ Sinkola:** 232; **Bob & Sandy Snyder:** 123; **Straus-Edwards Architects:** 37 top; **Suburban Water Gardens:** 29 top; **Ungers & Kiss, Architects:** 20 top; **Doug Walter Architects:** 17 bottom; **Ward-Young Architecture & Planning:** 210; **Polly Weber:** 28 top

ACKNOWLEDGEMENTS

We would like to thank the deck designers who graciously allowed us to reproduce their plans and the homeowners who allowed us to photograph their decks. Thanks also to John Champlin for his valuable assistance, and Piedmont Lumber Company and Peter Kyle Construction for supplying tools and materials for our photo shoots.

index

Page numbers in **boldface** refer to photographs.